refutes facile ideas of 'convergence' but sees hope in unexpected places, for example in the consensual tradition deriving from pre-European Africa in what are often glibly dismissed as primitive tribes.

This is a book which combines a broad perspective through time and space with a highly-informed and detailed view of our own world. It sheds a strong light on some of our most important dilemmas.

Robert Conquest is the author of a wide range of books on historical, political, cultural and other themes, including a number of classic studies in the Soviet field. He was educated at Winchester and Magdalen College, Oxford (MA, D.Litt). He served in the Army and the Foreign Office (OBE), and has held Fellowships at the London School of Economics; Columbia University; The Woodrow Wilson Center for Scholars, Washington; Stanford University; and elsewhere. In 1979 his *Present Danger*, on immediate issues of foreign policy, was published. He is at present working on a book on Western unity.

WE AND THEY

ROBERT CONQUEST

We & They

TEMPLE SMITH·LONDON

First published in Great Britain in 1980
by Maurice Temple Smith Ltd.
37 Great Russell Street, London WC1

© 1980 Robert Conquest
ISBN   0 85117 184 2

Printed in Great Britain by
Billing & Sons Ltd.
London, Guildford & Worcester

Acknowledgements are due to The Woodrow Wilson
Center for Scholars of the Smithsonian Institution,
Washington, DC and to the Hoover Institution on War,
Revolution and Peace, Stanford University, for much
help and discussion; also to *Encounter*, in which some
of this material first appeared.

Contents

FOR

Margaret Thatcher

dux femina facti

Preface

We are in the midst of a conflict of cultures and psychologies far deeper than any mere competition between political forms or opinions. And this conflict, which until fairly recently was sporadic or localised, has now come to dominate the world scene.

A true understanding of the nature and profundity of this present crisis can only be reached through the perspectives of history and of political philosophy. Originally this book was designed to go into ·more historical detail and to analyse other views in the field at some length. But of the various ways in which the matter could be treated, it seemed to me that the overwhelming necessity was to make it a 'public' book for the ordinary reader, to develop its main thesis as clearly and fully as possible, without worrying at the bones of argumentative particulars, and to give the great historical perspectives with only so much detail as would establish and support the framework of my argument. I cover long stretches of world history, obviously without exhaustive treatment of particular cultures or periods. To outline the origins of, and the relationships between, the different political organisms which have flourished and still flourish on this planet is not to make an academically formal statement of political philosophy. There is indeed, (and this is a point I develop in a different context), an erroneous notion of systematising in much current writing on politics which is often worthless, sometimes worse. At any rate, what follows is a discourse, not a 'dissertation'.

Readers will note two major omissions, made for different reasons. First, I have not.dealt with China, either ancient or modern.

I believe that a general analysis in terms of this book is possible, and necessary too; but after much reading and some writing, I decided that an adequate treatment of that variant of political culture would have to await further study. Since that decision, events there seem to have astonished even life-long students of the country. Second, I had originally intended to attempt a typology of the revolutionary and other psyches. After (again) much reading, from the psycho-historians to such sources as Himmler's unpublished diaries, I concluded that no such typology is convincing and fell back on general description and impressionistic detail.

In avoiding the academic approach, I have nevertheless used quite a number of quotations. But, generally speaking, these are included less as evidence—or ballast—than on Montaigne's principle: 'I quote others only the better to express myself.'

I am concerned here not with the immediacies of foreign policy, with which I have dealt in my *Present Danger*, but with the origins and nature of the forces that find us at present in a situation in which it is as if two great liners were bearing down on each other on a collision course: a collision course, moreover, in deep fog—the fog of illusion, the fog of ignorance, the fog of fallacy, the fog of factiousness. The more clearly we see, the better our chances of survival. And the main source of difficulty and danger in the world today seems to be the misunderstandings in our minds about the nature of world politics, and in particular a sort of intellectual parochialism, combined with a lack of political perspective, which prevents people from grasping fully the enormous differences between the political cultures, the political psychologies, the political motivations whose representatives divide the globe.

And so, I put a conception of history, and of our present predicament in history, before the public, in the assurance that it has not been fully and explicitly put before and that it should prove useful both intellectually and as a practical guide to the world today, in its larger context and in its immediate dangers.

Stanford, 1979   R.C.

PART ONE

Origins and Directions

CHAPTER 1

Definitions of Civilisation

Central to the world's history is the existence of an active and long-standing contrast between different types of political culture, covering all those relationships, activities and attitudes in a community which we can very broadly define as politics. And the most useful distinction appears to be that between the 'civic' and the 'despotic' cultures. In the 'civic' culture the polity is articulated and decisions are made (in principle at least) in accordance with a balance of interests, through consultation with and acceptance by various sections of the community; while in the 'despotic' culture, the decisions are taken by a single man or a single group and the population is merely a passive element.

I am not seeking to find a formula or claiming to interpret the whole of world history, but merely taking what appear to be those crucial characteristics of the cultures of the various areas of the world which constitute an essential thread and which differentiate most basically between great general types.

Our cultures grasp us with a thousand invisible fingers. The characteristics of individual countries, even, are of an enormous complexity; the details which give them savour and body, which pull them into one, are often not merely fantastic, but also contradictory. To consider France under Louis XIV and his two successors, to think of the religious controversies of seventeenth-century Russia, is to find oneself amongst an incredible intricacy. And again, each country is inhabited not only by its citizens, but also by ghosts and by phantasms from imaginary futures or saints from lands outside time. Even as to the details, Boswell remarked truly of English history that if it were not so well attested, no one could believe it. The same is true of France — perhaps even more so. Political and social cultures are not simply 'systems', as some political theorists imagine, patterns arbitrarily erected or demolished in any given area by administrative or economic *fiat* to suit a set of ideas. They are, above all, rooted in the consciousness and habit of generations.

The contrast between our current versions of the despotic culture and the civic culture is the modern crux, but it can be seen in a world historical perspective. Political Man in different systems is not just basically the same creature holding different theoretical opinions, but rather a life-form which has evolved into radically different phyla, each with deep-set attitudes, historically determined over long periods (and subject to natural selection as between different temperamental groups). So that, for example, the present Marxist-Leninist ruling elements in the USSR are actually unable to see the world under categories different from their own. They and their motivations and probable actions are not to be understood by projecting on to them our own notions of natural behaviour. The centuries-old tradition of post-Mongol Russia (as we shall later develop more fully) produced a system of unlimited despotism, with a tendency to universal expansionism. This was somewhat modified by two generations of Europeanisation after 1860; but this Western tendency was destroyed by the Revolution which, moreover, grafted onto the old despotic tradition a newer, messianic-revolutionary despotism with explicit pretence to world rule.

Cultures have had, as they still have, enormous intrinsic momenta, and they cannot be rapidly turned in new directions. The processes involved are long ones; it takes generations for a civic culture to emerge from a despotic environment and, equally, generations to destroy previously existing civic attitudes. In his great chapter on the English Revolution of 1688 Macaulay writes of the French Revolution that 'had six generations of Englishmen passed away without a single session of Parliament', then we too would have needed years of blood and confusion 'to learn the very rudiments of political science', and been equally duped by childish theories; and have equally 'sought refuge from anarchy in despotism, and been again driven from despotism into anarchy'. Six generations: even though France had started not too far from the English style and had by no means become *totally* uncivic. Even Marx talks of fifty years being necessary to teach his 'proletariat' to rule, while the Maoists have spoken in terms of a hundred or two hundred years as the time required to change social attitudes in a truly radical way. At any rate, we must avoid being too sanguine about the early blossoming of new cultural styles in areas where history has rooted others.

My broad division between civic and despotic cultures is not the only way to look at the development of society. But both historically and from the point of view of the most substantial and dangerous differences and misunderstandings between current forms of polity, it seems the crucial one. Not, of course, that there is any idea here of pure forms of state. There are, or have been, despotisms in the course of transition to civicisms, and vice versa. There are, or have been, old imperial despotisms which, on the contrary, have contained a powerful build-up of revolutionary-despotic elements. There are, or have been, despotisms which contain both the revolutionary and the civic potentials, in conflict. (And it is in this context that we shall later need to examine the possible development of a civic culture from the present Soviet order.)

The despotic type of culture divides naturally into two general types. First, the traditional, 'imperial' system, in which it is assumed that the true form of the state has already been achieved; and second, the messianic-revolutionary type, which seeks by an act of will to bring history to an eschatologically predetermined conclusion. The history of the latter tradition expressed itself at different periods in the most highly regarded terminology of the time—as Theology in the sixteenth century, as Reason in the eighteenth, and as Science in the nineteenth and the twentieth, each being, in fact, a closed and false 'scientism', but each appealing in turn to the intellectuals of the time.

It will be seen that this main division into civic and despotic involves treating the matter of political cultures in a rather different light from the usual. For example, the civic culture, though containing the possibility of democracy, is not necessarily 'democratic'. And though containing the potentiality of the 'open society', it is not in itself, or necessarily, definable as such.

This may to some degree avoid the various confusions of the contrasts more usually put forward between 'democracy' and 'totalitarianism' or despotism. The notorious ambiguities of the word democracy do not arise: nor do its distorting emotional charges.

Moreover, while democracy can be made to seem, however illogically, to amount to a claim to a complete libertarianism, civic culture does not. Democracy is almost invariably criticised by revolutionaries for the blemishes found in any real example, as compared with the grand abstraction of the mere word. With a civic culture it is more clearly a matter of a basis on which improvements can be made. For a civic society is a society in which the various elements can express themselves politically, in which an articulation exists between these elements at the political level: not a perfect social order, which is in any case unobtainable, but a society that hears, considers and reforms grievances. It is not necessarily democratic, but it contains the possibility of democracy.

In England liberty long preceded democracy. And indeed, it could be argued that only those who already practise consensual politics are equipped to make democracy work; or, to put it another way, that democracy cannot spring fully formed and viable out of the depths of despotism, but needs a transitional period, as Solzhenitsyn urges in the case of present-day Russia. (The confusion of liberty with democracy is a strange one. When one hears, as one not seldom does, an Englishman in a pub saying indignantly, 'It's a free country, isn't it?' he is in no way referring to his right to elect the government, but merely to his right to say what he wants — and he knows it. There seems no reason why more sophisticated folk should not also see this.)

The civic order includes the 'future': that is, it is open to it. As Macaulay acutely remarks, the Declaration of Rights, though it did not in itself establish a number of the liberties later won by the English people, did not give dissenters full equality, prohibit the slave trade, reform the representative system, secure the liberty of the press, nevertheless contained 'the germ' of all these good laws, and also 'of every good law which may hereafter, in the course of ages, be found necessary to promote the public weal, and to satisfy the demands of public opinion'. In fact, it established an open-ended system, under which 'the means of effecting every improvement which the constitution requires may be found within the constitution itself.' Or to put it slightly differently, the general principles then established, or rather reaffirmed, were imperfectly realised in the then state of affairs, for the practical reason that the political nation was not ready

to approve of them; but their future development, barring the overthrow of the system, was guaranteed by the fact that their lack was
progressively felt in each case to be an anomaly rather than a legitimate and natural result of English principles. The reformer — the
corrector of wrongs — was always to feel at a moral advantage, and
his opponent to plead merely practical difficulties and the unripe
state of public opinion — pleas not without their force, but all the
same admittedly limited and temporary.

There was, in fact, a built-in tendency in the civic order to extend
itself to those originally excluded from it: whether because of their
belief, like the Catholics, or for economic class reasons, like the bulk
of the working class, or for reason of sex, i.e. women. The history of
English constitutional progress has been that of making these ex-
tensions. These groups were, it is true, assimilated piecemeal into
the system against considerable inertia. It may be argued that
gradualness ensured the thoroughness of the assimilation.

But it is also the case that, partly owing to the anomalies resulting
from the very archaism in the system, the working classes were not
by any means totally excluded even before the Reform Bills. In the
London and Middlesex constituencies, and in Preston in Lancashire,
the franchise was already wide, and it was generally understood that
these constituencies indicated the feeling of that section of the people
not elsewhere represented. Moreover, the more general civil liberties enabled a good deal of pressure to be brought to bear on voters
by the non-voting sectors of the community. Both the threatening
aspect of the 'mob' and the kisses of the Duchess of Devonshire played
their part. Again, the fact that the premier duke of England was a
Roman Catholic was only one of the various ways in which that
particular minority could exert its influence. Such things may be
thought to be among the advantages arising from the inconsistencies
inherent in a non-dogmatic system.

To make such generalisations, to put forward such broad categories to cover the variety of political orders, is—let us repeat—not
to deny all sorts of intermediate and transitional cases. Nor, as we
have said, is it to ignore the mere idiosyncrasies, as they may appear
to be, in the history of the cultures of various countries: these
apparently superficial and sentimental matters, in fact, are often of
great influence, usually in reinforcing the traditional consensus
(or otherwise) of the country in question.

It is not very rare to come across people in the West who are unable to believe that other cultures can be, in any real sense, uncivilised if they can be shown to produce architecture, opera, ballet, drama and so forth on an impressive scale. Even in relations between states, we find 'cultural exchange' sponsored or handled by Westerners who seem to imagine that a political amenity is thereby achieved.

We must distinguish between the various uses of the word 'civilisation'. As is often pointed out, China has been 'civilised' for millennia. That is to say, it long ago achieved a civil order. But it never rose to the higher degree of a civic order. Cultures may win our admiration for the advanced development of their administrative arrangements, but political civilisation proper is another matter. A state with a complex organisation may yet be primitive at the level of articulation.

Something similar applies to the erection of great buildings. It used to be believed that the 'Old Empire' of the Mayas, in the Peten area, died out owing to a migration to northern Yucatan, where the 'New Empire' then arose. It is true that the great temples and buildings ceased to be used and disappeared under the jungle. But we now realise that the peasant culture which had supported these cults continued as before: they just stopped going in for architecture, just as pyramids petered out in Egypt after the earlier dynasties. Quite highly organised communities may exist without towns. There was nothing that could be called a town in Ireland until the Danes founded Dublin and the other settlements in the tenth century.

Large buildings at least imply a fair-sized and mobilisable work-force. When it comes to the purer arts, no necessary connection between high achievement and an advanced social order exists at all. The paintings in the Altamira caves are as accomplished, as brilliant, as any that have been produced since. Yet there is a reasonable sense in which we may feel that the Stone Age hunters were all the same less 'civilised' than at least some of their less brilliant successors on the same continent.

It is a similar delusion of the generally educated that politicians they approve of are more cultured, or more concerned with culture, than their alternates. But political culture does not run *pari passu* with 'culture' in the aesthetic sense. Abraham Lincoln was incomparably more advanced in political civilisation than any Romanov or Hapsburg, in spite of all the ballet and opera of St Petersburg and Vienna. Or, if we feel that some special exception should be made for the fan not only of Artemus Ward, but even of the far worse Petroleum V. Nasby, on the grounds that Saginaw County could hardly be expected to produce the culture of the old metropolises, we can retort first that Lincoln was extremely well read in the political culture, and we can anyhow destroy the dubious and shaky special plea by turning to England and noting that, while the Tsars were at the Bolshoi, British prime ministers (Rosebery, for example) would be at the Derby. And it was Nero, was it not, rather than Vespasian, who was so keen on the arts?

A curious little volume might be made of the poems of Stalin, Castro, Mao and Ho-chi Minh, with illustrations by A. Hitler: and this last name should remind us that the much-touted slogan 'When I hear the word "culture", I reach for my revolver,' was uttered by a fictional member of the SA, the Nazi radical, egalitarian wing crushed in the blood purge of June 1934; and that, on the contrary, Hitlerism proper (like Kaiserism) swarmed over Europe to the accompaniment of vast claptrap about *Kultur* and its preservation from Anglo-Saxon and Slavonic hordes. If it comes to that, the first truly 'cultured' man in English politics was the revolting Tiptoft, Earl of Worcester, translator of Cicero, patron of Humanists, the purity of whose Latin brought tears to the eyes of Aeneas Sylvius himself, but who is known to political history, according to different criteria, as the 'Butcher Earl', owing to his record as impaler of prisoners and slaughterer of infants, new phenomena in medieval England. We have a horrid example to moderns in the incredible eulogy of him by Caxton after his death as supreme 'in science and moral virtue'.

At any rate it ought to be possible to dismiss from our minds the idea that any necessary correlation, individual or collective, exists between artistic culture and political maturity.

It is clear that in the political sense the civic community is (regardless of such questions as material or artistic achievement) empirically recognisable at once as more evolved than any form of despotism. And more complex too, in that the system of political relationships is incomparably more intricate, while despotism is the simpler and more primitive method.

The civic cultures of the West, where an open mind has in principle been encouraged, have taken the lead over recent centuries in virtually all important invention. The despotic cultures copy the civic ones in all those elements which they think they can turn to their benefit.

There has been little trade the other way. The reason goes deep.

There is a hierarchy of types among the social animals. Lowest come the colonial invertebrates, such as the corals, in which polyp buds off from polyp, remaining connected by filaments of tissue, with each polyp fulfilling various specialised functions such as tentacles or stomachs, almost as if forming a single animal with no individual sphere of action at all. The social insects are not physically connected but are linked by communication (mainly odours) and have very limited individual flexibility, though the individual can survive for a time in isolation. The social animals, like baboons, have far more individuality, recognise each other as individuals and can play a variety of roles, sometimes in rotation. Human beings go further still in the same direction in various obvious ways.

One may similarly note the hierarchy of human societies, in which the lowest give the least scope to individual action, the least variation in attitudes and the narrowest limits to opinion.

The product of the higher form of political order was variety in unity. As W. H. Auden puts it (summarizing Whitehead, in *The Portable Greek Reader*):

> Civilisation is a precarious balance between barbaric vagueness and trivial order. Barbarism is unified but undifferentiated; triviality is differentiated but lacking in any central unity; the ideal of civilisation is the integration into a complete whole and with the minimum strain of the maximum number of distinct activities.

In its most important aspect, the civic order is that which has created a strong state while still maintaining the principle of consensus which existed in primitive society. Such an aim involves the articulation of a complex political and social order. The strains cannot be eliminated but can be continually adjusted.

For let us insist again that the civic order is of a higher and more developed type than the despotic, that the carrying through of the older adjustments into the higher form of state organisation is a remarkable feat, a continual and fruitful dialectic of the tendencies of state power and the interests and rights of individuals and groups. It has only been achieved by the Western type of culture.

The history of the civic culture has, of course, witnessed many instances of attempted usurpation of control by one group or other. Some civic cultures have perished, or virtually perished, in this way, after promising starts. Others, as we shall note, have fallen into a comparative stasis of despotism, from which only a 'revolution' could rescue them. In others (in particular, in England) the tradition has been maintained, with occasional lurches and recoveries, through Anglo-Saxon times and, presumably, from the prehistoric originals.

CHAPTER 2

The Consensual Tradition

Pre-technological societies, as is now realised, had all sorts of different arrangements and customs. What they had in common was, in fact, their size, and points directly arising from that size, such as inter-familial relations, which were solved in various ways.

Of necessity, a consensual relationship existed in these primitive societies. Engels was right in finding a co-operative type of order in the general prehistoric condition of man. The economic reductionism which makes such co-operation primarily an economic matter distorts the nature of this primitive communalism to the hard category of 'primitive communism', seeing the situation as in essence the mere absence of economic classes. In fact, the economic side, even in primitive society, where the pressure of need might be thought greatest, clearly did not play this supposedly dominating role in human relationships, where family, magic and general cultural attitudes were if anything predominant. If it comes to that, even the 'social' organisation of the higher apes does not seem to be dominated solely by feeding habits. Perhaps Marxism comes into its own somewhere lower down the evolutionary scale. . . .

Nor, of course, did society evolve further merely or primarily for 'economic' reasons. It now appears that the more or less egalitarian Neolithic order could not be maintained after the population of a given community rose above a fairly small figure. As the anthropologist Anthony Forge puts it (in *Man, Settlement and Urbanism,* ed.

Peter J. Ucko, Ruth Tringham & G. W. Dimbleby 1972), 'homo sapiens can only handle a certain maximum number of intense face-to-face relationships, successfully distinguishing between each.' This maximum figure seems to be around four or five hundred. Common sense and the experience of schools, army units and so forth would suggest the same. The reasons for change were thus strictly those associated with the impossibility of maintaining purely personal relations with larger numbers, together with the fact that specialisation could begin to emerge when numbers were large enough. At this point a 'chiefdom' type of organisation arose. The change was thus not, as the Marxists suggest, due to a food surplus making slavery economically feasible: examples supporting the above thesis but quite incompatible with the Marxist one are widespread — for instance, on Easter Island and among the Cherokees.

The rise of 'chiefdoms', and later of a variety of legal and political forms, did not of necessity mean the end of the older communalism and consensualism but rather its rise to a 'civic' level. To the natural articulation between individuals or families was added a more complex articulation between local communities and between interest groups; eventually a true executive arm complemented and made possible the survival of the new complexities. Thus, as the social order became more complex, and larger, we may again agree with the Marxists that formal law and central state organisation became necessary. From this time on we may trace in every civil order the struggle between the civic and the state elements.

Naturally, the machinery of power attracted, to put it at its simplest, those who liked power. In many areas the older relations gave way to despotism; this depended on local circumstances. But it was not a matter of economic or cultural level: Egypt and later Mongolia became despotisms; Attica and later Jutland retained an articulation of citizenry.

Primitive consensuality was rarely able to survive for long the evolution of highly organised, larger state forms: yet at a very advanced state of chiefdom, among the Saxons in the forests of Germany (as among the Six Nations of the Iroquois and other sophisticated 'tribal' societies), a type of civic relationship persisted. The civic co-operative element in the Anglo-Saxon society is continuous from primitive times.

In its most important aspect, the civic order is that which has created a strong state while still maintaining the earlier principle of consensus. It was the Western European nation-state which provided the possibility — no more — of political society on a scale which was neither too small (as with the Greek city-states) nor too large (as with the Eurasian empires). This was partly a matter of geographical luck.

'Participatory' democracy, at least normally, nowadays means not the participation of everybody so much as intervention by activists, busybodies and those with plenty of time to spare. Perhaps in the smaller Swiss cantons, and in the town meetings of the small communities of backwoods New England, some remnant of the older communalism remains, but in the larger world we are, at any rate for the time being, better off with the present system of awarding the job of managing policy to one or other of the groups of rival contractors we know as political parties. On the whole, the employment of experts, under suitable supervision, seems inevitable. The problem of making sure of the competence of the alternative parties (and not only the competence but also the sanity) is another matter.

As is indeed obvious, there are elites in all orders, including democracy itself. Outside very small groups, any political formation involves some form of leadership, with either a large or a negligible element of consent. Pareto notes that power is always, to some degree, in the hands of minorities. And all political organisations have a tendency to fall into the hands of oligarchical hierarchies (a tendency which Robert Michel asserts as a law). In the consensual state order these are nevertheless obstacles which can be overcome, society as a whole possessing the means to exert the necessary pressures, if in an untidy, belated and incomplete way.

There is, of course, nothing new in the idea that our liberties derive from early times. Montesquieu saw the origins of the English Constitution in the woods of Saxony. There were many nineteenth-century writers in America as well as Britain who traced modern liberties — and indeed virtues of every kind — to a rather mystically conceived German origin. What aspirations to free society there might have been in France, Spain or Italy too were attributed to Franks, Visigoths, Lombards: but the Anglo-Saxon heritage above all was derived from the ineffable purity of the noble savages of Germany, noted since Tacitus' time. Bancroft even traced the early American institutions to the forest Teutons, calling the early Virginians 'Anglo-Saxons in the woods again'! (And all this was further complicated by that other wonderful German invention, Protestantism.) A strong racial tone emerged, which tended to discredit even the mere fact of continuity in the English tradition.

Of course it is ridiculous to claim any special merit for the Anglo-Saxon culture because it was the first to develop (or rather to maintain) the civic level of state. If ours were to succumb, there are other sources of a consensus civilisation from which it could again emerge. It is not necessary for us to be overbearing about our heritage; it is a matter of luck we are born into it. All the same, why should we not repeat the words of Naboth, 'Jehovah forbid that I should give unto thee the inheritance of my forefathers'?

It has often been pointed out that appeals to past tradition, which have always marked English history in particular, have usually been appeals to bogus history. This is true, but only in a rather superficial sense. Seventeenth-century parliamentarians appealing to Saxon liberties against the Norman oppressor are easy to laugh at. Yet they had the nub of the matter. The memory is blurred, idealised, wrong in a number of respects; but it contains in this slightly distorted form the idea of the rights of Englishmen, and the truth that these rights in a general sense are rooted in the remembered tradition.

Since the collapse of Rome there has never been any significant period in Britain when the state was strong enough to enforce its will without considerable concessions to the rights and liberties of important sections of its subjects and without reliance upon consent.

By later standards the early rights and liberties were, as we have said, defective and incomplete. But their continuity proved a solid foundation for their extension century by century, always in accordance with the principle involved in their existence.

The special characteristic which gave rise to an English society different from those on the Continent was that the English conquest of Britain was piecemeal. It was not a question, as in France, Italy or Spain, of united barbarian armies under their acknowledged kings simply taking over a country. The piecemeal progress of the English meant that individual settlements sprang up, of varying origins, incorporating the indigenous populations, having the same or similar laws and customs and (eventually) acknowledging one or another small king. The groupings on a fairly small scale remained the traditional basis of the nation, which was thus created from below rather than from above.

Moreover, the society was loosely knit and, as Dr John Morris has put it in *The Age of Arthur,* 'its numerous intermediate gradations avoided polarisation between the extremes of over-mighty nobles and servile cultivators'. Even at the nadir of serfdom, the old tenures remained, and 'the yeoman and the franklin, the gentry and the squire were numerous enough and sufficiently secure to retain control of their own localities, and were thereby enabled to grant or withold the revenues of the central government'. While the popular assemblies of other nations withered in the Middle Ages, Parliament survived because 'it became the organ of lesser local lords and of their urban equivalents, whose interests repeatedly aligned them with the peasant against the demands of king and baron'.

The Germanic nations which came to Britain had various political customs. While the Angles had had 'kings' for several centuries, the Saxons had not. All the Saxon 'townships' had their own rulers, and general meetings were held once a year 'where the leaders met with twelve nobles and as many freedmen and bondmen from each township. There they confirmed the laws, judged important legal cases, and agreed upon the plans that would guide them in peace or war during the coming year'. (The Saxons remaining in Europe did not, in fact, have a permanent monarchy until the ninth century. This Saxon lack of commitment to central institutions greatly annoyed the Frankish conquerors, who had difficulty in making arrangements with a wide variety of local authorities. And it was a Saxon, Odoacer, who took the step no barbarian had hitherto ventured to take, that of simply abolishing the Western Empire.)

The effect on the American political culture of the special circumstances of the Frontier has, of course, been much discussed since the end of the last century. The idea of the determining effect of small communities owing a general allegiance to government on the coast, but beyond its effective protection and compelled to rely on their own common initiative, clearly has much to be said for it in accounting for the special circumstances of American democracy. It is interesting to reflect that this was in a sense a re-enactment of the original spread of the English settlers in Britain. That, too, was on the whole piecemeal. It was only after considerable areas had been settled for some time that they 'sent for kings' to the Continent — which is to say, under the circumstances, organised themselves into states.

In both the English and the American cases, it was not, of course, a matter of traditionless man evolving broad new administrative forms to suit the circumstances. Both Americans and Saxons built their new communities on the basis of the traditional laws and rights as they remembered them. In England from that time on, as Dr Morris puts it, 'Custom has expected that men of suitable standing should be heard before decision is reached; society has frequently disagreed about which men should be heard when, but when it has reached agreement, governments that ignored agreed opinion have been denied obedience and revenue.' Local tenures and local institutions 'trained English society to respect governments that co-ordinate and to discipline governments that rule by command'.

These attitudes maintained the flexibility of our society, with an easier movement of ideas and smoother social change than was possible in most of Europe. Above all, it became possible to correct a powerful central government, which was still obliged to observe the restraints of custom: 'Time and effort shaped a tradition of firm leadership and light rule.'

Our conception of English history is distorted to some degree by the idea of the Wessex monarchy as representative of the Saxon epoch. But the domination of Wessex was an episode, covering a period when a comparatively centralised military effort determined the shape of the state, in the epoch of the Viking invasions. *The Anglo-Saxon Chronicle* is in effect propaganda for the idea of a general Wessex supremacy over centuries, achieved by suppressing the far more fundamental and in the long run more fruitful rule of the extraordinary Mercian kingdom. (Indeed, the comparatively loose and easy original organisation of Wessex itself, with its sub-kingdoms, is also to some degree lost in the official account.)

The gradual movement of the Mercian occupation, the comparatively peaceful incorporation of British populations, provided much flexibility. Settlements varied from military colonies (mainly directed against the Northumbrians) to groups of individuals, groups following chieftains, individual farms; and the same is true, to a lesser degree, of other parts of England.

Apart from Mercia, the older English kingdoms for various reasons were somewhat peripheral to the main development of the country. Kent, which was rather exceptional in that it took over the old administrative system, as on the Continent, remained a coastal strip largely cut off from the main development, as did Sussex. The powerful and long-settled kingdoms of East Anglia were also largely isolated by the fens and forests. The great warrior kingdom of Bernicia (and the eventual Northumberland) ruled scattered subject populations in the wilder north and though capable of military conquest in the south, could never establish dominance. Wessex, too, for a long time remained a half-Celtic border state in the area between the Solent and the Severn Estuary.

Mercia, centred on the settlements south of the Trent, spread over the heartland of Britain. Until its very last period it remained a highly flexible state, with great devolution of powers to local authorities. It spread westward by this piecemeal type of settlement. And it is a curious fact that though its western frontier was the one with the greatest physical contact with the Welsh, it was very seldom at war with them.

Though there was military tenure in the normal feudal sense, its importance rapidly decreased in Mercia and in all the southern kingdoms. Hereditary tenures by payment, or something approaching them, in one way or another tended to replace these, as they did again after the brief exception of the early Norman period.

The (up to a point) systematising genius of William the Conqueror led to surprisingly little disruption of the local and communal customs and jurisdictions. Indeed, the inevitable pluralism of power of the true military tenure which now briefly prevailed tended if anything to force the king to a certain dependence on the older structures to counter his strong vassals. There is much more to be said on the subject than this. Nevertheless, the Common Law eventually prevailed, and the various attempts of kings to turn local administrations into centrally appointed bureaucracies in the long run came to grief.

There have been many occasions in English history when the executive has become too powerful by comparison with the communities. Offa, by removing the under-kings and centralising the Mercian empire, had a temporary success but effectively wrecked the system. The Angevins, in their attempt to replace local administration by royally appointed sheriffs, likewise failed in the long run. Until the end of the nineteenth century, with the exception of Cromwell's major-generals, even the most tyrannical executives did not substantially interfere with local government.

Generally speaking, great and successful rulers in England have been those, like Edward I and Edward III, who worked within the laws and customs, sought co-operation rather than submission from the representatives of the cities and counties. In turn, from Magna Carta on, the community rarely called into question the essential powers of the executive, though particular kings might be, and were, removed. These were those monarchs, like Edward II, Richard III and James II, who sought to extend the power of the state at the expense of the community. And the balance in each case was restored by a constitutionalist counter-revolution.

For the civic tradition of Britain has fairly often in the past been faced by more dynamic, more modern 'waves of the future'. In Yorkist times the attempt was made to instal in England a stream-lined, Renaissance-style despotism (complete with the torture and treachery of the Sforzas and the Borgias). In Stuart times came the attempt to turn England into one of the new Divine Right monarchies on the French model, again to the accompaniment of illegality and torture.

The point is that an executive can be strong without being intrusive in areas in which the community, or a large part of it, resents its presence. This is the key distinction to be made between Elizabeth I and her successors. To say that the Tudor state was as dominant as that of the Stuarts is to miss the essential. Generally speaking, it did not, and that of the Stuarts did, try to impose itself on areas of life (including the economic) which the community thought inappropriate. The state monopolies of James I's time remind one strongly of similar state operations in Britain in the past generation. This is true even to the extent of the appointment to leading positions (accompanied by peerages) of prominent adherents of the executive power.

The advantages of a strong executive have always included the maintenance of legal order. Bede tells us that in the days of Edwin of Northumberland, in the seventh century:

> If a woman with a new-born babe then wished to walk across the land from sea to sea, she would come to no harm . . . King Edwin so considered his subjects' comfort that when he saw clear springs by the highway, he had posts set up with bronze cups attached for the refreshment of travellers, and no man dared . . . or wished . . . to touch them beyond his need.

Similarly, we are told of William I that a man carrying a bag of gold was safe in the realm wherever he went. This last point may remind us that free enterprise requires firm laws and is by no means, even in principle, the free-for-all it is represented as being in some propaganda.

A society cannot be in any true sense civic if there are not lesser communities within it which have their own life and vigour. Thomas Aquinas puts forward what he calls the principle of subsidiarity: that nothing should be done by the larger and superior body which can be done by the lesser and inferior one. That is to say, the state should do nothing that can be done by the community, and the community nothing that can be done by the family.

From this point of view, experiments such as that of the Stuarts can be seen as an attempt (parallel with the more successful ones being made in France and elsewhere) to use the power of the executive to destroy the civic nature of English society. This was finally defeated by the Revolution of 1688, just as George III's attempt to do the same thing in his American territories was destroyed by the Revolution of 1776.

In a sense, since primitive times there has thus always been in our society this major contest between the civic, mutual interadjustment of man and man and the despotic imposition of the will. But apart from the occasional total breakdown of restraint at the very top, usually affecting only a limited ruling class, a system of rights and obligations has persisted, or at least the principle of it has.

This does not involve any fatalism about 'national characters'. But it does imply that these are not to be changed — in the right or the wrong direction — without time and difficulty.

CHAPTER 3

Europe and Elsewhere

Europe is an area in which civilisation and anti-civilisation have clashed for centuries. It is not part of the purpose of this book to trace the whole of Western or of world history even in outline, but some relevant points illustrating the complexity of this struggle may be sketched.

Only in England (and in a few other countries) did the old civic consensuality persist — and even there not without interruptions, though these never endured quite long enough seriously to shake the deepest attitudes. On the Continent the record is a good deal spottier. In most of the former Roman Empire, as we have said, the conquest by barbarians had not been a piecemeal, community-level affair, but a matter of nations under organised kingships taking over the apparatus of the Roman polity.

Yet even in continental Western Europe (partly because the areas and the economics were suitable and a feudalism of mutual balance arose; partly because the barbarians brought in at least some of the old chiefdom content of kingship; partly because Rome itself contributed the remnants of law and the beginnings of Christianity) a civic element persisted to a certain degree and showed a capacity to revive even after long and destructive disaster.

The purest despotisms of the traditional type had arisen in the East and similar lands, where small peasant populations supported little in the way of economic or social classes except for the centralised bureaucracy and deified ruler responsible for irrigation, taxation and war (and in such cases as post-Mongol Russia, in a large territory without natural frontiers, where a vast and centralised defensive effort was needed for survival). The despotisms that had arisen in Europe (the Hellenic and Roman empires) had different roots.

The Hellenic world, and later Rome, deteriorated piecemeal from a civic to a largely despotic society, rather as, in the sixteenth and seventeenth centuries, the monarchies of France and Spain gradually suppressed much of the old civic content of their own societies. This aspect of the Hellenic and Roman empires reflects the partial intrusion of the despotic tradition into an area which had previously contained a large and often dominating element of civic and legal order — the change accompanying the establishment of large-scale states where the frontier provinces were several weeks' journey from the centre.

In the Greek cities civic-ness had been maintained more by the balance of power between interests than by devotion to a civic principle. Rome, until the last century of the Republic, was far more of a consensual and civic society than most or all of the Greek city-states. In them, or some of them, the vote and the assembly operated; but the victory of a faction seldom led to accommodation. The principle of struggle (*agōn*) was important, even metaphysically, to the Greeks and in their endless revolutions may be thought to have played something of the same destructive role played nowadays by the dogma of 'class struggle'. The arrival of the 'critical' attitude to the state was so overwhelming that, among the educated classes at least, the traditional and unconscious ties of society often became disastrously weak.

Rome, on the other hand, developed a firmly based constitutionalism, slow and plodding by Greek standards but founded on generations of experience. The Licinian Laws, which gave the *plebs* the right to highest office, involved a bitter struggle lasting for five years. But it was finally solved under the constitutional arrangements, avoiding the bloodshed which would have been inevitable in a Greek city.

In Rome the very success of the political system provided those huge reserves of expansionist energy which turned the city into an imperial state. And in the then conditions of slavery this produced (as with Athens before it, but on a larger scale) a boom in what were little more than piratical slave wars, with an influx of unassimilated and heterogeneous slaves distorting the older economy in a way not truly comparable with the more institutional and social slavery, such as it was, of the old river empires.

From the time of Marius and Sulla constitutionality suffered a series of breakdowns. The vast new territories coming under Roman rule, the great armies that had to be kept in existence over long periods, stretched it to the utmost. Yet a remnant of legality remained. Greek political theory, and the general idea of standing back and looking at the state, was of course known to the Romans, and they consciously founded institutions and consciously created political arrangements, though equally appealing to historical rights and precedents. Legal development proceeded, even when it was being overlaid by despotism, right through the Principate.

By the time of Diocletian a new arrangement, the institution of an Oriental-style despotism, seemed to imply reversion to a pre-critical epoch. But, in fact, though the monarchical despotic principle prevailed and the 'critical' element was severely depressed, nevertheless a complete orientalisation was impossible.

The rise of Christianity, with its association with the state on the one hand and its development of certain social ideas and forms of its own on the other, also provided a 'critical' milieu. Theology, in succession to Greek philosophy, was a highly intellectual exercise, quite unlike anything associated with pre-critical religions. The great monastic movements of the fifth century were themselves an important social phenomenon, and even a social criticism. Christian doctrine is often to be found emerging in hostility to the social order. Church leaders were already capable (as with Columba) of outfacing the secular rulers on their own ground.

The notion of individual right under the law was never wholly lost. As Giovanni Sartori puts it in his *Liberty and Law,* 'Roman jurisprudence did not make a direct contribution to the specific problem of political freedom, but it did make an essential indirect contribution by developing the idea of legality whose modern version is the Anglo-Saxon rule of law.' The concept, with its high abstraction, may be thought to have strengthened, even in Britain, the practical consensual arrangements of the Welsh and the Saxons alike. And to some degree, even though Roman law on the Continent gave authority greater powers than the Common Law permitted it in England, its element of equity may still be felt to have contributed there to a persistent, if less successful, civic thrust.

As a result of feudal mutuality, Christianity and the influence of Roman law, the later despotisms of Western and Central Europe never became quite unmitigated. And by the latter part of the nineteenth century, this never quite abandoned notion of the *Rechtstaat* prevailed over most of the continent: finally (from the 1860s) even, as an import, in Russia.

The feudal style of civic order, with its system of rights and obligations, was powerful in many parts of Europe where it was later crushed — for example, in Aragon. The despotisms which arose in the fifteenth to seventeenth centuries were traditionalist rather than messianic: they amounted to the concentration of political power at the centre, and usually under the old dynasty, with the general elimination of the older popular elements. In fact, as Karl Mannheim points out, the 'democratisation' of the late Middle Ages was followed by a retrograde tendency in which European society became 're-feudalised'. The condition of the peasantry in the France of the thirteenth century was better than in the France of the eighteenth century; just as the Russia of 1910 was better than the Russia of 1970.

Till Philip II, or Louis XIV, the civic element was still putting up a struggle, just as in England, till William III, the despotic element in Britain still seemed capable of victory.

The general effect of the victory of 'absolutism' in France from Louis XIV's time was to prevent political and economic evolution, in marked contrast to the splendid, if flawed, period in British history from the 1690s to the 1760s. In France the Revolution can be seen, from a constructive point of view, as the release of tensions, like a sudden slip in the San Andreas Fault, so that the long overdue emergence of the market economy in the countryside could eventuate. It could be and has been argued that the excesses were in some sense unavoidable, and that by the time of the Third Republic France had gradually settled down to a situation already achieved by Britain. According to this view, the Commune was the last temblor of the catastrophe.

Unfortunately, the mere fact that a civic tradition had been so largely destroyed, and a revolutionary messianic tradition had had such a run for its money, left the latter too powerfully embedded in the French consciousness for safety, particularly when, as we see today, it is possible for international totalitarian traditions from backward countries to provide support and encouragement to the local product.

One of the leading contemporary historians of the French Revolution has told me that Burke did not understand it. In a sense, this is clearly true. And nor did Robespierre. Indeed, it could be argued that in some respects no contemporary at all understood it, since detailed investigation of who was doing what and why naturally did not take place at the time. Experts were not polling the people of Poitou.

So, Burke did not understand the crises of the rural market and so forth. What he did understand was Utopian political mania and its inevitable results.

For regardless of all considerations of its inevitability in given circumstances, or of its possible benefits in the long run, the catastrophic type of revolution is an event *sui generis,* carrying with it its own specific stigmata.

For a revolutionary situation brings to the surface not (or usually not) the people who might, even through a temporary dictatorship, control the process and leave the country prepared for the future which would follow these catastrophic events as their true and natural result. It brings to the fore not people relevant to the future but, on the contrary, people relevant to a Utopia outside time.

The countries with a 'feudal' style of society had been through different experiences. In Russia consensual feudalism was totally destroyed by the major and long-lasting disaster of Mongol rule. In France the emergence of the Bourbon autocracy was not as devastating. Remnants of the old institutions remained, and arbitrary rule was to some extent held back, particularly in certain provinces, by the survival of law. Nevertheless, generations of despotism had produced the despotic habit both among the rulers and, as it turned out, among that decisive section of revolutionaries which, deprived of civic roots, turned to millenarian fantasy. The history of France since then has been that of a long, and not invariably or ever totally successful, attempt to restore the civic society.

In Germany a similar development of autocracy, mitigated only, in certain areas, by the smallness of the political units, had its effect immensely worsened by the frightful catastrophe of the Thirty Years' War, from which (it has been said) the German mind never recovered. We hardly need to be reminded of the survival of the old autocratic trend and its combination, by the horrible genius of Hitler, with the radical millenarian tendency.

Similar things might be said about Italy and, in general, about all the countries of Europe except Britain, Holland and Switzerland. . . . In a sense, indeed, Marx himself recognised this, when at various times he exempted England, America and Holland from the necessity for a violent revolution, even though this implied that the countries of classical capitalism were precisely those which were the exceptions to Marxist principle.

We should note one peculiarity which distinguished the English Parliament, almost from the medieval start, from most of its then equivalents on the Continent: the representatives of the shires and cities sat together as a single chamber. The merchants and the knights were thrown into collaboration. For there were two partially separate civic trends. In the newly developing towns specific liberties and independences were needed for the development of trade; in the countryside the traditional desire for consultation and order remained.

The cities, if inadequately supported by the countryside, might gain the independences they needed, become richer and more flourishing, and yet succumb to internal instabilities and autocracies based on the very rich, or become victims to bands of semi-professional soldiery attracted by the wealth. As in ancient Greece, the Italian cities succumbed one by one, revived, succumbed again.

One of the few areas where the civic order prevailed almost uninterruptedly was Switzerland. As has been pointed out, on the face of it the country had none of the qualifications for statehood, let alone for a stable civic order. It lacked ethnic, cultural, economic and later religious unity. It was a strange alliance of small communities of farmers, cities, minor feudal lordlings, each generally supporting the others, in a network of rights and obligations built up piecemeal. But this very pluralism meant that, apart from England, Switzerland was the main repository of civic permanence. Wordsworth's

> Two Voices are there; one is of the sea,
> One of the mountains; each a mighty Voice.
> In both from age to age thou didst rejoice,
> They were thy chosen music, Liberty!

is a slight but not intolerable exaggeration. Elsewhere it is particularly striking to see the Iceland of the saga period, a country with no state machinery whatsoever, nevertheless forming into a community of settlements scattered over a huge area under the shield of a traditional Law, often broken, but always eventually prevailing.

Geographical detail played a large role. We have only to think of

Britain on its island, of Holland behind its marshes, of Switzerland in its mountains. Economic geography is also relevant — but it will not be necessary to repeat old and widely known facts.

Apart from this, it does appear equally fortunate that these original small civic states were not sooner or later overwhelmed from outside by the superior power of the despotisms. Partly this may indeed have been sheer luck. But it is also true that the civic states produced a disproportionate level of invention, technique, perhaps initiative in a broader sense, which time and again balked a more powerful adversary, as when the *Revenge* 'justified her designers'.

Consensuality has indeed been latent in, or has penetrated and influenced, countries far outside the Anglo-Saxon, or the European, sphere. The civic political concept and practice has arisen on its own in other cultures; while in some parts of the world the Western variant has been incorporated in older local traditions. But, however one looks at it, outside this civic culture one can only speak at present of various forms of barbarism, some being dead ends based on traditional ideas of despotism, others being the product of newer styles of closed dogma, though often the new dogma will similarly be seen to interact with the earlier despotic traditions of a given country.

A reasonable division of the world would take into account, first, those countries where democratic stability has been achieved — in effect, the Anglo-Saxon lands with a handful of others in North Europe and elsewhere; second, countries such as France, Germany and Italy, where the democratic tradition is strong, but where the forces of barbarism and dogma have also shown their power in the fairly recent past; next, those countries, to be found all over the world, where the influence of the democratic idea is powerful, though perhaps not so deeply rooted. And even in the countries we may define as politically barbarian, we can distinguish between those in which the regime is simply imposed by outside forces, those which, however rooted in despotism, yet contain visible elements of democratic yearnings, and those where little or none of such promise is at present visible.

It is not, of course, the case that political liberty is not feasible outside the English-speaking culture or even outside Western Europe. A few South American countries maintain a democratic stability. Governments have been changed by election in Ceylon, in India, and elsewhere. All the same, it will surely be agreed that the stability of the roots, in some of these countries at least, is weak. That is not to say they cannot be strengthened.

It is equally true that there are states all around the world which, if not yet developed to the stage of political liberty, are yet in various modes of transition, or potential transition, towards it. We should not necessarily condemn in the abstract corrupt or dictatorial beginnings of assimilation to the democratic culture. On this criterion a backward, 'feudalistic', 'reactionary'-looking group may be preferable to a militant band of officers and intellectuals who wish to replace incipient 'democracy' with a modern totalitarian dictatorship.

The persistence of the Western civic tradition, on the basis of fairly small nation-states carrying through that tradition from tribal times, had little parallel in a large part of Asia. There, on the contrary, large-scale despotic empires to a decisive extent destroyed the older tribalisms and eliminated, or at best froze, their 'political' traditions. Some of the smaller Asian states may, however, be thought to retain a scale (often reinforced by an ethnic solidarity) which could eventually take as a graft (or have already done so) the civic traditions developed elsewhere.

In Africa, on the other hand, 'tribal' societies with a genuine consensual tradition existed over most of the sub-Sahara area almost up to the present day. On the face of it, development like that of Western Europe would be easy and natural.'Tribal'is nowadays usually used as a hostile adjective. But, in fact, these societies, whatever their formal organisation, were conducted largely on a basis of discussion and consensus. It might be argued, though it would require greater knowledge of the subject than I myself possess, that such 'tribalism', if it can indeed be transformed and used as a basis for a more modern style of state, remains a major hope for large parts of the continent. And, however mistakenly it turned out in practice, it is fairly clear that Kenyatta's original conception of Mau-mau was in one sense an attempt to use tribalism for this purpose. It is, of course, true that (as in Western Europe) there were polities of despotic character in Africa — in the south, for instance, where, at various times of war and the mass movement of peoples, tribal communities have been virtually destroyed, leaving groups of broken men to be incorporated (as with the Zulus) into new nations tribal in form but despotic in character, and in the Niger Basin in the eighteenth century, where social collapse and distortions were produced by the Arab and Western slave trade. But it may be doubted whether these centralised

dynastic states lasted long enough, for the most part, truly to eradi-
cate the *traditions* of consensus. On the other hand, the present
states of Black Africa, with very few exceptions, have no *ethnic* unity
(the major exception, Botswana, appears as a model of non-violent
and consensual development). Most inherit the frontiers arrived at
on a pragmatic basis between the French, the British and the other
colonial powers. The unity of these states reposes not on any ethnic
basis, but on a political, bureaucratic and commercial trans-tribal
class or caste.

A curious development from this is the abandonment in Africa
of the principle of self-determination: in Katanga, in Biafra, in the
Ogaden — wherever an attempt has been made to secure self-determination, the principle of the inviolability of the artificial frontiers of
the new African states has outweighed it.

An important point, though perhaps not decisive, is that the unity
of many of the post-imperial states is thus strongly determined
by the use of a non-national language. There is nothing new in this.
In Hungary, up to the nineteenth century, Latin was the official
language, and it must at least be given part of the credit for holding
together the disparate races (Magyar, Romanian, Croat, Slovak)
which formed the Hungarian kingdom. When Magyar nationalism
and the Magyar language supervened, the other nations became the
perhaps inevitable agents of the eventual break-up of the state. The
position is the same today in much of Africa and Asia. English and
French form the bond in many areas. The attempt in India, in particular, to impose Hindi, while understandable enough, has already
had fissiparous results. (On the other hand, while the fact that many
states of Africa use the English or French languages by no means
implies any automatic reliance on Britain or France, nevertheless,
combined with the traditional links, the languages certainly constitute a closer tie than otherwise subsists between Africa and the
West or any other part of the world and hence link the continent
with examples of advanced economy and polity.)

Basic African communities and similar 'primitive' social arrangements may thus be regarded as societies which were in a sense civic,
though they were not 'open', and may be thought to contain the
possibility of becoming 'open' in a way that the Asiatic despotisms
did not. Yet this may, after all, have some implications when it comes
to the type of state likely to be most promising in a continent like
Africa. For if this virtue resides in tribalism, it might seem that

African states should not be conglomerate, as they are now, but should be based on actual nations. Otherwise (or so it could be argued) the political processes within such states are not seeking new versions of the traditional forms of balancing interests, but are tending rather to a struggle, or at best a bargaining, between political intellectuals projected from different communities; which is not to say that in some cases the sound tribal traditions might not be transmitted through an acceptable federalism of the component nations.

For, admitting that the present boundaries are often very artificial, one cannot say that groupings of diverse, and to some degree, hostile, ethnic elements automatically exclude favourable development. Britain itself has emerged from a long interaction between different racial groups. Indeed, to narrow it further, Scotland arose (not without conflict, indeed) out of the merging of four different stocks (five, if one counts the Norse element). And the Swiss case is even more relevant. It would be worth examining some of the perspectives, under this conception, for the development of democracy from the 'tribal' forms, often now suppressed but still with their own vitality, in Africa.

To the extent that, on the contrary, despotisms (particularly of the new 'Marxist' type) prevail, the economic basis for serious advance would also be largely absent. Bryan Magee has pointed out in *Popper* that the reason why the

> dozen odd countries with the highest living standards are all liberal democracies, is not because democracy is a luxury which their wealth enables them to afford; on the contrary, the mass of their people were living in poverty when they achieved universal suffrage. The casual connection is the other way round.

Which is to say that just as the USSR is technologically parasitic on the West, precisely because it is the Western political culture that is the condition of technological advance, so the states of Africa would tend to remain in the same condition to the degree that they became Leninised or otherwise decivilised. As is notorious, the 'Third World' demand for aid from the West, though constant and powerful, has produced little sign of a rise of independently prosperous economies, in spite of the enormous investment (that is, except in a few cases like Singapore, which has become prosperous by relying on not aid but investment). Which is only to say that a society can make serious economic progress in the modern sense if it provides conditions which the world's capital can utilise.

Apart from the profounder questions of the civic tradition and its connection with a developing economy, it is also the case that it is unlikely that dictatorships will be enlightened enough to maintain conditions suitable for investment. And this is particularly so when the ideologies going the rounds regard the investor as natural prey.

It is equally true that mere aid is unlikely to achieve important results. For the maintenance of new politico-commercial elites, far larger in numbers than the state can normally afford, often depends greatly on access to this money.

Unlike Africa, in South America we find countries which, generally speaking, appear to be nation-states. One or another Latin language is normal to a high proportion of most of their populations, and they are within areas which are distinguished each from the other by a certain 'national' differentiation. As against this, it may be urged that in many of these countries the civic roots have been weak. They did not in any case base themselves on Indian tribalism, and in important areas that tribalism had anyhow already given place to despotic empires. The Spanish immigration was not from the most civically developed part of Western Europe; it took place, after the first turbulent years, under central bureaucratic control; and in most areas the liberalism was an import of nineteenth-century Europe rather than a natural development.

It is sometimes said that the consensual politics of developing countries can be practised under a 'one-party democracy'. Our Saxon and Scandinavian ancestors went in for a good deal of discussion of the issues before the community without 'party' organisations. The same seems to be true of at least some well-studied tribes and tribal confederations. The political sophistication of the Iroquois may have been rather exaggerated, but in any event the constitution of the Six Nations was a complex method of securing agreement by debate and consent. In these cases one cannot ordinarily speak of a party system (though there might be a war 'party' and a peace 'party' over long periods among the Senecas and Mohawks). And if a similar level of discussion could be obtained under a one-party system in modern circumstances, this would not be a bad defence of the non-totalist, one-party system, *faute de mieux*. In some cases this seems a genuine perspective.

But, in general, defenders of the one-party system in the up and coming states do not take this line. They fall back rather on the

Fascist notion of a single national party expressing the national will in a mystical sort of fashion, particularly in the case of 'nations' fortuitously fenced in by former imperial boundaries.

A couple of generations ago, it was everywhere felt that the Western democratic model was the most advanced. Semi-feudal monarchies claimed to be looking forward as far as possible to the eventual development of the same system. Dictatorships in the least advanced parts of the world proclaimed themselves as transitional stages in their evolution in that same direction.

After the establishment of the Leninist regime in Russia, there was a change. It became acceptable for a regime to proclaim itself advanced and forward-looking while openly modelling itself, at least to some degree, on the Leninist conception. Thus we see military dictatorships, which even thirty years ago would have been thought of as signs of backwardness and instability, presented as progressive in themselves and not requiring the excuse that they are preparatory to the system of the advanced countries. The new political primitivism of communist-style politics is thus assimilated to the traditional despotisms of the Third World.

There were, it is true, as there still are, states like Turkey, where occasional military dictatorships still aim at the eventual assimilation of their country to the Western model and a hand-over to the constitutionalists. There still are quite a number of one-party regimes (like that in Tunisia) which do not claim metaphysical justification; that is to say, they do not present a one-party state itself as the most modern and most admirable form of state. Lacking ideological self-righteousness, they hold out the hope of evolving into something different.

But, more commonly, the regressive dogmas of Leninism have provided 'modern' sounding justifications for a retreat from reason and progress in the Third World. This can yet be halted. One of the requirements would be a firm and forthright lead, both political and intellectual, from the advanced democracies themselves.

CHAPTER 4

The Despotic Tradition

When we turn to non-consensual, 'command' society we find that it too goes back— if not as far as our own, at least to the beginning of recorded history. The original centralised despotisms, in the valleys of the Nile, the Tigris-Euphrates and the Indus, arose from the needs of a centralised irrigation system. There are indeed important differences between the regularly flooding Nile and its regulation and the more erratic rivers of Mesopotamia, and enormous differences between the continual troubles of the refractory city-states of Sumeria and the rare but extreme disasters of centralised Egypt. As with every general point one may make about human history, the detailed reservations and nuances tend to trap one into abandoning the argument in favour of complete differentiation. Yet the central points, it seems agreed, remain: the great increment of benefit from a unified economy covering huge areas; the rise, through necessity, of a sizeable central bureaucracy; the distancing and elevation of the rulers; the concentration of the local chiefdoms' scattered mana into a single god-king.

Other and later despotisms arose on a different basis: perhaps at first, as has been suggested, through mere imitation; through the degeneration of consensual republics into vast slave-trading empires; and, later (the Russian case) as a consequence of the mere necessity for centralisation in providing and supplying armies, on an open frontier, of a size far greater, and for far longer, than any feudal consensualism could ever manage.

Under the traditional, and to a considerable extent the retraditionalised, despotisms, a 'pre-critical' attitude prevailed. No one could envisage a different order of things. There could be risings, anarchy, civil war, but the aim was always a new pharaoh or tsar.

But a new totalist tradition arose early: the possible establishment on earth of a new but perfect despotism with revolutionary and transcendental aims. In a Rome which made no traditional call on the loyalties of its newly conquered slaves, in an ambience where the 'critical' Greek ideas had entered a social debate already not far removed from consensual chiefdom, came Spartacus and the idea of the City of the Sun. There were individual Utopians like Nabis of Sparta. In a Jewry conquered but refusing to abandon its claim to be the chosen race, millenarian sects arose.

Despotism thus presented, in effect, two forms of Utopia, one for the future and one for the present. The former is easier to picture in glowing colours, but we need not forget that Marx's teacher, Hegel, was quite capable of representing the Prussian state of the early nineteenth century as the perfect realisation of the Idea. Generally speaking, despotism is represented either as in principle perfect, or as heading for perfection: as a system divinely ordained, or historically determined, or scientifically correct.

When we look at the millenarian revolutionaries of the present century, we are too apt to regard them as a new (even a typically 'modern') phenomenon. This is only because there was a long period when they were rare in Europe. In reality, the attitude is an old one, and this new 'revolutionary' despotism, far from being new in essence, is merely outside recent Western experience. In fact (apart from the particular nature of the verbalisms), it is a revival of previous millenarian despotic movements of, for example, the fifteenth century in central Europe or of the T'ai-ping in nineteenth-century China, which, equally, (a) promised to bring history to a conclusion and (b) guaranteed achievements so high that all oppressions were justified to bring them to pass.

Current despotisms, or a certain array of despotisms, have done no more than partly confuse the issue by a veneer of modernity. That is, the new radical revolutionary movements which erected the post-1917 despotisms have created backward, pre-civic polities, but have used the phraseology of 'science'. Their backwardness is to some extent concealed by this employment of a modern style of justificatory jargon; in fact, they are just a variant of atavism.

It is most remarkable how strongly the writings and actions of the revolutionary-messianic type resemble each other down the centuries. And, of course, revolutionaries have admitted, or rather exalted, the resemblance. Norman Cohn remarks (in later editions of *The Pursuit of the Millennium*) that Communism and Nazism are inclined to be 'baffling for the rest of us' because of the very features they have inherited from an earlier phase in our culture, now forgotten, but still appealing to more backward areas of the world. In such countries as Russia and China the apocalyptic view has been 'appropriated and transformed by an intelligentsia which, alike in its social situation and in the crudity and narrowness of its thinking, strikingly recalls the *prophetae* of medieval Europe'.

As Cohn points out, both Nazis and Marxists themselves often proclaimed their affinity with the millenarian demagogues of the period of the German Peasant War, claiming that these were men born centuries before their time; but, as he says, 'it is perfectly possible to draw the opposite moral—that, for all their exploitation of the most modern technology, Communism and Nazism have been inspired by phantasies which are downright archaic'. (Cohn might have adduced as a truly striking confirmation of his view of the shared traditions of Communism and Nazism the fact that Florian Geyer, hero of Engels's *The Peasant War in Germany*, also gave his name to an SS Division.)

As with the chiliastic movements of centuries long past, modern revolutionaries have, as Cohn points out, pictured the coming society much as did their medieval predecessors: 'as a state of total community, a society wholly unanimous in its beliefs and wholly free from inner conflicts'. And each in turn 'claimed to be charged with the unique mission of bringing history to its preordained consummation'. Cohn notes with special point:

> And what followed then was the formation of a group of a peculiar kind, a true prototype of a modern totalitarian party: a restlessly dynamic and utterly ruthless group which, obsessed by the apocalyptic phantasy and filled with the conviction of its own infallibility, set itself infinitely above the rest of humanity and recognised no claims save that of its own supposed mission.

A certain confusion can be seen on both sides in the fairly common assertion (equally commonly denied) that Communism is a sort of religion. Of course, it is perfectly true that Communism cannot be called a religion in any ordinary sense, and if all that is meant is that it attracts, in some cases, a fanatical devotion, the same could be said of attachments to nation, to regiment, to football team. On the other hand, Communism may be thought to be like religion, or like some religions, in that it nourishes the conviction that human history tends eschatologically towards its destined end.

Of course, we are always promised by revolutionaries that *their* revolution will be free from the defects which have attended every previous one. Their remedies and precautions are somewhat lacking in substance, but by abjuring the experience of all real cases, they put themselves in the happy position or being beyond, or below, argument. 'Criticism is almost baffled in discovering the defects of what has not existed; and eager enthusiasm and cheating hope have all the wide field of imagination, in which they may expatiate with little or no opposition' (Burke, *Reflexions on the Revolution in France*).

The present situation is, of course, unique, like all previous situations; and the particular polities now existing equally have their own singular and specific characteristics. Nevertheless, there is nothing novel about the existence of a civic culture in some countries and a despotic one in others; nor, among the latter, of the temporary emergence of political orders claiming the 'messianic' power to bring history to its final end. Present ones may seem novel to us, not only because they have not, in the immediately preceding epoch, played much of a role on the world scene, but also because present-day political eschatology is couched in terms which, on the surface, seem to be assimilated to certain political dialects of the established civic cultures, and even, by a logical confusion, to constitute no more than an extreme and total case of ideas operating normally in the civic order.

It was not until modern times that messianic despotism contrived to hold power for more than a few years. Modern techniques have, of course, made it possible for despotism to be taken to the extreme and held. The 'Ghengis Khan with a telegraph' whose arrival Herzen feared has already been among us in more than one guise.

The old traditionalist despotisms had certain advantages. If long-established, they could rely on the people identifying them with the country as a whole; they had partly adopted themselves, partly imposed on the people, unconscious sentiments of solidarity, if not precisely of community. The new, revolutionary despotisms had opposite advantages; coming when their predecessors had finally antagonised vast sections of the population, they could present themselves as the new, the only, alternative (just as in *Animal Farm* all repugnance to the new regime is blocked by the cry 'You don't want Jones back'). They could rely, at least for the short intervening period while they consolidated, on generous impulses to justice. And they could nourish, at least among a section of their followers, the mystique of a new (party) solidarity.

The revolutionary despotism, persisting, incorporates the habits of the older despotism it has succeeded. Indeed, if we compare the Russia and Britain of today with the Russia and Britain of 1830, we will note that in Russia the previous institutions had been destroyed and new ones created, to the accompaniment of the physical destruction of the earlier classes and elites, mass 'social engineering' slaughter generally, and so on; while in England the institutions and the elites evolved in what is, on the face of it, a far milder and less complete fashion. Yet the Russia of today is far more like the Russia of 1830 than the England of today is like the England of 1830.

It is, indeed, a characteristic of radical totalitarian movements—at any rate of successful ones—that an incorporation of 'reactionary' methods of nation-binding has given them extra power and appeal. As George Orwell points out, 'the idea of National Socialism which Hitler brought to fruition was one of the most appealing demagogic inventions of the twentieth century', while the true German 'Nationalist' movement under Hugenburg achieved little and the various 'internationalist' Socialist bodies were ineffective.

In the war the Stalinists too turned to the resources of a national socialism for survival. Not only were all the old paraphernalia of tsarist officerdom and history brought into play, but anti-Semitism (usually noted for the first time in Soviet official circles in 1943-4) was also resurrected from the tsarist past.

A revolutionary despotism is, for several reasons, almost bound to institute, sooner or later, a terror on a scale not to be found elsewhere. First, of course, it is obvious enough that any radical dictatorship with a programme involving the destruction of whole classes or races is bound to rely on a larger degree of terror than a merely 'reactionary' regime needs. But beyond that we should consider an even more profound point: a radical revolutionary regime comes to power after its predecessor has lost the minds of the thinking classes in campaigns of 'critical' argument; and the whole revolution, including the new ruling party itself, is highly charged with the idea and the habit of making politics the subject of critical thought and debate. On the other hand, the whole intent of the revolution is to institute the rule of infallible messianic theory which alone has the right and power to bring history to its single, foreordained end. And this implies a complete reversion to pre-critical society, in which it is impossible to exercise the judgment on the form of state. Plainly, this is conceptually a very difficult task and must involve the destruction of the whole attitude which the revolution once deployed against the former rulers. It can only be done effectively by a most thorough use of terror against the revolutionary class itself.

Primitive and ideological polities tend, moreover, to endless expansionism, on universalist (sometimes, though not always, theological) grounds. The messianic despotisms have almost automatically included the expansionist notion that they were designed to prevail over all mankind.

Despotism, especially 'scientific' ideological despotism, which appears to be the rational, ordered form, in fact contains greater elements of irrationality than our own culture. Ours, it is true, usually involves an attachment to ancient rights on a piecemeal, and even sentimental, basis not easily amenable to rationalisation. But it also contains the element of debate and argument, as well as a feeling of deeper and less conscious needs, even if these have not been susceptible to adequate verbal elaboration. Despotism contains within itself all the elements of a more extreme irrationality: the elimination of real debate and criticism and the idolisation of premature political perfectionism. In fact, the backwardness of modern despotisms resides not merely in the parallels which may be seen between them and the bureaucratic empires of the past, but also in the factors thought to constitute their modernity.

CHAPTER 5

Reality and Rationalisation

Society is less malleable than simple-minded revolutionaries and others suppose. George Orwell wrote, in his essay, *England, Your England, that*

> it needs some very great disaster, such as a prolonged subjugation by a foreign enemy, to destroy a national culture... England will still be England, an everlasting animal stretching into the future and into the past, like all living things having the power to change out of recognition and yet remain the same.

But a similar point could be made of any culture, at any point in history. For the moment let us note the case of Czechoslovakia, where the events of 1968, after twenty years of high-powered political distortion, prove the comparative inextirpability of civic habits in another area where they were well established.

There are some remarkable examples of the continuity of cultural elements through century after turbulent century which might have been supposed to destroy them. A symbolic example, nevertheless very striking, is the great White Horse of the White Horse Vale, carved on the downs near Uffington some two thousand years ago, which would have disappeared very quickly had it not been kept clear, and in its unchanged Celtic form, by sixty or seventy generations of successive strains of locals.

As Burke notes, the great fault of every sort of arbitrary rule is the superficiality of imagining that political and similar difficulties can be disposed of by main force. This is, he points out, in a famous passage in *Reflexions on the Revolution in France,* laziness and evasion:

> Amicable conflict with difficulty obliges us to an intimate acquaintance with our object, and compels us to consider it in all its relations. It will not suffer us to be superficial. It is the want of nerves of understanding for such a task, it is the degenerate fondness for tricking shortcuts, and little fallacious facilities, that has in so many parts of the world created governments with arbitrary powers. They have created the late arbitrary monarchy of France. They have created the arbitrary republic of Paris. With them defects in wisdom are to be supplied by the plenitude of force. They get nothing by it. Commencing their labours on a principle of sloth, they have the common fortune of slothful men. The difficulties, which they rather had eluded than escaped, meet them again in their course; they multiply and thicken on them; they are involved, through a labyrinth of confused detail, in an industry without limit, and without direction; and, in conclusion, the whole of their work becomes feeble, vicious and insecure.

Orwell similarly remarks of the 'mental coarseness' of revolutionaries, who 'imagine that everything can be put right by altering the shape of society'. He might have added that there is something infantile or childish in the whole revolutionary-despotic approach, which is, in effect, based on the simple-minded attitude 'If I were King. . . .', that it only needs a well-intentioned man in power to solve everything by mere decree.

In despotisms of whatever style politics properly speaking can hardly be said to exist. There are the skills of intrigue among a narrow group of those closest to the instruments of power; but though on a more impressive stage, these are exercised within limits appropriate to a parish council. Administrative skills may, indeed, be very highly developed. But these again, though necessary in any state, do not themselves constitute the substance of politics. Real politics is an immensely untidy art, dependent more on the habits of a culture and the experience of centuries than on any political science or on concepts worked out in the abstract in studies or reading rooms.

The first true studies of politics, in particular that of Aristotle, were already historical; that is, they (or the best of them) were not abstract speculations but were based rather on several generations of experience in a score of real political units. It is no accident that both of the greatest writers on politics (the other being Machiavelli) had experience of, or immediate access to, a large number of variously ruled states. It is perhaps not to be wondered at that a professor, separated by thousands of miles of space (or reams of paper) from any but the most indirect and misinterpreted notions of other types of polity, should come to shallower conclusions.

A delusion common even in the West, at least among academics, is that 'social' problems in particular are susceptible, in principle, of being solved by political decision. It is this error which has led many backward countries further and further into the grip of incompetent terrorists. Each time a solution imposed by force has, after all, failed to improve matters, it is thought that the fault is merely that insufficient power has been put behind it. If one more refractory social group is liquidated, if party discipline is tightened and all shirkers and compromisers adequately dealt with, then next time all will be well. We should have learned by now from these unfortunate 'social experiments' that there are problems which cannot be dealt with even by the maximum application of political power.

But even genuine social improvements may be unacceptable if imposed by force. Frau Heydrich has told us (*Sunday Express,* 8 August 1965) that her husband 'introduced higher education and health insurance and raised the standard of living' and that the British had him killed because he was, in this way, winning over the Czechs. Similar errors are being made today.

Of course, it is true that (usually) despotisms have to some degree to take into account the feeling of the various classes of the public: but to take them into account as forces outside the system, like the weather or the incidence of snow in the Ural mountains—that is, in a purely passive capacity. Revolutionary states have in no case succeeded in transforming their cultures so much that they can relax the pressures or bring the populace into the polity. The situation is particularly unlike that foreseen by Marx, who held that the revolutionary state, through a dictatorship of the proletariat (a phrase by which he did not in any case imply the rule of a minority machine), would start to 'wither away' immediately. In all the revolutionary countries the current structure of society can only be maintained by the constant pressure of the administrative organs holding everything in a state of special strain. They are left regarding as the central moral principle the mere protection of their own rule. By definition, this is the ideal system, no longer requiring objective justification (or only perfunctorily) as with the legitimists of the declining period of the European monarchies.

Revolutionaries, and some reformers, speak of 'radical' change. It is worth remembering that such change is not necessarily *greater* than those associated with the gradualist approach. Cutting the tap-root is in one sense *a lesser* operation than lopping off a number of dead branches. To pursue the metaphor further, it is also much easier to kill a tree, and requires considerably less knowledge of dendrology, than effectively to prune it. Two things distinguish political civilisation from its obverse: first, the realisation by all major parties in a state that their own coming to power should not be regarded as permission totally to reorganise society according to formulae, wholly to ignore the sentiments of a large minority or to crush other views; second, the realisation that no abstract formulae for reorganising society, as distinct from amending specific faults, have any validity.

One of the most misleading ideas of modern times is that of 'democracy', in the sense of the absolute right of the temporary electoral (or merely legislative) majority to impose its will. The British system, in particular, lends itself to this excess—or at least, the exaggerated notion of the 'sovereignty of Parliament' does. Not that this is the right interpretation of our constitutional arrangements. As C. H. Sisson points out, the essential of the monarchy, of the continuity of Her Majesty's Government, is that it represents the past and the future as against the government provided by a brief House of Commons majority supported by 38 per cent of the voters.

The pseudo-'democratic' implication is, first, that the minority has no rights in a 'democracy' except at the will of the victors and, second, that the inhabitants of the past and future have no rights either — the brief cross-section of a culture's present moment can destroy the past and commit the future.

As against this, the practitioners and thinkers of the real politics of the continuing community have always held, in Madison's words (*The Federalist Papers,* No. 51), that 'in a society under the forms of which the stronger faction can readily unite and oppress the weaker, anarchy may . . . truly be said to reign'. Again, in the tenth Federalist Paper, he defines as a faction 'a number of citizens, *whether amounting to a majority or a minority* of the whole, who are united and actuated by some common impulse of passion, or of interest, adverse to the rights of other citizens, or to the permanent and aggregate interests of the community'. Other founders or re-founders of the American system, like Jefferson, were equally clear about the danger of the 'tyranny of the majority'.

The principles of democracy include the absence of fanaticism. It is no part of the democratic culture that a government elected by a bare majority, or even by a fairly large majority, is thereby empowered totally to reconstruct the social and political order by sacrificing the minority. Michael Oakeshott notes that for some people government is 'an instrument of passion; the art of politics is to inflame and direct desire'. For others, which is to say, in general, for those who have a traditional regard for the unity and continuity of a culture, the business of government is something different: 'to restrain, to deflate, to pacify, and to reconcile; not to stoke the fires of desire, but to damp them down', on the grounds that, as Oakeshott puts it, 'the conjunction of dreaming and ruling generates tyranny'. For it is a basic principle of true, as against despotic, politics that it is more important for the civic system as such to be unshaken than for particular measures to be opposed or insisted on to the limit. A democratic community enjoying political liberty is only a possibility when the attachment of the majority of the citizens to political liberty is stronger than their attachment to specific political doctrines. And this is to say that on many controversial issues a certain comparative apathy must prevail amongst a large part of the population. But apathy cannot appear a virtue to the man who has committed himself to an intellectually elaborated scheme or policy.

In a famous investigation of the politics of the small town of Elmira, New York, in the 1950s, the scholars concerned (Paul Lazarfeld, Bernard Berelson and William McPhee) were at first surprised by the results. The democratic processes had worked very satisfactorily in the town for a very long period. So, on theoretical principles, the researchers expected to find the citizenry well-informed about political issues, with firm and clear-cut opinions. They found, on the contrary, that the majority were fairly ill-informed and fairly apathetic. They concluded, after admirable heart-searching on their own part, that this was the condition for a working democracy. On the other hand, it may be urged that the instability of many of the Greek states was due to the devotion to politics of all concerned and that, to a lesser degree, this has been the cause of many of the difficulties met with in France in the last fifty years — though it is suggested that the ideological enthusiasm of the French electorate has been to some extent compensated for by the cynicism and apathy of the deputies themselves.

Dean Acheson remarks of the 'moral values of Graeco-Judaic-English thought' that they are, in particular, capable of accepting the mixed motivation of real individuals and peoples without lapsing into cynicism or Utopianism. And political civilisation is not primarily a matter of the good will of leaderships or of ideal constitutions. It is, above all, a matter of time and custom.

All the major troubles we have had in the last twenty or thirty years have been caused by people who have let politics become a mania. The politician should be a servant and should play a limited role. For what our political culture has stood for (as against the principles of total theorists and abstractionists) is the view of society as a developing and broadening of established liberties and responsibilities, and the belief, founded in experience, that in political and social matters long-term predictions, however exciting and visionary, seldom work out.

Nor is an abstract 'libertarian' principle of much use in real life. Since a political order of a consensual type depends on the maintenance of a strong mediating state, since liberty and law are mutually dependent, it follows that when state and law are threatened by immediate danger, they have the duty to defend themselves, even at the cost of a temporary suspension of particular rights.

People forget what a remarkable thing it is that in our countries we have these rights and liberties. Civilisations have existed for thousands of years in which there was no trace of the mere idea of criticising the government, of being secure from arbitrary arrest, of having a fair trial (or even a fairish trial, or even a trial at all), of printing almost anything one likes, of voting for one of a number of candidates for public office.

The maintenance of liberties, the principle of the accommodation of various interests, the preserving of balances, imply totally different aims and attitudes in the civic politician from those prevailing among revolutionaries and despots. It would be impossible for a representative of those cultures to see that the highest praise possible to confer on a statesman in an advanced society would be in the nature of what was said (by Macaulay) about Halifax: that he was 'the foremost champion of order in the turbulent Parliament of 1680, and the foremost champion of liberty in the servile Parliament of 1685'. It is a good thought that he was one of the key men in securing our liberties, as against the rigid doctrinaires who have presided over the revolutions producing the dreadful regimes of the twentieth century.

Critical thought on politics, beginning with the pre-Socratics, provides a major contrast between our society and the despotisms. As we have already suggested, a most useful conceptual distinction, up to a point, is that between 'pre-critical' (what Popper [in *The Open Societies and its Enemies*] calls 'abstract') societies and the 'critical' ones which, in some cases, followed. In the first, as the phrase implies, the existing arrangements are taken as the natural order of things. And this, of course, applies both to the primitive consensual and to the despotic conditions. Until the time of the Greeks the form of the state was largely or wholly taken for granted. The motto of pharaohs and so on had been in effect, 'We're here because we're here because we're here because we're here.' The sudden outburst of Ionian thought, which subjected the whole universe to enquiry, was soon reflected in an almost totally unrestrained application of reason to the social order and to social behaviour.

As with all grand and fruitful concepts, there are qualifications. It is clear that the Chinese political philosophers, and some of the statesmen and emperors who followed them, had to a certain extent at least made the effort to stand outside the subject and to make (sometimes to implement) radical transformations. (And the little we know about such incidents as Akhnaten's reign in Egypt show that 'critical' temperaments existed, even if only as sports, in the ancient empires.)

But just as it succeeded in creating a strong state without destroying the consensual, only the Western type of society has (so far) deployed the critical attitude without destroying the older loyalties. In this it has been hampered by those concerned to rationalise and verbalise everything, right from the time of the Sophists, who sought to make every attitude and action the product of pure reason and treated as null and negligible the old half-conscious bonds and myths uniting society. But, in fact, the bonds of social order did not become fully conscious; nor could they, any more than the evolution of the consciousness or self-awareness by which the human being distinguishes himself from other animals in any way eliminated the personal unconscious.

Political civilisation is deeply rooted in the tradition of generations. It is modern in that it is open to the search for undogmatic
solutions to unforeseen problems. But it is a modern style which has
not (or not yet) deprived itself of the power of the ancient loyalties
and could not survive if it did.

The post-critical political culture, except to some degree and in
certain areas and periods, has contrived since it emerged to preserve
the unconscious or 'myth' basis of the state while exercising the
critical faculty in politics. And this is the essential of any genuine
progress. As Whitehead put it: 'Those societies which cannot combine
reverence for their symbols with freedom of revision, must ultimately decay.' Men who do not deny their past are wiser than men who
do or who try to. As Burke noted in his *Reflexions on the Revolution
in France,* in the English Petition of Right.

> The parliament says to the king, "Your subjects have *inherited*
> this freedom", claiming their franchises not on abstract princi-
> ples "as the rights of men", but as the rights of Englishmen, and
> as a patrimony derived from their forefathers.

Selden and the other learned men who drew up the Petition were
aware of theories about 'the rights of man'. But they preferred to
ground themselves soundly upon experience rather than on speculation. Something of the sort could be said about the American
Founding Fathers. Arthur Schlesinger, Sr, says of them that they
were 'men of vision without being visionaries'; Carl Bridenbaugh
that they were 'men of intellect, not intellectuals'.

Our political culture depends less on the conscious will of its
citizens, or even on the political institutions which have been found
to provide a suitable mechanism, than on the whole drift of habit
and tradition. As Aristotle put it (in *The Politics*):

> There are plenty of instances of a constitution which according
> to its law is not democratic, but which owing to custom and way
> of upbringing is democratic in its workings; there are likewise
> others which according to law incline towards democracy, but by
> reason of custom and upbringing operate more like oligarchies.

One does not transcend one's culture; one simply deserts it.
Patriotism is, as Orwell remarked, for better or for worse. Stephen
Decatur's famous formulation 'Our country! In her intercourse
with foreign nations, may she always be in the right; but our country

right or wrong' does not state a general abstract principle, but only asserts that in a society of the Western democratic type involvement is inextricable. Those who go outside it are not, in fact, judging from a superior position. They have merely cut their roots. Their attitude is by no means purely rational and moral, but merely a rationalisation of hostility towards their own homeland.

Patriotism is assured, fully rooted in the unconscious and its assumptions, derived from the general traditions in the society working in each psyche. The new nationalisms associated with ideologies are a more artificial product. With them the mere possibility of being 'wrong' does not arise: their 'right' is actually *defined* in terms of their own allegiance. It is necessary to whip them up continually; in war their soldiers require constant hate propaganda.

And here we may note a 'contradiction' in the modern messianic despotisms. Their movements were once, in an important sense, the product of critical rather than pre-critical attitudes. Yet they are now, as we have said, in the position of having to restore the pre-critical attitude as far as their own ideas and organisation are concerned. The dust must be swept back under the carpet, the djinn restored to its bottle. But this is a staggeringly difficult task, both conceptually and administratively. Conceptually it can only be done by extravagant double-think, highly deleterious to the minds elaborating it; organisationally it requires an unprecedented exercise of force, far more than was ever needed by traditionalist despotism. It seems to be partly for this reason that the new-style rule, which needs every possible form of psychological support, turns to the older traditions of its country's imperial despotism.

PART TWO

Despotism Today

CHAPTER 6

Formative Pressures

In our own time the division between the despotic and the civic political cultures (and political psychologies) is more than ever the dominant factor in world affairs. It manifests itself, above all, in the confrontation between the Soviet order and that of the West. Recent advances in communications and in weaponry have brought these opposing cultures into a most immediate, constant and dangerous contiguity. At the same time, the extent and profundity of the differences between them are masked by various superficial phenomena.

The first and most obvious of these is the fact that the Marxist type of despotism, for historical reasons, uses a vocabulary deriving from the Western culture. Its spokesmen sound as though they are saying the same sort of things that we are. It is even the case that the communist countries have shadow institutions resembling those of the West: 'parliaments', 'elections', 'trade unions', and so on—even 'national self-determination'.

At the same time, Western judgment has been misled, partly for internal reasons, partly as a consequence of infection by essentially despotic ideas, towards *étatisme*. For, once it is accepted that the state is able to solve all social problems, the communist despotisms tend to appear simply to be doing that on a particularly grand scale.

A further cause of misunderstanding lies in the fact that many of the basic attitudes of our or any other culture are more or less 'instinctive', or at any rate not always conceptually formulated at any abstract level. The recent increase in the quantity, and decrease in the quality, of education has produced a large class sufficiently well-educated to grasp simple political and social formulae, but not to take the next step and see that even the most attractively packaged formula does not, in fact, accord with the complexities of reality and the unpredictabilities of the future.

It is not so much that the Soviet system is in principle difficult to understand as that those of us brought up to the habits of mind of a totally different culture and tradition find it difficult to make the intellectual effort required for that understanding. In particular, the difference between the consensual political order that has existed in the West for centuries and even millennia and the old despotic orders as of post-Mongol Russia (and similar states) on the one hand and messianic revolutionary despotisms on the other forms a psychological and conceptual barrier which requires a good deal of breaking down.

I do not believe that a true understanding of the Soviet order can be deduced from either its formal 'structure' or the details of its operation. They are not, indeed, to be ignored: but it is rather in the central motivations of those who operate the system, and their attitudes and general methods, that we shall discover (if we can discover at all) the elements that make that system what it is and so different from those to which we are accustomed.

Before considering the Soviet political culture in this way, it may be appropriate to say a word about the other countries of the Soviet bloc, if only to stress that, for both historical and cultural reasons, the communist despotic tradition has put down no roots in these countries. Communist governments have been imposed by force. But as soon as the full rigour of terror has at all relaxed, there have been national, and in particular worker, outbreaks (as in Berlin in 1953, in Plzen in 1953, in Poznan in 1956, in Hungary in 1956, in Czechoslovakia in 1968, in Gdansk in 1970, in Radom in 1976). These prove that the failure of totalitarian ideas in these countries has been total. Even those (or many of those) who had, on purely argumentative grounds, accepted communism in the thirties, were affected by the reality of their own countries, the unreality of the communist solutions —above all by the lies — and went through a revulsion. This applied to Imre Nagy after long training in the USSR, to Dubček, to thousands of others duped by words, but capable of retrieval by facts.

If one wanted to see, in a more general sense, not the revulsion of actual communists, but the feeling of the whole thinking class of an East European country, one could hardly do better than look at the letters of the leading Polish intellectuals in 1976. These were not the men who had been, at one time or another, forced to flee for their views, but the core of those who had stayed. The great thing to notice in their manifestos is that they do not even take communist apologetics seriously. The whole tone of the declarations assumes that the silliness or phoniness of the regime's notions is conceded by all.

The Soviet Union itself is a different matter. We have spoken generally about the 'messianic-despotic' culture. But like all real polities, that of the USSR is *sui generis*, and we should consider its specific characteristics.

In this area, we are in the position of having to proceed not according to any fully established laws, but by the application of historical experience in a more intuitive way: that is, in effect, by analogy. But no analogies from the past can be wholly applicable to the Soviet situation. We are, after all, in the presence of a modern technological economy that is subject to change at a totally different sort of tempo, and with qualitatively different effects, from those which characterised *politically* comparable societies in the past. Nor are analogies from the present wholly applicable either, since the Soviet political structure is critically different from that of *economically* comparable societies. Above all, it is not to be apprehended under categories suitable to quite different political cultures such as our own.

But it has its historical roots and its general principles: in part the entire Russian background, and in part the specific communist political and ideological present. Its ruling elite are the products of centuries of history, of personal and collective experiences, of indoctrination, and of psychological suitability to surviving those experiences and accepting that indoctrination. (Chekhov writes of Russia's 'heavy, chilling history, savagery, bureaucracy, poverty and ignorance . . . Russian life weighs upon a Russian like a thousand-ton rock'.)

Until the Mongol invasion the Russian principalities were going through a 'feudalism' not greatly different from that of the West. It is true enough, as has often been pointed out, that the heritage of Byzantium and Orthodoxy was different from that received in the Catholic and Romano-barbarian West. Nevertheless, an element of consensuality persisted, in part deriving from the Norse tradition of

Russia's early rulers, and the princes could never pretend to act without consultation with and the consent of other elements in society.

The Mongol period which followed was totally different from those of other countries under other conquerors (Spain under the Arabs, Bulgaria under the Turks). As Tibor Szamuely summarises in *The Russian Tradition:*

> The Mongols were rather different from other hordes of Asiatic horsemen that had ravaged Europe during the preceding millennium. They had not only a superb military organisation . . . but a state that, despite its size, was far more efficient than any contemporary European administrative system. They also possessed a very definite set of socio-political ideas.

> The Mongol empire was, in fact, a state grounded on an ideology, an early example of a phenomenon to which the world has since become accustomed; it was not just a state among other states, but, to use an apt description, an *imperium mundi in statu nascendi,* a World-Empire-in-the-Making. Its object was the establishment, by means of a series of wars, of a system of universal peace and of a world-wide social order based on justice and equality. . . . These ideas were embodied in the great Mongol law code, the Yasa, which uncompromisingly laid down the fundamental principle: 'There is equality. Each man works as much as another; there is no difference. . . .'

> The Mongol concept of society was based on the unqualified submission of all to the absolute, unlimited power of the Khan. Every member of society was allotted from above his specific position, to which he was bound for life, and which he could never desert, on pain of death. The Khan was not only invested with unquestioned authority over the lives of his subjects: he was also sole owner of all the land within his domains, and all other persons could hold land only on conditions of temporary tenure. In his role as supreme land proprietor the Khan stood as the embodiment of the principle that all the land in the empire of the Mongol World-Conqueror was to be devoted to the interests of the State, i.e. of the entire community.

Unlike the original European feudalisms, which were in part the product of the virtual disappearance of money and were based on contributions in kind, the Mongols demanded of their Russian fiefs a purely monetary tribute. The subordinate princes of that part of

Russia which the Mongols did not occupy directly had no experience of the type of state required for this purpose; they took its principles directly from the Mongols' own. Not merely its principles, but almost every petty detail of political ritual, vocabulary and even dress. The new Russian state, after the defeat of the Mongols, had an intensely Christian and national character, but was firmly set in the political ways it had learnt from the khans.

Thereafter, the Great Russians (and particularly those originally united under Moscow) lived in an almost permanent state of mobilisation, as the frontier against the continual menace from the steppe. For hundreds of years the threat was permanent. Moscow was sacked by the Crimean Tatars as late as 1571. As a result, Russia had always to keep what was, by the standards of the time, a huge army on the frontier till winter made the routes impassable to raiders. Unlike the brief campaigns of feudal levies in Western Europe, this military service was permanent and universal. Some 65,000 men (it is estimated) were regularly called up, a very large army by comparison with those raised in periods of crisis in France and Germany, which then had considerably larger populations than Russia: the French army at Crécy, the largest hitherto seen in feudal Europe, was 12,000 men, and the Germans could not raise as many as 20,000 to face the great Turkish invasion.

The Russian effort was a killing one. As the great historian Pavel Miliukov wrote, 'Compelling national need resulted in the creation of an omnipotent State on the most meagre material foundation; this very meagreness constrained it to exert all the energies of its population —and in order to have full control over these energies it had to be omnipotent.'

As Trotsky also put it, not only Russian 'feudalism' but all the old Russian history is marked by its 'meagreness': the absence of real cities, the fact that in its attempt to compete with 'richer Europe' the Russian state 'swallowed up a far greater relative part of the people's wealth than in the West, and thereby not only condemned the people to a two-fold poverty but also weakened the foundations of the possessing classes', whose growth was 'forced and regimented'. (The periods of swift industrial growth, both under tsarism and in Soviet times, he notes as being, in fact, the result of that very backwardness.)

And, of course, effective defence entailed expansion.

Rigorous centralisation was enforced over huge territories. Even when it took a year for an order to reach its recipient, even on very petty matters, the decisions were made in Moscow. On the other hand, naturally enough, the great distances made it far more difficult for the scattered subjects to bring any influence to bear on the capital, or to coordinate complaints into any general movement.

The dangers and the distances were exceptional features, leaving their own stamp on the community. (So, clearly, was the extreme climate: a point not to be forgotten when one considers that it is now felt by historians that ancient Athenian politics developed different-ly from those of Thebes, only fifty-odd miles away, since the better weather of Attica led to street and doorstep discussion of an evening when the inhabitants of rainer and mistier Boeotia would be in their houses. One can certainly insist on the even more striking effects of fifty degrees of frost.)

The autocracy of the period between the Mongols and the Emancipation, extreme by most standards, was not (if only for want of the technical possibility) anything like as complete as the post-revolutionary settlement. Nevertheless, it contained some major elements which have persisted, or have revived, under the Soviets. For example, it was the common observation of foreign observers that while the old merchant cities of Novgorod and Pskov, which had emerged beyond the Mongol reach, were regarded by the Hanseatic cities as particular-ly credit-worthy, this trait disappeared on their annexation to Mus-covy. The Hanse now forbade all credit to Russians. It was observed that cheating became endemic. An Englishman of the time gives as a reason that, unable to rely on the future, the Russians thought only of immediate advantage, a point confirmed by a German observer. Under such a style of autocracy, there was no real security, since the state could at any moment take everything away. That is to say, a complete change in economic attitudes was produced by, and solely by, the form and attitudes of the state.

This was true throughout. The British Ambassador to St Peters-burg in Catherine the Great's time remarked: 'The form of govern-ment certainly is and will always be the principal cause of the want of virtue and genius in this country, as making the motive of one and the reward of both depend upon accident and caprice.'

For as Ronald Hingley succinctly puts it (in his *The Russian Mind*), Russia 'never possessed a politically influential upper, middle, or any other class; never any powerful corporate body able to exert irresist-ible pressure on central authority'. Or as a Soviet official told K. S. Karol, correspondent of the *New Statesman* (1 January 1971):

Our country has no civil tradition. The taste for association, for organising communal life together, for getting to know each other and taking decisions together, never really existed in Russia. Between the czar and the moujik there was nothing; equally, between one moujik and another there was nothing except for essential personal relationships. We were and we remain a huge body, colossal even, but shapeless and deprived of articulation, of that political fabric on which the modern states of Europe were built.

The political class has always been merely the servant of the executive; the idea that the Law gives the common man rights not only as regards his fellows, but actually against the executive was unknown.

This Russian state tradition was not the only social and intellectual tradition in Russia. As Solzhenitsyn has pointed out, Russia has at one time or another given birth to important civic developments. Pre-Mongol Russia, Kievian Russia, with the traditions of Slavic tribalism and Norse law, had developed along lines comparable with European feudalism. The great merchant republics of north-west Russia were grand examples of the urban civicism then beginning to emerge in many parts of Europe. But the new model state at Moscow crushed them thoroughly, as it had crushed the remnants of Kievian feudalism.

The independent element in Russian thought and organisation continued to manifest itself: in religious life, particularly in the monasteries, which long maintained a sturdy independence of the state; in the popular initiatives at the beginning of the seventeenth century; in what might have been a proto-parliament, the Zemsky Sobor; after the religious reforms of the mid-seventeenth century, in the persecuted but bitterly resistant Old Belief, which was never assimilated to the state.

Again, on and beyond the borders of the central state, serfdom came late or never. By a process of natural selection, the freer minds swarmed to the border areas to form the Cossack regions of the Ukraine and Siberia. In the Ukraine the Republic on the Waterfalls had an organisation of a strictly consensual type and was only crushed late in Catherine the Great's time, leaving behind perhaps a more independent spirit in the area (as noted also in Siberia) than in central Russia. And finally, among these non-despotic areas of the old Russian culture, one has to mention the village community *mir*. This institution has been so greatly misunderstood (for example, by Marx, but even by people who have not got the actual facts wrong) that perhaps not too much should be made of it. In one sense, no doubt, as an important school holds, it constituted an assembly of those without rights whose aim was to settle the dividing of their obligations to their superiors; it was thus an organisation for the convenience of the state. In this it would be comparable with the village communities of the oriental empires. Nevertheless, one can also see in it, within certain limits, a true development of civic consensual action.

The Russian state tradition which prevailed, on the other hand, was based on the intensive and total serfdom of the main regions of Russia and on an increasingly rigid grip of the autocracy and its bureaucracy. The tradition was founded in the Mongol and post-Mongol periods but came to its full fruition from the time of Peter the Great. It was in reaction to this tradition that the Russian revolutionary tradition, its mirror image, emerged. The Enlightenment and the great legal and political reforms from 1860 to 1905 created the proper basis for a different evolution. Yet the state tradition of autocracy powerfully persisted.

It was reflected in a competing autocracy of revolution from Pestel in the 1820s on. Moreover, though there is a sense in which the despotic revolutionaries of Russia, up to and including Lenin, were 'Europeanised', this was at the superficial level of verbalisation and the acceptance of 'Science' as the modern equivalent of the theology and reason which had justified the messianic revolutionaries of the sixteenth and eighteenth centuries respectively; it was not the product of any change in the substance of the old urge of the Muenzers and Robespierres to bring history to its divinely appointed close. As Berdyayev remarks in *Vekhi*, among Russian revolutionaries 'Scientific positivism, and everything else Western, was accepted in its most extreme form and converted not only into a primitive metaphysic, but even into a special religion supplanting all previous religions.'

As early as the 1850s liberal-minded Russians were noting the despotic tendencies of the revolutionary intelligentsia. Herzen even made the extraordinarily prophetic remark, 'I believe that there is some justification for the fear of Communism which the Russian government begins to feel: Communism is the Russian autocracy turned upside down!'—a formulation to be repeated, specifically of Lenin and his Party, by Rosa Luxemburg half a century later.

The period from about 1860 to the Revolution is nevertheless a fascinating example of the development of a despotic society in the direction of a civic one. The abolition of serfdom, the establishment of a fairly independent judiciary, the (eventually, after the 1905 Revolution) beginnings of a parliament, with opposition members, an increasingly free press—all with the oscillations of any real process— had begun to establish in Russia the basis of a truly civic society. As Pasternak puts it (*The Paris Review* No 24, 1960), in the 1840s, though serfdom was obviously obsolete, no tangible hope was to be seen; in the 1860s 'liberal landowners have appeared, and the best among the Russian aristocrats begin to be deeply influenced by Western ideas'; and in the 1880s came 'the birth of an enlightened and affluent middle class, open to Occidental influences, progressive, intelligent, artistic'. The Russian Enlightenment, not yet sufficiently translated into political action, had emerged. Unfortunately, as we have said, at the same time the revolutionary movement or attitude, based on the habits of autocracy, was also coming into being, proclaiming (just as Tsardom itself had, at its hardest) a perfect society rather than a real one.

For the truly creative minds of Russia had a less sanguine and a profounder view of the revolutionary future than, it may be thought, is to be found among Westerners of a more facile time. In addition to Dostoyevsky's tremendous setpiece, we find this strain continually. Lermontov, writing in 1830, already speaks of the fall of the monarchy leading to terror, plague and famine from which a ruthless tyrant, 'The Man of Power', will emerge. On the eve of the Revolution Alexander Blok also foresees the fall of the emperor, people speaking of freedom in the public squares; but out of the chaos, instead of freedom, he sees the rise of 'the people's subduer — dark and evil and cruel', driving them 'to unknown abysses, as if they were herds'.

Chekhov's encounters under Tsarism with the intolerance of leftwing journalists led him to an understanding of the effect that revolution would have on Russian literature:

> Under the banner of learning, art and persecuted freedom of thought Russia will one day be ruled by such toads and crocodiles as were unknown even in Spain under the Inquisition. Yes, you just wait. Narrow-mindedness, enormous pretensions, excessive self-importance, a total absence of any literary or social conscience: these things will do their work . . . will generate an atmosphere so

stifling that every healthy person will be nauseated.

The communist regime thus based itself, insofar as it soon went back to the principles of autocracy and bureaucracy, on all that stood for serfdom and despotism in the Russian state tradition. But, and here again is a point which Solzhenitsyn has made very powerfully, it brought in the new element of totalitarianism, an absolutism that really was absolute, and demanded the submission of all those elements in Russian life which even Nicholas I had not found it possible to crush. At the same time, it reduced all public morality to that which enabled the ruler's will to prevail, again going far further than any of the tsars. Even Ivan the Terrible had his moments of repentance and regret. As Stalin was to remark ('humorously', as the Soviet press put it) 'God stood in Ivan's way,' since he would repent for a year after liquidating a great feudal family, when (Stalin felt) 'he should have been acting with increasing decisiveness.'

Thus the Soviet regime was in part a monstrously exaggerated product of the bad section of the old Russian state tradition, eliminating from it all its ethical limitations; and it was at the same time the most complete of absolutist messianisms, deriving from, and bringing to fruition, a far more extreme non-Russian concept.

Lenin's revolution tapped to some extent the aspirations of those who hated the old despotism to instal a new despotism. It was precisely the achievement of the Leninist autocracy to destroy the inchoate civicism of the past half-century in Russia. And, on the international scale, it produced a division between the civic and the despotic cultures that was sharper and more extreme than had ever yet been seen.

It is a good deal more than mere rhetorical comparison or the enlistment of vivid metaphor to point out how much the Communist seizure of Russia resembled that of the Mongols hundreds of years before. In both cases societies which contained or were developing considerable elements of civic consciousness were overwhelmed by a united, centralised, disciplined, military-style body of men devoted to a non-Russian ideology with totalist claims. In fact, the idea, common for generations, that the Western civilisation would (like the Roman) be destroyed by barbarians (but, in our case, consisting of 'internal' Goths) leads one to note that in the case of the Russian culture the 'internal' Mongols appropriate to it now showed their hand. Spengler saw already that Soviet Communism, though itself an import, des-

troyed the innovations dating back to Peter the Great and opened
the way to the more primitive Russo-Asiatic forms, concluding that
the country had been taken by a 'horde' called the Communist Party,
with its chieftains and its khan.

At any rate, it should be noted that what has been found in Russia
since 1917 has, *politically* speaking, been almost entirely a regression.

The Soviet regime is the first in which a 'messianic' despotism has
established itself and lasted several generations. In the course of this
consolidation, it has increasingly incorporated the inheritance of the
traditionalist despotism of Russia from the time, in the mid-thirties,
when Stalin began to reintroduce the ranks and the uniforms and the
other paraphernalia of the earlier phase. I would argue that a messianic
dictatorship can never achieve even moderate stability unless, after
the first years at any rate, it subsumes into its own attitudes and
actions many of the characteristics of the traditionalist despotism of
its country's history. This does not replace, but rather gives psychological ballast to, the new style of rule and expansion. Such, anyway,
has been the case. It is, moreover, a striking fact that the leaderships
of communist parties which have succeeded in consolidating their
power have everywhere fallen into the hands not of the cosmopolitan
theorists, but of men who have had local political traditions deep in
their bones. The Soviet attitude (in international affairs particularly)
is sometimes thought to be 'merely' that inherent in a powerful Russian state. Once more, it is true that the foreign policies of successive
rulers of any country are to some extent determined by its geographical position, size, and strength, so that there are bound to be
important resemblances. Yet to assert that the Stalinist and post-
Stalinist order was *no more* than a re-establishment with different
formalities of the Tsarist tradition of the time of Nicholas I and earlier,
fails on several counts.

First, old-style Tsarism was despotic but not totalitarian. No monolithic party machine permeated the whole state. The central political
dogma of despotism was not subject to rigorous and detailed official
interpretation in every sphere. The oppression which sustained the
regime was on an incomparably smaller scale than that of the Stalinists. The ruling ideology, while certainly tending to exalt Tsardom
above all other political forces in the world, and to justify its expansion, was not overtly and completely committed to universal rule.

The conscious regression to certain aspects of Tsarist despotism
came just at the time when the remnant of Europeanising, democratic

and critical tendencies in Russia that had survived within the Leninist regime had been finally crushed. Politically, as we have said, the setting up of the totalitarian one-party state by Lenin in 1917 marked the end of the progress toward a civic order which had begun in Russia in the 1860s. But within the Communist movement itself, and among the surviving intelligentsia, a tradition of critical thought (an inevitable concomitant of the dispute between revolutionaries and the regimes they had overthrown) still survived. The destruction of this tendency was Stalin's main achievement in the 1930s. And when the Communist Party had become no more than an uncritical mechanism of despotism, it became appropriate to use *all* the psychological and other resources of the general despotic tradition.

On this view, the Stalinist purges were necessary to the preservation of the regime. The most profound problem was precisely to establish in the Soviet Union the 'pre-critical' society of ancient times, in which the ideas and wishes of the rulers were to be accepted as infallible by a 'modern' society. But Lenin and his Party had come to power in part with the encouragement of an extreme 'critical' attitude towards the previous order; and those trained in such an attitude were unable to switch it off on demand. One of the requisites for the maintenance of one-party rule was the destruction of that party.

There are those who argue that the critical element to be found in Lenin's time is a sign of a 'democratic' side to Lenin, and that Stalinism marked an unexpected and unnecessary change. It is perfectly true that none but a Marxist or other doctrine-bound historian can regard developments as *inevitable*. Still, Stalinism was what actually evolved from Leninism; and in spite of the large-scale changes, it remains clear, first, that without Stalinism and Stalin himself, the one-party state would have eroded and collapsed in the early thirties, as even Stalin's opponents in the Party conceded ('If it were not for that so-and-so . . . everything would have fallen into pieces by now' was a comment in the *emigré* Trotskyite *Byuleten Oppositsii*) and, secondly, the system Stalin imposed was in all essentials that which Lenin had in mind and had only temporarily shelved for tactical reasons. It is true that the Party in Lenin's time, though ruthlessly suppressive of all other forms of political life, was full of argument, close voting, even organised factions until Lenin himself banned them; while in Stalin's time it had become a monolithic organisation with a single voice. This too may be seen as a profoundly logical development, inherent in the whole nature of messianic revolutions of the Lenin type, whose essence lies in single-minded orthodoxy and totalitarian rule. Revolution is inevitably bound up with inciting minds to criticism of the previously existing system; but the establishment of any despotic-messianic regime inevitably involves destroying the habit of criticism on which it was obliged originally to rely. Seen in this light, Stalin's inner-Party terror may be taken as the natural means of destroying the persistent, but now obsolete, critical attitudes among the revolutionary elite itself.

When it comes to the 'democratic' element allegedly to be found in Lenin, it is difficult to see much in this claim, except the fact that, given the then 'critical' situation in the Party, he had to proceed to some extent by persuasion and vote-gathering within the Central Committee. His whole attitude (right back to the time in the first years of the century when he told Trotsky that, regardless of the formal position, the editorial board of *Iskra* should run the Party over the Central Committee's head) was to disregard 'democracy' in any real sense: he dissolved the Constituent Assembly, openly said that he did not recognise 'labour democracy' if opposed to the Party line, suppressed the other socialist parties, crushed the peasant and worker revolts of the Kronstadt period. Within the Party he produced the situation by 1921 in which (as Sapronov noted) local Party committees were virtually appointed from the top, and in general created the regime in the Party which ensured the rise of Stalin.

This is not the occasion to discuss in detail the 'Second Civil War' against the peasantry, forced collectivisation, famine, millions of deaths and millions of deportations. At any rate, by 1933 the peasantry had been beaten into submission, all Stalin's former rivals for power had been removed, and the Party had been hardened—to the extent, as Bukharin put it, of 'dehumanisation'—in its campaign against the rural population.

During the crisis years 1929—33 the general unpopularity of the Party and its policies became intense. The Party itself reacted by closing ranks, tightening discipline and increasing 'vigilance'. Even members who had had their qualms about Stalin began to feel that but for his ruthless willpower in leadership, the total defeat and disaster which sometimes seemed to threaten would have overwhelmed them. It is true that several 'anti-Party groups', and in particular the right-wing one responsible for the 'Ryutin platform', took the view that the crisis was due to Stalin's leadership, so that a change at the top and a switch from extreme policies was what was required to save the country. But Bukharin, Rykov and Tomsky, the genuine leaders of the

'Right' who, under any other political system, would have led the large but inchoate opposition, submitted throughout to Party discipline, and Stalin had no trouble in crushing the minor dissenters.

By the beginning of 1934, however, things again began to look a little easier. The collectivisation struggle was over. A number of new industrial centres were beginning to produce adequately. And the political unity under a single leader which is traditional in times of extreme crisis, began to look a little less necessary. In one sense, indeed, Stalin retained an enormously powerful position as the victor in the recent struggles. On the other hand, though all non-Stalinists had long since been removed from the Politburo, within the Stalinist faction itself powerful support began to emerge for a reconciliation with the population, a relaxation of the extremes of discipline.

This manifested itself first of all in the success of moves by the new 'moderates' to block the execution of members of the various 'anti-Party' groups. Sergei Kirov, Sergo Ordzhokonidze and others intervened in several of these cases and secured majorities in the Politburo. When the 'Congress of Victors' (the XVIIth Party Congress) assembled in January 1934 discussions seem to have taken place, of which we have only scrappy and incomplete accounts, which Stalin himself, at any rate, seems to have interpreted as an attempt to remove him from the General Secretaryship of the Party to some other post of great prestige but considerably less power.

Instead, he (logically enough) launched the Great Purge. I will not here describe the three fake Moscow trials, or examine the circumstances of the labour camps in which in 1937—8 at least eight million prisoners were probably held, or detail the mass executions in the Central Committee, the Communist Party, the army and the population as a whole. I have examined all these at length in my book *The Great Terror*. It will be sufficient for my purpose at present to take all that for granted and to insist merely on two decisive elements of the Purge.

First, its unprecedently massive scale. During the Stalin period it is hardly possible that less than twenty million people perished, and the figure may well be a good deal higher. The Party itself lost half its members. So did the officer corps, in particular the experienced men. The most interesting figure, perhaps, is the one that emerges from the Soviet census of 1959 where, of the purged generation, the proportion of male survivors, compared with female, is far and away lower than that of the generation which provided the fighting troops in the War! (See *The Great Terror,* Appendix I.)

The second great characteristic of the Purge was falsification and secrecy, what Pasternak called 'the inhuman power of the lie'. We hardly know of a single case, or a single trial, where any of the charges bore any relation whatever to reality. It was a fake on a gigantic scale. And among its products was the silencing, the atomising of society. As the writer Isaac Babel put it, 'Today a man only talks freely with his wife — at night, with the blankets pulled over his head.' It was this atomisation that left in Russia only one effective social mechanism: the Stalin *apparat.* And this was now thoroughly cleansed of the 'critical' element and had become a complete, even instinctive, servant of despotism.

In this aspect, the purges may be seen, as we have said, as destroying that part of the Party which a residual Europeanisation had affected. The present Soviet leadership is derived from those social strata which were never influenced by liberalisation or the Enlightenment. As several thoughtful observers have noted, they come from households either of peasants or of an urban working class just out of the villages. The current generation of rulers is, moreover, the first that is entirely the political product of the Soviet order. Khrushchev and Molotov, whatever their convictions, still had in them the memory and, to some slight but unavoidable extent, the influence of pre-Soviet (even non-Soviet) ideas.

Furthermore, the selection process which produced the present ruling class was a quite astonishing piece of forced evolution. The thin slice of the political spectrum which came to power in 1917 was, in the 1930s, sliced ten times thinner. From the point of view of political (but not only political) psychology, a very special type emerged.

The membership of the present Politburo, both old and young, owe their careers to the Terror. Kosygin and Brezhnev were among the few surviving *apparatchiks* to fight their way up through the political slaughter-pens of the party machines of Leningrad and the Ukraine. Moreover, it should be remembered that official statements (as in, for example, Yu. P. Petrov, *Party Construction in the Soviet Army and Fleet 1918-1961,* Moscow 1964, p. 301) formally decreed that all who did not adequately denounce others were themselves among the guilty.

We must, in fact, bear in mind that a new political species was created at this time. Since 1917 the political talent of the whole country, outside the adherents of a single doctrine, had been excluded; in the years that followed all but one nuance within this narrow section of the political spectrum were equally reduced to oblivion. In the actual years of the Terror, however, a new principle, in many ways more restrictive still, was applied: even those who fully agreed with the official line were disposed of if they did not exhibit absolute servility and the total renouncement of any other loyalty, even of qualms of conscience.

As Dr Alexander Weissberg, the physicist, noted (of Ukrainian industry, but the point applies more generally):

> A few months later their successors were arrested too. It was only the third or fourth batch who managed to keep their seats. They had not even the normal advantages of youth in their favour, for the choosing had been a very negative one. They were men who had denounced others on innumerable occasions. They had bowed the knee whenever they had come up against higher authority. They were morally and intellectually crippled.

The new Stalinist institutions were based on these principles and manned by these characters.

CHAPTER 7

The Party Mind

The USSR has advanced further than any other order into a condition in which (as in principle in all despotisms, less so usually in practice) the shape and the actions of society are determined by the political and other ideas in the minds of the rulers.

A highly articulate and explicit statement of the essential communist attitude in these matters was made by a member of an earlier generation, Gregory Pyatakov, just fifty years ago. Meeting a former Menshevik friend, N. V. Volsky-Valentinov, in Paris, he burst into an excited harangue:

> According to Lenin, the Communist Party is based on the principle of coercion which doesn't recognise any limitations or inhibitions. And the central idea of this principle of boundless coercion is not coercion by itself but the absence of any limitation whatsoever— moral, political and even physical, as far as that goes. Such a Party is capable of achieving miracles and doing things which no other collective of men could achieve. . . .

The Soviet order is thus characterised above all by the subjectivist world view of its ruling group. Nor is this a matter of mere intellectual conviction, the acceptance of one 'ideology'. Their attitudes go much deeper than that. They are unable to see the world in any other way. They were trained in, and are a product of, the lower levels of a dogmatic millenarian sect, which has destroyed the remnant of critical thought existing within it.

The main characteristics of their attitude, simply put, are these. First, it is a way of seeing the world which is in the very strictest sense dogmatic; that is, it accepts the idea that a final philosophy, political philosophy and theory of society have been devised; and that the nature of the perfect human order which will prevail throughout the future is known and can be realized by theoretically prescribed methods. That is, it is a closed system of thought, and one which, being 'true' in contrast to the falsehood of all others, implies a closed society. As a result, in Solzhenitsyn's words, 'The primitive refusal to compromise is elevated into a theoretical principle and is regarded as the pinnacle of orthodoxy.' Second, this way of thinking implies that the political leadership, and political considerations generally, are on a higher and more comprehensive plane than all other elements in society and are empowered to make the final decision in all fields. Third, it is based on a view of history, and of the world in general, which sees struggles and clashes as the only essential mode of political or any other action. And long practice in putting this principle into operation has generated an attitude so deeply ingrained as to be almost automatic. Fourth, the dogma's universal applicability throughout the world is equally deep-set. All other political orders—even 'communist' ones which deviate in any significant way from that of the USSR (for example, Dubček's Czechoslovakia or Mao's China)—are in principle illegitimate and should be destroyed when tactically convenient, just as aberrant political or other views within the USSR are subject in principle to total suppression.

It is a matter less of an 'ideology' as such than of an inability to think in other categories. But ideology must not be dismissed. Suslov, Ponomarev and others have often provided not merely public but also confidential analyses, in the most scholastic terms, both at home and to foreign communist parties; one example is the confidential Soviet advice proffered to the Syrian Communist Party (*Ar-Rayah,* 26 June 1972), which insisted that there was no such thing as an Arab nation, and that this, though 'politically harmful', must be accepted as good Marxism-Leninism. The Russians went on to urge that not Arab unity but the establishment of socialism piecemeal in various Arab countries was the 'principal target'.

And what could be a more vivid example of the extent to which considerations of ideological struggle influence the Soviet leadership than the demands put by them to the Czechoslovak Politburo at Cierna-nad-Tiszu in 1968? Of the five demands, four concerned the removal of specific individuals from Party positions or the suppression of specific active groups. The fifth, however, was for a guarantee that the Social-Democratic party should not be legalised. This was the sole point of long-term political principle involved; its significance should be obvious.

Again, apart from the mere power of the apparatus, the sole rationale of the disastrous collective farm system of agriculture (of which we shall speak later) is ideological.

More generally, the acceptance of a closed ideology of absolute certainties provides the justification for rule, the mortar for the bricks of power and ambition. It is a further profound reason why their attitudes are so different from our own.

The revolutionary attitude, with its corollary that nothing is more important than making specified changes in society, implies above all this primacy of politics. Since intense political conviction does not necessarily accompany expertise in other fields, this usually means that 'radical'-sounding theories are more likely to be voted for by the Central Committee or other revolutionary ruling body than less commonly known and less emotionally impressive (though better supported) ideas.

This politicising of all decision-making in the USSR continues to have highly unsatisfactory results. The Party and governmental machinery now dispose of a wide variety of skilled and expert groups in most fields. The common experience has been, and still is, that when such a group presents the often highly complex elements in a given problem, the political figure dealing with it, even at Politburo level, becomes baffled and annoyed and turns instead to some self-appointed expert with high doctrinal claims, great confidence and an apparently clear-cut plan to outflank or break through the difficulties.

The system, far from tending to rationality, places a premium on quick and spectacular results, however obtained. A. N. Larionov, First Secretary of Ryazan province and a full member of the Central Committee for many years, promised in Khrushchev's time to double his province's meat production in a year. He and his associates succeeded in this by slaughtering all the milk cows and breeding stock, buying (with illegally diverted funds) cattle from other provinces, and so on. Larionov, by now a Hero of Socialist Labour and holder of the Order of Lenin, had to commit suicide in 1960 when the truth came out. He had many imitators in other provinces.

Nor was this merely a Khrushchevite aberration. Ten years later, under full Brezhnevism, we find similar things. One of dozens of examples was a great efficiency drive in agriculture in the Kokchetav province (*Kazakhstanskaya Pravda,* 15 February 1970). This took the form of enforced specialisation, by which sheep, cattle and so forth were concentrated in the areas thought best for them. As a result, villages where sheep farming had been practised for centuries were left with no sheep, and dairy farms were suddenly filled with hordes of them. Pigs, however, were the greatest sufferers. They were banned on all except a few specialised farms, the rest being slaughtered immediately. As a result, meat, milk and food production in the province fell drastically. The peasantry, for the first time, had to import food. The local meat factories refused to buy pigs except from the special farms, which had not got round to producing any, so the pigs left in private hands had to be marketed in provinces hundreds of miles away. . . .

Again, it has been stated publicly (*Literaturnaya Gazeta,* 18 March 1970) that while in the decade before the Revolution a million peasants from European Russia were successfully and prosperously settled in Kazakhstan as a result of the policies of the arch-enemy of the Revolution, Stolypin, the vast influx of people in the fifties and sixties who came to exploit the same area left a dust bowl, from which even those earlier settlers finally fled, as well as their successors. Soviet correspondents drove through scores of abandoned villages. The point of this is that no amount of failure has induced the rulers even to consider the old and successful solution of building up an independent peasantry. But it goes even further: the *practical* error was the failure to leave land fallow—just what is to be expected when operators are under political incentive to produce a maximum this year and not worry about the next. And this error still persists, even after this huge lesson.

A high proportion of the members of the Central Committee, and particularly the senior ones, have an educational background which may go part of the way to explaining the semi-educated impression which so many of them give. It is associated with the curious phenomenon of having had primary and 'higher' education but having missed secondary education. They thus missed a solid background of instruction in their teens and went through higher education (usually technical or political) without it, having been selected for this later phase in their education simply on political grounds.

The general quality of thought of the Soviet elite, apart from the dogmas of Marxism, seems to be the consequence of a half-baked mish-mash of general ideas. A whole series of pseudo-sciences has been found compatible with Marxism, ever since the time of Marx himself, with his addiction to phrenology. That Engels was a follower of Lewis Morgan's anthropology, respectable at the time, is understandable. That he incorporated it into his classic *The Origin of the Family,* and that this has remained established dogma for later generations of Marxists, is another matter. In the 1930s some ill-considered ideas of Maxim Gorky's were erected by Stalin's right-hand man, Andrei Zhdanov, into an allegedly scientific aesthetics, 'Socialist Realism'. (During the 1956 'thaw', the old Polish writer Slonimski explained the method. Nothing which is not progressive can be beautiful: so people proved that Notre Dame was progressive or, 'if more convenient', that it was not beautiful.) Again, from the thirties until 1950, when Stalin suddenly changed his mind, the crackpot linguistic theories of N. Marr, who held that all language derives from the four sounds 'rosh', 'sal', 'ber' and 'yon', were declared essential to orthodox Marxism, and linguists proper, such as Professor E. D. Polivanov, disappeared, together with their supporters.

The story of Lysenkoism will be known to most readers. Lysenko owed his long triumph, almost equally damaging to agriculture and to science (and scientists), to having as his main supporter a man skilled in the manipulation of Marxist terminology, I. I. Prezent, who had no difficulty in proving genetics reactionary and its practitioners enemies of the people. Less well publicised are such men as V. R. Vilyams, another crackpot agricultural scientist, whose views were accepted and whose opponents were silenced or shot in the thirties. His sphere was soil development. He promised fantastic increases in fertility (up to tenfold from particular plant mixtures in crop rotation), taking the view that the texture of the soil was the only really important factor and that no soil which was not of suitable texture could be made fertile even by irrigation and fertilisation. No genuine experiments supported this notion, and its success was due to two factors: attractive promises and the branding of other views as Trotskyite. His leading opponent, Dr Tulaikov, was arrested in 1937 and died in one of the White Sea camps in 1938.

In matters of human physiology and psychology, things have always been worse yet. Lenin, in a well-known letter to Maxim Gorky (written in November 1913) advised him to avoid Bolshevik doctors:

'really in ninety-nine cases out of a hundred doctor-comrades are asses
. . . but try on yourself the discoveries of a Bolshevik—that is terrifying.' (But Lenin himself, after all, had refuted the voluminous and
subtle philosophical works of Mach and Avenarius, after having read
or had in his possession, two of their books, twelve hundred pages in all,
for two and a half days.) And when he died, prominent Bolsheviks—
his Commissar for Education Lunacharsky, and Krassin—seem to
have hoped that 'science' would eventually progress to the level of
bringing him back to life again.

A whole series of crackpot medical theories were taken up. A mira-
culous medicine produced by Professor Schwartzman enjoyed brief
vogue in the Party leadership around 1930. It was followed by a similar
'new' medical method invented by the unfortunate Ignaty Kazakov,
who was shot in 1938 as one of various doctors responsible for killing
the head of the Secret Police, Menzhinsky. It was then publicly stated
that there was 'a small group of important people' at that time under the
impression that they were being helped by him a great deal. There had
even been a special meeting of the Council of the Peoples' Commissars
to discuss the 'Kazakov method'.

In 1949 a further phoney called G. M. Boshyan generated wide
state and Party support for some fraudulent work on the crystallisa-
tion of bacteria and other notions connected with the origins of life,
always a theme of special interest to the followers of pseudo-sciences.
But perhaps the most regressive pseudo-biological craze was that of the
work, illiterate even by Lysenkoite standards, of the aged Bolshevik
woman O. B. Lepeshinskaya. In her twenties, in the 1890s, she had
attended some courses for medical assistants. But since then she had
nothing to do with medicine or any other science until some time after
the Revolution, when she suddenly became a 'biologist'. Her *bêtes
noires* (fortunately for them, both foreign and dead) were Virchow,
the great student of cellular pathology, and Pasteur. Lepeshinskaya
took the view that cells were much overrated, and she deduced from the
dialectic and from some obsolete remarks of Engels's that albuminous
matter without cellular organisation had life and metabolism. In 1951
her ideas were compulsorily propagated by decree of the Ministry of
Education. Lepeshinskaya also contributed to another great concern
of the leadership: rejuvenation. Her method, a simple one, was to dis-
solve a bag of ordinary soda in one's bath. Another parallel piece of
work on something approaching personal physical immortality was
that conducted in a Romanian 'laboratory' much favoured by Stalin.

From 1957 to 1962 the Leningrad Party leadership sponsored a quack cancer cure, the 'Kachugin method', which the medical profession was only able to put a stop to as the result of a turn in the political struggle, though the victors at this time happened to be keen Lysenkoites, so that science lost a good deal on the roundabouts. However, the Lysenkoist view that genes were a 'mystical' hypothesis with no visible material basis, more or less arguable in the 1940s, has been impossible to sustain in the age of the electron microscope, which has shown them in physical detail.

Fashions change: there is now, for example, a good deal of well patronised work (of a type not well regarded even by open-minded members of the Academy of Science) on extra-sensory perception. . . . But the idea that Marxism-Leninism provides politicians with a foundation for arbitration from above between the sides in scientific controversy remains unchanged.

Further, the conviction that Marxism is a 'science', while providing Soviet Marxists with suitable justification for their beliefs, also intruded into their world more refractory and less easily disciplined aspects of the scientific attitude. And every time that they were, in fact, proving themselves right by mere doctrinal assertion, they had to do it in a way which appeared 'scientific', thus setting up yet another strain in the Party mind. As the (then) Polish Communist philosopher Leszek Kolakowski remarked of the post-Stalin Party: 'You have values that change profoundly every day, and every day they are proclaimed as final. . . It is a peculiar cult which preaches monotheism, but every day has a new deity to be worshipped.'

The principle of accommodating science to a particular metaphysic, rather than leaving it to act autonomously, seems bound to produce distortion. And then the notion that Marxism is a basic, universal science leads to the condition in which many people professing it feel that they are already fully educated and, in effect, capable of judging any subsidiary studies without adequate humility or adequate work. The addiction to miracle cures, a longing for quick results and dramatic short-cuts and solutions in every field, seems also to be a reflection of the revolutionary temperament.

Solzhenitsyn's account of the terror in *The Gulag Archipelago* has many virtues. One of them has, perhaps, not been sufficiently noted. Unlike other accounts (such as my own *The Great Terror,* or Koestler's *Darkness at Noon*) he shows the terror operatives not in the comparatively serious way in which they have been treated elsewhere, as people who, however monstrous, think of themselves as fulfilling the demands of history, but as self-serving degenerates. It is salutary to remember the narrow-minded philistinism which marks the whole phenomenon.

Who are the ruling elite among whom such irrationalities have flourished?

In France, during the reign of Louis-Philippe, there was an official distinction between the population as a whole and those entitled to take part in politics, the *pays légal*. In the USSR the entire system is, in practice, a matter of political rights being confined to a limited number of citizens — not even to the membership of the ruling party, for the great bulk of the Communist Party itself has virtually no influence on decisions and exists as an instrument of the leadership in the same way as the other mechanisms of the state. The communist *pays légal* (that is, those citizens who are entitled to discuss matters of state policy at all), is in fact confined to a few thousand. Members of the Bureaux of Provincial Committees, together with equivalent Party workers from the army and elsewhere, number something between five and six thousand. There are, in addition, about eight thousand Party workers attached to those Bureaux as professional activists, and they may have some minimal influence. The full membership of the Provincial Committees is about twenty thousand, and if we double that to include, as before, the equivalents in the army and similar organisations, we may stretch to the total to about forty thousand people who are in some very slight way involved in political discussion at the extreme periphery. The whole *Nomenklatura* is believed to number about fifty thousand. More realistically, discussion proper takes place among the members of the Politburo and the Secretariat, with the members of the Central Committee exerting influence on a lesser scale.

Institutions are the creations of political minds imbued with a particular political psychology. In turn, they are adapted only to that particular political psychology; and, generally speaking, they themselves generate, one might say, a political-psychological field which over a term transforms those employed in their apparatus (to the degree that recruits are not already largely adjusted to it) into a suitable cadre.

Every time conditions allow a Soviet writer to delineate the *apparatchik,* we get the same picture, from Vladimir Dudintsev's 'Drozdov' in *Not By Bread Alone* in the mid-fifties, through the characters in

For The Good of The Cause, to the recent *Ivankiad.* Perhaps even more telling is the direct account of personal experience of the veteran and respected writer Konstantin Paustovsky:

> The new caste of Drozdovs is still with us . . . there are still thousands and thousands of them. . . Recently I took a trip around Europe on the steamer *Pobeda.* In the second and third classes there were workers, engineers, artists, musicians, writers; in the first class were the Drozdovs. I need not tell you that they had and could have absolutely no contact with the second and third classes. They revealed hostility to everything except their position, they astounded us by their ignorance. They and we had completely different ideas about what constituted the prestige and honour of our country. One of the Drozdovs, standing before 'The Last Judgment', asked: 'Is that the judgment of Mussolini?' Another, looking at the Acropolis, said: 'How could the proletariat allow the Acropolis to be built?' A third, overhearing a comment on the amazing colour of the Mediterranean, asked severely: 'And is our water back home worse?' These predators, proprietors, cynics, and obscurantists, openly, without fear or embarrassment, carried on anti-Semitic conversations worthy of true Nazis. They were jobbers, quite, quite indifferent to anything else. . . .

I once said to a Soviet academic that it was hard for us to see what benefit the Soviet rulers derived, or even thought they derived, from their handling of the Panovs. It was to the state's advantage either to let them out or to stop them going, instead of which, for a year or two, Moscow attracted disgust and rage throughout the West by refusing them exit visas and firing them from the ballet and so on, and in the end let them out after all. My Soviet colleague said that it was quite simple. He himself had, with considerable general nastiness, been refused an exit visa for a conference abroad he was supposed to be attending, and when he had gone to his delegation's farewell party an official handed him his passport, properly visaed, with an offensively patronising remark. So he went after all, but with no affection for the authorities. The motive, this academic explained, was simply to show who was in charge, to demonstrate to the citizen that he depended entirely on the whim of the bureaucracy. When it comes to ruining the odd life, breaking the odd treaty, violating the Constitution and so on—why, these are even more striking demonstrations of who's who and what's what in the USSR.

The anti-Semitism which, from about 1943, has become so in-grained in the attitudes of the Soviet elite is, of course, another sign of an alien (to us) intellectual-moral standard. This is not to deny that it has a rational component: for clearly the stubborn and cosmopolitan Jewish culture is notably unassimilable to the totalist state. But in the earlier Soviet period this was coped with by the suppression and per-secution of movements or institutions such as the Zionists, the Bund, the Rabbinate, without a specifically anti-Semitic component, which represents a gross mental degeneration. In the late forties a friend of mine was employed as tutor to the son of a leading Balkan Communist, returned after many years' exile in Moscow. The boy, a bright and in-telligent child of nine or ten, made an interesting comment on the dif-ference between the life of children like himself in Moscow and that of children in his new home. Here, he said, the boys chased and generally persecuted cats, which was not the case in Moscow. On the other hand, his new friends paid no attention to sparrows, while 'in Moscow, we call them Yids and kill them.' It was almost universally held that Alexander Shelepin was the most 'intelligent' and highly educated of the Soviet leaders. When he came to Britain early in 1975 he had to face a small Jewish demonstration up at Leeds and, in front of the Press and in the evident belief that this was effective demagogy, he said to the demon-strators that they had been paid £5 by Zionists to come, and he would pay them £10 to go away. . . .

The Soviet leaders are capable of behaving with amenity in inter-national affairs, of being on their best behaviour, on certain occasions. At their meeting with the Czechoslovak Communist leadership at Cierna-nad-Tiszu in the summer of 1968 the arguments were heated, sometimes to the point of having to be broken off. But this did not prepare the Czechoslovak leaders for Soviet conduct when they were arrested a few weeks later, subjected to violence and paraded as prison-ers before the jeering Soviet leadership. As one Czech put it, it was no surprise to find that the Russians were narrow-minded, but it came as a shock that they should turn out to be 'vulgar thugs', who were not above making anti-Semitic cracks into the bargain. Yet the coarse-ness and the narrow-mindedness are aspects of the same attitude.

There are, in lands long subjected to oriental or quasi-oriental despotism, certain other habits and standards of conduct that are dif-ferent from our own. Marshal Rokossovsky, who was arrested and badly beaten during the purges of the 1930s, was released and given a high command later on. Moreover, he even retained his affection for the system under which he had suffered: not just communism, but Stalinism, which he defended in the Polish Politburo against the majority of the Party's leaders. A parallel might be found in the treatment by the Byzantine emperor Theodore Vacates of his logothete George Acropolita, whom he had publicly beaten in the presence of the troops, only to recall him a few days later to his seat on the council. Such an act would not have been possible in the Western countries, then or later, any more than it would have been in Classical Greece. . . .

One of the key demonstrations of the true Soviet attitude came on 22 February 1978, Soviet Army Day. Dimitry Ustinov, Minister of Defence (and formerly Stalin's Minister of Armaments), addressed an audience of six thousand, the Soviet elite. He made two highly favourable references to Stalin and was each time interrupted by prolonged applause. The applause was, moreover, reported in *Pravda* the next day.

This was a frank and open demonstration of the views and allegiances of those who rule the Soviet Union. The Soviet philosopher G. S. Pomerants acutely remonstrated a few years ago: 'to restore respect for Stalin, knowing what he did, is to establish something new, to establish respect for denunciations, torture, executions. Even Stalin did not try to do that. He preferred to play the hypocrite. To restore respect for Stalin is to set up a moral monstrosity by our banner. . . .' Ustinov's public proclamation, certainly with his colleagues' approval, of the true allegiance of the Soviet leadership, makes it clear that de-Stalinisation, of which so much was once said, has failed to take.

This formal re-Stalinisation is intellectually, morally and historically unjustifiable in any sense: but it is justifiable ideologically and institutionally.

The Italian left-wing Socialist leader Pietro Nenni, who had always been a good friend of the Communists, wrote confidentially to Suslov after Khrushchev's 1956 'Secret Speech' that any destruction of the Stalinist myth must also call in question

the judicial and political structure of the state, the very idea and practice of one-party government, and the conduct of economic and social affairs — in short, the entire system. . . What is more, despotism and abuse will rear their heads again tomorrow as they did yesterday, if the denunciation of the 'shameful facts' of the Stalin era is not followed by a full and complete restoration of democracy and liberty.

When Khrushchev fell, eight years later, Nenni published this letter, adding the comment that the new coup proved the point that 'the good will and good faith of human beings, even those endowed with exceptional personalities, are powerless against the vices of the system'. As Pierre Garaudy, the former French Communist leader, puts it:

> Not only did the criticism of Stalin, from the start, remain within these limits, but the weight of the structures and of the apparatus forged over a quarter of a century of bureaucratic centralism very quickly eroded the human choice: criticism was not pushed to the point where it would have permitted a radical change . . . in reality, the present Soviet leaders hastened to turn back the page, and less than ten years after the XXth Congress, the criticism of Stalinism was completely interred. The leaders who constitute the essential framework of the Party and the State were formed by Stalinism and given position in Stalin's time on the basis of the criteria of the epoch: acceptance of official dogmas, the carrying out without discussion, at every level, of directives come from above, and centralised, bureaucratic and authoritarian functioning in all institutions.

It is of course by no means an either/or situation. The institutions and the political psychology are fitted to each other, and a substantive institutional change would be evidence of a change in political psychology. Democratic centralism was a device invented by Lenin to ensure, as far as possible, that he would have in his hands a disciplined nation that would do what he told it to do. It nevertheless seems plausible to regard the questions of political culture and political psychology as, in a general sense, more basic than institutional ones.

Formally speaking, the merely administrative organs of the USSR are not as strange or new as is often claimed by apologists and opponents alike. Even at the most superficial level, it is notable that Lenin made no serious effort at all to carry out his policy of 'destroying' the bourgeois state. All the elements of power within it, such as the police, had been destroyed by his predecessors, while the administrative structure he simply took over intact. The present state machine is, apart from the rise of new departments to suit new problems, as elsewhere in the world, a continuation of the old (even down to such details as the 'collegium' system in the ministries), just as, in spite of political incrustations and perversions, the Russian educational system remains based on those of traditionalist Germany; even the law, though more distorted still, betrays the same origins.

On the other hand, the sheer post-revolutionary bulk of the organs of administration and compulsion, and their permeation through the layers of state, party and police machines, constitutes something new, deriving from the overtly totalist claims of the messianic-despotic order, and wholly comparable with the brief Utopian state blueprints of earlier centuries.

Although the Soviet system is formally and theoretically describable as totalitarian, or totalist, we all know that these terms, though not to be avoided in general, are bound to need modification when applied to particular cases.

First of all, the system cannot work as its designers hoped, because it is based on a closed-minded and fallacious notion of politics and of human psychology, and on economic error. Moreover, if it be regarded as an Orwellian state in principle, it is an Orwellian state without the full courage of its convictions. Perhaps the most obvious way in which powerful ideas that contradict the whole concept of the Leninist order are permitted to penetrate the consciousness of the population is through the reprinting of Russian classical literature, all of which, with negligible exceptions, in effect teaches non-Leninist attitudes. There are other spheres in which a lack of true totalism has awkward results: for instance, in Soviet treatment of the nationality problem. Rosa Luxemburg, it will be remembered, was totally opposed to any grants of national autonomy in the proletarian state. The Leninists, on the other hand, chose the method of encouraging it up to a point, while suppressing aspects of it which seemed disintegrative, as if national feeling, that wildcat of whose worldwide rages we are all aware, could just be 'fixed' like some old tabby.

Then again, the Soviet rulers (and, ironically enough, this became particularly true in the Stalin period) wished to appear, for certain purposes, to be respectable liberals.

So that there are two separate types of institutions in the USSR, the genuine and the phantom. The latter, which includes such phenomena as the Supreme Soviet, complete with 'elections', is given enormous attention, to the point of lunacy. The Russian word for election (*vybor*) conveys, as ours does, the idea of choice. The ballots carry careful instructions about crossing out all the names but one — but there is only one name. Yet the whole ceremonial is conducted with vast publicity, massive meetings and hearty congratulations to the winners in a way that is hard for us to credit.

Then there is the equally fictitious framework of the 'autonomy' of the various republics, which, though two of them rank as members of the United Nations and several others have foreign ministries, have no foreign representation; of which the key police and economic ministries are, even formally, under Moscow control; which do not, even as a legal fiction, own their own natural resources, control their planning, trade, education, defence and many other matters. All this fakery has two disadvantages. First, it is obvious nonsense, and can only be believed by an effort of doublethink which cannot but have a deleterious effect on the party intellect. Second, in certain cases such formal structures may display an unwelcome vitality, as with the 'sovereignty' (which was never intended to be taken seriously) of Poland, Hungary, or Romania, where on occasion the shadow institutions have taken on substance after all, something which, in conditions of extreme crisis, could conceivably happen in the USSR itself.

When one considers, as crucial evidence of the culture's political psychology, the official attitude to truth, some of the phenomena strike Western readers as extravagant to the point of comedy; and so they are. Carlyle saw that there were certain scenes in the French Revolution which could only be described in comic terms — the reception of Anacharsis Klootz's 'Delegation of the Human Race' by the Convention, for example. There are, similarly, what appear to us to be elements of high lunacy among the communist phenomena.

Nevertheless, the deep concern of the rulers to manipulate or suppress undoubted facts is very powerful and revealing evidence of their whole attitude to the world (perhaps the most revealing of any) and so worth developing here in cumulative detail.

On almost everything printed in the Soviet Union can be seen the note 'Passed for press, on date so-and-so' and beside it the number of the censor concerned, consisting of a letter and five figures: for example, M-54321. This is to be found in books and magazines, newspapers and posters, even on tram tickets and postcards. The only exceptions are a few papers with important foreign circulation, such as the *Journal of the Patriarchate* on the one hand and *Pravda* (published directly by the Central Committee of the Party) on the other.

Glavlit (believed to employ about seventy thousand censors) derives its current functions from a decree of June 1931, which delegated to it the duty of exercising 'all aspects of politico-ideological, military and economic control', with power to suppress any form of anti-Soviet propaganda, the disclosure of state secrets and pornography. It has the right not merely to censor but to confiscate, and it controls the import and export of literature and the actual existence of publishing houses and periodicals. (Article 72 of the Customs Code refers to 'items liable to examination by Glavlit organs').

There are Glavlit representatives attached to all periodicals and publishing houses throughout the country, though lately, in some cases, the editor himself has been made the Glavlit plenipotentiary and is held responsible for censorship.

When it comes to books, the procedural details are well worth recording in the interests of understanding the Soviet ideological bureaucracy. There are two stages of control: 'preliminary' and 'subsequent'.

Before a printing house can accept an order to print, the manuscript must be accompanied by the permission of the local censorship organ. The printing house must then enter details of the order and all subsequent stages in the process up to final publication in a book which must be registered with the local police.

A first proof is supplied. The editor and the Glavlit representative write in all necessary 'corrections' and the proof is returned to the printer stamped and signed. The printer makes the necessary changes, and the corrected copy is now inspected and signed by the editor, while the Glavlit representative signs, dates and stamps it on each sheet as 'licensed for printing' (each sheet also bears the number of the licensing certificate). This completes 'Preliminary Control'. The licence to print is valid for three months only. A new licence must be obtained if any changes are required or if the work is transferred to another printer.

'Subsequent control' goes as follows. The printer may now run off twenty-eight 'pilot copies', and this number must not be exceeded. Pilot copies are immediately despatched for examination and final censorship to: (a) the Plenipotentiary of the Council of Ministers of the USSR for the Safeguarding of Military Secrets in Printed Materials; (b) the Director of Glavlit; (c) the Publishing Sector of the Department of Agitation and Propaganda of the Central Committee of the Party (Agitprop); (d) the Police Ministry; (e) the Ministry of Defence. (Agitprop receives four additional and the Police Ministry three additional pilot copies of all 'artistic, socio-political, children's and instructional literature'.)

Three pilot copies must also be sent to the publishing house which originally placed the order, and one copy, stamped 'This corresponds with the copy licensed for printing', to the publishing house which licensed the work for printing. The publishing house now returns one pilot copy with a certificate signed by the editor responsible or the director giving the printer permission to print the edition. The first copies of this edition must be despatched as 'obligatory copies' to the Police Ministry and the Central State Book Chamber.

Release to the public, however is not authorised until permission is given by the local representatives of Glavlit. Such authorisation can be obtained only when the printing house has produced: (a) the proof copy that was signed by the local representative of Glavlit for printing; (b) the card bearing the necessary stamps confirming the despatch of the pilot and obligatory copies; (c) one copy of the printed work bearing the publishing house's stamp. 'This has been read for release to the public' and signed by the editor responsible.

The censor retains a copy and marks another 'Release to the public is permitted' and sends it back to the printer. Until permission is received, no copies other than the pilot copies can be issued. When permission is received binding and distribution can begin.

Printing may be stopped at any moment during this tedious process by Glavlit or its organs by telephone, telegraph or letter. When this happens all printing automatically ceases, printed books or sheets are placed in carefully locked rooms pending special instructions, and not a single copy is issued except to Glavlit functionaries. On receipt of written instructions to confiscate a book, the entire printed and bound edition is sealed by the Glavlit representative. Removal and destruction of the edition is arranged by Glavlit.

The principles on which Glavlit operates depend on political decisions at the centre. On important occasions the Central Committee's Secretaries responsible for ideology intervene; while the Central Committee Departments of Science and Culture and of Agitation and Propaganda give regular instructions to the responsible editors of the press. For, of course, censorship is only part of the huge apparatus of the political control of expression.

More generally, however, the process by which an author gets a book published is one which involves the entire machinery of the publishing houses as state organisations in their own right. After a manuscript is accepted, it is edited, according to the *Model Statute on Preparing a Manuscript for Publication,* 1967, Article 47, 'with the aim of advancing the ideological, scientific and literary qualities of the work'. The *Statute* notes that the author has the right to reject the suggestions of the publishing house and 'to defend his conception and views if they are founded scientifically, do not contradict the interests of the socialist state, the principle of party-minded literature and the task of protecting state secrets'. If the editor and author do not agree, their differences are 'decided by the leadership of the publishing house'. The author may appeal to the next higher agency and to the ministry concerned. But, of course, these are all parts of the same state mechanism and bound by the same political requirements, so that it is only in borderline cases that an author may occasionally have a subordinate official's opinion reversed. If the author fails to accept the editor's suggestions, once confirmed, the contract is rescinded and the manuscript rejected.

The publishing houses do not, in any case, have much independence *vis-à-vis* the higher organs of the cultural bureaucracy. For example, they are required to submit, for the approval of the higher agencies, 'a draft of the annual thematic plan of works to be published'. Moreover, those higher agencies have considerable organisational and financial powers, including the right to hire and fire and to award cash premiums to editors and others.

There is, incidentally, an inducement for an author to write suitable themes in the first place, in that if he agrees to produce 'literary works on historical-revolutionary topics', he is entitled to the maximum fee and to a 50 per cent advance.

In addition to the state mechanisms of censorship and of editing, the Party is explicitly given rights of control at various levels. It directs, for example, the work of the State Committee for Publications and provides directives on the limits of discussion and criticism. And this is only to deal with printed matter. Of course, all other forms of communication are treated similarly. For example, a decree of the Council of Ministers, signed by Kosygin and dated 31 August 1972 (*Collection of Decrees of the Government of the USSR,* No. 19) adds the following sentence to Article 73 of the *Regulations on Communication of the USSR:* 'The use of telephone links (inter-city, city and rural) for purposes contrary to state interests and public order is prohibited.'

All this is, of course, relevant to the question of the free flow of ideas, now being advocated as a necessary corollary of any really meaningful detente. . . .

When we come to the substance of what is suppressed, we are on even more extraordinary ground. A new edition of the most generally used

Russian dictionary (Ozhegov's) came out in Khrushchev's time: *khrushch,* a type of beetle, had been described in earlier editions as 'deleterious to agriculture'; this phrase was now deleted. However, on Khrushchev's fall in 1964, a Soviet opera company was in Milan playing *Boris Godunov* : it issued a new programme, in which a minor character in that opera, Khrushchev, became merely 'a boyar'.

Soviet encyclopedia-ing is a well-known illustration of the Soviet political mind. I have cited as examples elsewhere the pages on the Bering Sea which were issued to replace those on Beria; the replacement of the entry for the fallen Chinese leader Kao Kang by entries for small African towns; the abbreviation of Malenkov's entry in favour of a small fortress, a railway engineer and a strawberry called *malengr*; the portrayal of Franklin Roosevelt as agent of capitalism and an imperialist warmonger in some copies and as a popular leader and an anti-Fascist warrior in others (the edition happening to roll off the presses in June 1941).

It has, of course, been conventional in the USSR for different groups to be given the credit first for the Revolution and the civil war and later for victory in World War II. Many of the genuine leaders of the Revolution still remain unpersons or play far smaller roles in Soviet historiography than they did in fact. Others disappeared from the records when they got involved in the Anti-Party Group in 1957 and were followed seven years later by Khrushchev.

Victory in World War II was attributed first to Stalin, who was helped to some degree, it was acknowledged, by various subordinates. Later those who had served on the State Defence Council, such as Malenkov, were given a very large share of the credit. During the brief ascendency of Marshal Zhukov, he and the Army won much ground from the Party in this field. Khrushchev's ascendency was marked by greatly exaggerated acclaim of his role, which had been limited, in fact, to being a political representative on the Ukrainian fronts. Nowadays, Brezhnev receives a hardly believable amount of the credit, based on his fairly humble role as political commissar of a single small army group. Dr Hingley tells us in *The Russian Mind* of the colossal mosaics embellishing the roof of the Komsomol Square Station in Moscow, where, until fairly recently, six of the nine Politburo members represented as Triumphant over Nazism had been whitewashed into ghostly outlines. . . .

The most vivid illustration of this attitude has, of course, been the manipulation of photographs, of which a typical example is the celebrated photograph of Stalin in exile in Siberia with half a dozen other revolutionaries. In the earlier version Kamenev is on his left; in the later he has become part of a tree. As I recount elsewhere (in *Present Danger*), this habit persists in Brezhnev's Russia, as evidenced by two recent photographs of cosmonauts, where a man present in one print has been transformed, in a second, otherwise identical print, into a door post. I describe there, too, the extravagantly comic (from one point of view) case in which a group photograph containing a prominent purgee (Faisulla Khodzhaev), then not yet but shortly to be rehabilitated, compromised by disguising him in a beard.

Such things are illuminating just because they seem so futile from a rational viewpoint. More obviously essential is the refusal to acknowledge the huge crimes of the Soviet past: a totally false account of the Katyn massacre continues to circulate; the victims of Kolyma are still left unrecorded.

The situation might reasonably be thought of as more or less psychotic, in that the present elite cannot permit itself to see undoubted facts. This contradiction cannot be very good for the minds (or the collective mind) of the rulers. As against Stalin's story that the victims of the Great Purge were pro-Nazi, and Khrushchev's story that they were the innocent victims of Stalin, the present rulers have developed the intellectually and morally scandalous solution of having no story at all. On this negative, suppressive side, the January 1973 issue of *Index* caused some stir in the world, largely owing to Leonid Vlamidirov's article on Glavlit's list of banned subjects. Many of these have been understood as natural in a tyrannical society: for example, the earnings of government officials, references to food shortages, references to the existence of censorship, reference to rising living standards in non-communist countries. Others, though regarded as bizarre, are at least a recognisable part of the now fairly widely understood, 1984-style mentality of the Soviet attitude to facts; for example, the ban on the names of a long list of unpersons. On the other hand, astonishment is still felt at the ban on any reference to rail or plane crashes or similar disasters, and even more to such natural disasters as earthquakes.

Different cultures have different attitudes to history. No doubt, as has often been pointed out, every type of society tends to interpret its own history and that of the world in terms that imply its own superiority or uniqueness. Nevertheless, history as it has emerged in the West is committed, in principle, to the elucidation rather than the suppression of facts. Indeed, it would not be going too far to say that the attitude of a political culture to history is one of the clearest indications of its whole nature.

We tend to forget that while it would be reasonable to describe it as the most advanced, the Western attitude is not the only one that societies have found natural. For example, the accounts of the achievements of various pharaohs, in a way quite unlike our own, are rarely concerned with them as individuals or with their particular feats, but rather treat them as merging into the ideal ruler performing more or less identical actions. The details, though recorded, do not have even a perfunctory relation to reality. At one time it was thought that genuine information was obtainable from such sources as the depiction of Pepi II and his victory over the Libyans, which carefully named the captured Libyan chiefs. However, we find captured chiefs with exactly the same names in inscriptions to Sahure two hundred years previously. In the same way, Ramses III carefully listed his conquests in Asia in what turns out to be a copy of his predecessor Ramses II's list, which in its turn is taken from Tuthmosis III's. It is not that the Egyptians were trying to conceal or invent anything; it is simply that for them the particulars were of no special interest, though some were needed to give body to the record. It did not much matter which.

This is not the same as the Soviet attitude, in spite of certain resemblances. It does, however, illustrate the variety of attitudes to fact which may emerge in different cultures.

It has been said that the truest information about Ancient Egypt is to found in its fiction, since the supposedly factual documents are designed to celebrate the triumphs and glories of the state and not to say what really happened. Something of the sort may be said of the Soviet Union. Professor Alec Nove (in his *Was Stalin Really Necessary? Some Problems of Soviet Political Economy*) notes that 'the best material about the village appears in the literary monthlies'.

It has seemed worth elaborating the official attitude to facts, since each point seems so alien to our preconceptions of the tolerable, even the probable, that the effect may be the more striking, the more able to illustrate a political mind different, very different, from our own. For these are not aberrations, but fair illustrations of the Soviet mind as a whole, of the attitudes of the Soviet political culture. It is that culture as a whole which is aberrant from our point of view.

CHAPTER 8

Social and Economic

Among other flaws, the Soviet system has the conceptual weakness that it was and is supposedly a vehicle for rule by the industrial working class. To believe this, as the rulers in some sense evidently do, must require the equivalent of an ideological lobotomy. It is, of course, notorious that workers' risings of a type that far exceeds anything seen in the 'capitalist' West have been endemic since the early sixties.

The system, as consolidated by Stalin and as maintained by his successors, is designed above all to prevent intellectual, national, social and other forces outside the *apparatchik* fold from gaining political or other expression. All fresh thinking and independent-mindedness among the intelligentsia is, to one degree of another, crushed by Party orthodoxy. The continuous purges of 'nationalists', within and without the Party, has likewise shown that the aspirations of the non-Russian peoples remain unappeased but contained by force. A question less frequently treated of is the extent to which social forces, the general aspiration of the masses, conflict with the regime.

It is notable that as against the position in the non-Russian republics, in which there have been many signs of a broad national solidarity, extending from the masses to the intellectuals (and even to a section of the Party), the intellectual resistance in Russia itself has largely lacked, until very recently, any contact with mass discontent. Indeed, almost the only known attempt of the Russian intellectuals to make contact with the working classes was the distribution a few years ago, by a group of dissident economists, of a leaflet exposing in popular terms the inequity and incompetence of the industrial system. Yet mass disturbances of a spontaneous type have been occurring for years, mostly in the provinces. While the campaign against the intellectuals in Moscow is highly visible to Western observers, however, the power of the authorities to prevent information about quite major incidents elsewhere from reaching the West is strikingly illustrated by the long delay which intervened before a first-hand *samizdat* account of the riots which took place in Brezhnev's home town of Dneprodzerzhinsk in June 1972 became available. Even the most general reports of these, indeed, took nearly three months to reach the Western press (see the *Washington Post,* 16 September 1972).

Dneprodzerzhinsk is a city of a quarter of a million inhabitants only five hundred miles from Moscow. When it comes to more distant and smaller locations, matters are even more difficult. It was only in June 1972, for example, that the French left-wing *Hebdo* was able to obtain, from a Soviet geologist who had been in the area, details of events that had previously been only very vaguely reported — the 1968 bread riots by miners in the small town of Khorol near Vladivostok, who carried banners reading 'No bread — no work' and of whom several dozen are reported shot when the militia restored order. Again, though there had been reasonably clear and authentic reports, it was only in 1972 that a student reaching the West gave a first-hand account of the strike wave in Sverdlovsk in the autumn of 1956!

If we omit from consideration the great revolts in the labour camps of Vorkuta, Inta, Karaganda and elsewhere in 1953 and 1954, the first mass disturbances recorded since the stabilisation of Stalinism in the 1930s began, in fact, in that politically stormy year of 1956. Sporadic strikes took place not only in such distant industrial cities as Sverdlovsk but even in Leningrad and in Moscow itself. In the autumn, in connection with the Hungarian events, there were mass demonstrations in the Lithuanian cities. But the most massive troubles took place in the Georgian capital of Tbilisi, and elsewhere in Georgia, on and after 9 March 1956. Tbilisi, particularly during the Khrushchevian thaw, was (as it still is) one of the most accessible of Soviet cities to Westerners. And at that time, too, the authorities were not as prepared as they later became to cope with, or to prevent the reporting of, such events. The city was virtually in the hands of demonstrators for some hours.

Ironically enough, the original complaint was against Khrushchev's rude handling of the Georgian Stalin: but the essence was local nationalism. There was even an attempt to send a telegram to the United Nations demanding independence. An appeal for a 'return to normal work' was broadcast. And later the Rector of Tbilisi University gave an interview to Reuters (17 April 1956) admitting that 'order was disrupted' by 'bad elements' who had exploited nationalism and shouted 'illegal slogans'. There had been 'casualties', he admitted, though he denied stories that hundreds of people had been killed. The death toll is not known but is believed to have been, at a minimum, several score. Army units were in action, as Khrushchev has told us. There were riots again in Tbilisi in 1972.

Nationalist feeling is a constant in the peripheral republics, and such demonstrations are merely the tip of a well authenticated iceberg. The entry of Russian workers into confrontation is a different matter. After the strikes of 1956 the authorities took a firmer hand. The next major outburst seems to have been the strike at Temir-Tau, where the workers at the Karaganda metal works came out in August 1959. The strike, involving originally the twenty thousand construction workers at the site, was prompted simply by bad living conditions. These had, indeed, been reported in the Soviet press as early as May, but nothing had been done about them. The strike developed into mass demonstrations. The militia were unable to restore order and the army had to be called in. Casualties are said to have been fairly heavy. On this occasion the authorities later admitted (*Kazakhstanskaya Pravda,* 28 October 1959) that conditions had been intolerable; the local Party officials and economic chief of the area were replaced. But at the same time it was made clear that police precautions had been inadequate, and the heads of both the KGB and the MVD of Kazakhstan were removed.

The next relevant events came in 1961 when, significantly for future developments, mass attacks were made on police stations in the towns of Murom and Aleksandrov in the Vladimir Province. Three men were sentenced to be shot for the Murom riot, and this was reported in the Soviet press (*Vechernyaya Moskva,* 17 August 1961). The original causes of this outbreak are not known.

In 1962 a series of major riots and demonstrations took place as a result of a decree raising meat and butter prices which was published early in June. While *Pravda* printed accounts of the enthusiasm of workers for the price increase, a large number of them failed to measure up to the government's ideal on this matter. There were disorders at several towns in the Rostov Province, and at Voronezh, Krasnodar and Grozny. The main outbreak came at Novocherkassk, an industrial city which produces locomotives and farm and mining equipment and is the seat of several technical schools. Large crowds of initially peaceful demonstrators, both workers and students, together with their womenfolk, assembled to demand explanations of the price increases. The militia seem to have accidentally wounded some participants with warning shots. Things then rapidly got out of hand. The militia lost control, government buildings were attacked, and it was with considerable difficulty that army units finally restored order; the death toll is believed to run into the hundreds (*New York Times,* 8 October 1962).

Nineteen sixty-three, the year of the disastrous failure of the grain harvest, saw a large number of strikes, while there were actual disorders in a number of important towns, in particular Krivoi Rog, Odessa, Ryazan, Baku and Omsk. At Odessa these originated with a strike by dockers, who refused to load butter for Cuba in protest at the rising price of food. The Krivoi Rog 'violations of public order' were referred to in the local press, and martial law and a curfew seem to have been imposed for about a week: in this case the violence started with an affray between soldiers and policemen, in which seven of the latter were reported killed.

Nationalist outbreaks also continued sporadically; though, as we have said, they raise a different issue, they are, of course, highly relevant to the whole question of police control, apart from their general importance in Soviet politics. On 24 April 1965 there were disturbances in the Armenian capital of Erevan. On 21 April 1968 a demonstration by Crimean Tatars at Chirchik in Uzbekistan was forcibly put down by troops and police. (No deaths are reported, but twelve Tatars were sentenced to terms in labour camps.) In May 1972 there were major nationalist riots in the Lithuanian city of Kaunas as the result of the self-immolation of the student Kalanta. The same month saw three days of disorder at Dnepropetrovsk in the Ukraine, in which Ukrainian nationalist feeling seems to have played an important part.

But a more important tendency, from the point of view of this conspectus, was to be seen in the great uprising in Chimkent on 10 June 1967. As we have seen, economic discontents had produced serious upheavals among Soviet workers. The Chimkent trouble indicated a certain change in the pattern. It was provoked by purely administrative, or political, action. A taxi driver arrested for a minor traffic offence was beaten up by the police (as appears to have been customary). Unfortunately, he died after he had been handed over, unconscious, to his wife. His colleagues roused the city; the workers attacked the police headquarters and sacked it and another police station, then marched on the local gaol four miles away. Before they could reach this objective, troops had been called in and the crowd was fired on for some time. The death roll, again, is believed to have been a minimum of several score. It was later announced (*Kazakhstanskaya Pravda,* 17 September 1967) that three men had been tried and executed for 'outrages' in Chimkent.

It seems clear that hostility to the authorities was much ingrained in Chimkent, a largely Russian-inhabited industrial city of 192,000 people. Interestingly enough, the beginnings of a certain political-style feeling against the authorities, expressing itself as it had not done since the 1930s, had been thought sufficiently serious to warrant articles in *Pravda* (25 May and 2 June 1967). Such articles, particularly in the Party's central organ, do not appear unless the 'crimes' or 'errors' cited are felt by the leadership to be of major and countrywide importance. These dealt with assaults committed by workers against men known to have informed the authorities about lax labour discipline and inflated production figures. The two incidents that *Pravda* took as its texts were in widely separated parts of the country, the North Caucasus and the Tula Province. One informer was killed, the other severely beaten.

The origins of the Dneprodzerzhinsk riots of 25 June 1972 were surprisingly similar to those of the Chimkent incidents. They started with two drunks being left to burn alive in a Black Maria when it accidentally caught fire. Members of their families saw that no effort had been made to unlock the door to free them. Again, large numbers of people (reportedly about ten thousand) were rapidly roused, and the local police and Party headquarters were sacked. Troops were finally called in and scores of casualties ensued.

The crowd that attacked the militia station raised the cry 'Fascists!', and after the attack on this station and on the building of the City Committee of the Party, it was the local First Secretary who called in the troops, of which three battalions were quickly deployed against the crowd. Dneprodzerzhinsk, though in the Ukraine, has a largely Russian working class and (as at Chimkent) the rising is to be regarded as a proletarian rather than a nationalist affair.

This is not the place to pursue the problem of the alienation of the Russian proletariat to the point of elaborating on the details of various minor signs of discontent and trouble which are reported from time to time in the Soviet press, nor to discuss the role of the official Soviet 'trade union' movement, of which a former head of the Secret Police was once abruptly appointed leader. The overlapping and mutually reinforcing role of nationalist and working-class complaint in the minority areas is readily apparent. However, the extent to which 'intellectual' dissidence itself penetrates should not be under-estimated. A pointer is given by a recent account of the expulsion from her job of a woman teacher in Moscow, whose offence was that she had been one of those who stood outside the court during one of the recent cycle of trials. Of the fifty-odd members of her branch of the teachers' 'union', about fifteen either opposed her expulsion or abstained. When one considers the pressures involved, it seems plain that a large section of this stratum, at least in Moscow, is potentially hostile to the despotism.

There is, on the other hand, much evidence to suggest that the higher 'intelligentsia' is generally resented by the workers as a privileged stratum. Teachers, and the Soviet 'intelligentsia' in the broadest sense, constitute a fairly large and important element. But in the context of mass discontent they appear to represent the limit of those affected, even indirectly, by intellectual dissidence, and they remain a special grouping in terms of social motivation.

When it comes to the strikes and riots which we have recorded, we were on different ground. First, it should be said that we have listed only *events which are reasonably authenticated.* Rumour suggests hundreds of others. Secondly, these are almost all cases which indicate, beyond doubt, that there is a great potential for trouble among the Soviet working masses. They have shown, time and again, a tendency to erupt in reply to unpopular economic measures and, in particular, to food shortages. And, over and above that, they have shown an easily triggered detestation of the police and of authority in general.

This is all the more remarkable when we note that these uprisings have all been spontaneous. In none of these cases were there organisations, particularly workers' organisations such as those that existed in Russia in tsarist times or exist in the West now, to give anything in the way of preparation to, or a lead to, the demonstrators and rioters.

It is also true that these outbursts have been sporadic and local. Nor have they shown much tendency (except in the minority republics which, as we have said, to a large degree constitute a separate case) to develop from particular grievances to general political demands. The Polish workers' riots in the Baltic ports in 1970, which brought down the Gomulka regime, equally started with economic and particular grievances. But no strict parallel can be urged: in Poland the political tradition was stronger in the first place and had not been extirpated over two generations; the feeling that the capital is far away and cannot be influenced is not relevant to the case of Poland; nor are Gdansk and Szczecin easily cut off from the attention of the world, as are Chimkent and Novocherkassk, where world opinion is not able to affect the issue, and where the authorities are a good deal less inhibited in their use of the machine gun and the tank to solve their problems.

Having made these reservations, it nevertheless remains clear that mass discontent is a potential source of trouble to the regime and perhaps even, in the long run, a pressure for revolutionary change. Lenin notes the conditions for revolution as being a combination of mass revulsion from the rulers and a disintegration of their capacity to rule. On the face of it, a spontaneous rebellion such as the food riots which brought down the tsardom in February 1917, is not to be expected. Nor has there yet been (except, again, in the minority areas) any major interpenetration and amalgamation of intellectual dissidence and worker discontent, such as that which destroyed the Hungarian communist regime in 1956.

However, we have so far only discussed the negative features, the factors discouraging a workers' movement (as apart from spontaneous outbreaks). In fact, there have been minor organised groups, such as the 'Young Workers' circle in Alma Ata as early as 1967 and others sentenced in Sverdlovsk and Kerch in the early seventies. In 1977 came the extraordinary 'Free Trade Union' of experienced miners and others, who for the first time flatly stated an independent position and spoke to the foreign press before being partially silenced by the KGB. And this is indeed a portent.

The mere existence of this vast potential disaffection is significant. So is the fact that (as Djilas puts it) the ruling class in the Communist countries is 'at the height of its power and wealth, but it is without new ideas. It has nothing more to tell the people.' All living tendencies run against the regime in combination. These elements suggest that despite its obvious organisational strength and its immense reserve of *force majeure,* if a political crisis at the top (of the type envisaged by Michel Tatu and Andrei Amalrik) were to get beyond a certain point, there are mass pressures in the country which might prove explosive. The people of Russia are the ones who, in Chesterton's phrase, 'have not spoken yet'; but they have, to put it mildly, murmured, and there are circumstances in which they might find their voice.

What has happened in the past ten or fifteen years in these Soviet cities has not been clearly understood in the West. But if we imagine similar events here — food riots, strikes, nationalist demonstrations in Warrington, Bristol, Cardiff, scores shot, hundreds arrested — we may form some picture of the social and political pressures involved. More important: such scenes, not very rare in the USSR, certainly indicate a basic weakness, even a philosophical error, in the position of the Soviet leadership. It seems clear that the Politburo takes these events seriously. The despatch of two of its own full members (and very senior ones, Mikoyan and Kozlov) to Novocherkassk during the riots there in 1962 was exactly on a par with the sending of two such representatives to Budapest in October 1956.

Perhaps more remarkable still, the mutiny of the Soviet warship *Storozhevoy* in November 1975 aroused little comment. But if such a mutiny, and such an attempt to take a vessel into a neutral port, had taken place in the British or US navies, would we not have heard a terrific outcry about the collapse of morale? Indeed, it was an extraordinary event and a remarkable symptom.

The social order of the USSR bears, in fact, little resemblance to the official conception of it, to the Party picture. Above all, it is both politically and economically class-ridden.

Even members of the ruling elite have, in some respects, fewer political rights than ordinary members of the adult population in the West. For example, they have no right to suggest that the economic and political system itself is faulty. Below them, with privilege and financial commitment to the *status quo* but with negligible power in a political sense, is the important stratum of members of lower committees, factory directors and so on.

From another point of view, a careful estimate of the Soviet

elite, considered in terms of real income, is given by Mervyn
Matthews (in his *Privilege in the Soviet Union*). He found that
approximately a quarter of a million people make 450 rubles a month
or more (a cleaner averages 70 rubles) and have access to secondary
benefits. Of these 95,000 are full-time Party officials, 60,000 state,
Komsomol and trade union officials, 22,000 managers of enterprises,
30,000 army, police, and diplomatic officials and 43,000 assorted
intelligentsia (academicians, lawyers, doctors, etc.). This class, so
estimated, amounts to 0.21 per cent of the labour force, or one
person in every 470. Professor Zygmunt Bauman (in *Problems of
Communism,* Vol XX, No. 6) contrasts the position of a capitalist
and a communist 'managerial class': the former does not owe its
rights to the political leadership, nor can it hold that leadership
generally responsible for its own predicaments. The latter is rooted
solely and exclusively in the political sphere, and its powers are
'politically granted, politically guaranteed and politically oriented'.
This is pointed up by the extent to which the privileged enjoy
perquisites deriving from their status rather than their pay, as
in feudal times. For in addition to high salaries, the Soviet elite
have access to an extraordinary array of hidden secondary benefits.
An extra month's salary ('the Thirteenth Month') is routinely given
as a bonus to most leading Party figures and some others. Important
officials in Moscow receive special extra payment in gold 'rubles',
with which they can purchase foreign goods in the state-run foreign
currency shops: several thousand are believed to benefit from this
so called 'Kremlin ration'. The foreign currency shops are also of
particular use to Soviet elite families, about eight thousand members
of whom have positions abroad and are able to exchange part of their
very high salaries in a form usable in these shops by relatives at
home. Then there are several thousand sinecures; for example,
those of the approximately fifteen hundred deputies of the Supreme
Soviet, who only have a few days' ceremonial duties per annum,
get 100 rubles per month and enjoy free travel.

There are special shops, 'distributors', to which only a few
thousand senior personnel have access. They sell, at prices which
are so low as almost to be fictitious, goods of high quality which
are not generally available. There are other, lesser, special shops
which sell to people living in privileged blocks of flats; their rates
are not necessarily cheap, but they provide high quality Soviet
goods unobtainable elsewhere. In addition, of course, there are

special high-grade restaurants for the Central Committee, the Council of Ministers and so forth. Finally, those in positions of power normally have access, through their personal relations, to distributing centres where they may obtain goods before they reach the general public.

The elite enjoy also special holiday facilities and, more important, special medical services. The Fourth Directorate of the Ministry of Health runs a closed system of hospitals and clinics far superior to the general ruck: registration for this goes with elite jobs. Leading political organisations have their own housing funds and run blocks of flats of high quality on behalf of their leading members. And so on.

Matthews points out:

> Another touchstone is the secrecy which shrouds the doings of the most favoured Soviet citizens. It is noteworthy that (a) words like 'elite', 'rich' are banned as a description of any Soviet social group, (b) no information whatever on higher salaries is printed for open distribution, (c) no official figures have so far been given for the national distribution of income, probably because this would reveal an unsocialistic degree of inequality, (d) scarcely anything is printed on elite lifestyles, or the benefits which an elite might enjoy, (e) there is nothing nearly as comprehensive as a 'Who's Who' in the Soviet Union. Given the amount of discussion of pay, differentials and lifestyles at lower levels, the obvious explanation lies in a complete censor's prohibition of the topic.

—as, indeed, recent evidence on Soviet censorship shows to be the case. These facts require an inordinate doublethink to accommodate in terms of proletarian rule.

Marx's dictum 'the proletariat have no country' was based on the idea that the industrial working class in his day had no stake in Western society and did not in any real sense form part of it. Nowadays such a principle should be differently applied. In the West the whole population is part of the political culture. Society is in principle identical with polity, and everyone is a member of his country or culture. It is in the USSR that polity and society are not coterminous. As we have said, the polity, the *pays légal,* consists (stretching it to its utmost) of a few tens of thousands of party and other officials, and the great bulk of society is excluded from it. In this sense, the

Russian worker can truly be said to have no country, not in the sense
that he is not a Russian, or is deprived of the legacy of the general
culture of that nation, but at least in the sense that the doings and
attitudes of his government, which has not in any way consulted
him or taken him into account except as a mere object, cannot bind
him. This constitutes a 'contradiction', as the Marxists say, a conceptual weakness in the Party mind which is unable to do other
than repress the notion, as well as a potential physical weakness over
the longer term. As Andrei Sakharov has said:

> It is paradoxical to hear it repeated that the intellectuals should
> subordinate themselves to a working class of which, in the USSR,
> they have long formed part. These declamations tend only to
> compel the subordination of the intellectuals (as, come to that,
> of the working class) to the central apparatus of the Party and to
> its officials who consider themselves infallible interpreters of
> the conscience of a working class theoretically in power, but
> which by virtue of this 'pre-established harmony' need never
> be consulted.

The proof usually advanced to show that the USSR is a workers'
state takes the form of pointing to various social benefits, albeit
not of such high quality as those reserved for the elite, available
to the industrial worker. Of course, social welfare (of which Bismarck
was the first effective legislator) is not in itself a product of socialism.
Yet even Russians who would not concede the rulers' claim to
represent the masses, even ones ready to acknowledge the great superiority of the West in terms of both standard of living and democratic
rights, often believe that only in Russia is there free education
and a free health service. A British doctor who had addressed a conference in Kiev some years ago wrote to *The Times* to say that even
the medical men there refused to believe in the existence of the
British Health Service. A friend of mine, interpreting for a Soviet
visitor, finally convinced her of the position of our educational
and health systems, upon which she burst into tears. All the losses
and sacrifices of fifty years had not given the USSR even that advantage. Many similar stories are told.

It is sometimes thought that the great expansion of the educational system is a product of the Revolution. In fact, the educational
plans already approved before World War I would have had about
the same result, the elimination of illiteracy by about 1930; it

was largely this pre-war plan which the Soviet government actually put into effect. The one area in which then unforeseen improvements have been made is in the medical and other social services. These are now found in most industrial countries, and it is hard to imagine that they depend upon any specific political system. But even in 1912 a comprehensive system of industrial insurance was already in existence in Russia, covering most industrial workers.

As to the standard of living, this is, in its essentials, lower not only for the peasant but even for the worker, than in 1914, as can be deduced from Soviet statistical manuals. Much that has been said more impressionistically confirms this fact. For example, Svetlana Alliluyeva says in passing that her grandfather, a skilled worker in Petrograd in the second decade of this century, had a four-room apartment—as she says, 'as much as a Soviet professor could dream of today'. Again, Khrushchev once mentioned in a speech that as a young miner during World War I (and of all workers, miners were allegedly the most exploited) he had a motor-bike. As Professor Pipes of Harvard lately summed up to a Senate subcommittee:

> The Soviet citizen today is poor not only in comparison with his counterpart in other European countries, but also in comparison with his own grandfather. In terms of essentials—food, clothing, and housing—the Soviet population as a whole is worse off than it was before the Revolution and in the 1920s. If one considers such intangibles as access to information and the right to travel as elements of the standard of living—as they should be—then the Soviet citizenry is positively destitute.

Peter Drucker remarks in *The Age of Discontinuity* that a time-travelling economist from 1913, knowing nothing of intervening wars and revolutions, would, on arriving in the present, find nothing not already included in his extrapolations for our time (apart from the industrial and commercial advances of Formosa, Hong Kong and Singapore), except perhaps the poverty of Russian farming. In fact, the last years of Tsardom saw the beginnings of the establishment, for the first time, of an independent and productive peasantry. In 1913 grain production ran at 820 kilogrammes per hectare. Fifty years later, after the Russian equivalent of the mechanisation revolution on the farms, it had gone up (officially) to 950.

Industrially, too, the rate of advance in tsarist times was among the highest, and projects then afoot would have continued this trend. A study actually published in Communist Poland (*Historyczny Proces Wzrostu Gospodarczego*, by Stafan Kurowski) shows with great thoroughness that even the production of steel, the Soviet favourite item, did not increase significantly faster under Stalin than in Russia's pre-World-War I industrialisation (nor than in Japan and elsewhere at comparable economic periods).

Thus much of the economic as well as the social claims made by the regime is mystical, though required by the needs of ideology. The real state of the economy, and prospects for its improvement, need a more empirical look, especially as regards the effect of the political culture on economic matters. For it is in the conduct of the economy that we find the crucial element in the devotion of the political culture to the principle that all problems can be solved by force.

As Burke pointed out in the eighteenth century, this means that they are never really solved. Local officials in charge of any industry or region are under both ideological and administrative pressure to produce the maximum output at all costs. As a result, the highest conceivable plan figure is the one regarded as most in accord with revolutionary principle and least damnable as evidence of right-wing or bourgeois timidity (or even sabotage): a phenomenon seen in Cuba, for example, as much as in Russia. In this atmosphere the administrator has no choice but to sacrifice everything to the immediate target, even if this means destroying resources necessary for the following years, let alone a mere bagatelle like pollution. After all, a provincial First Secretary who does well in this sort of competition may figure that by the time next year comes he will have been transferred to another post and his successor can take the blame for what happens then.

As Solzhenitsyn puts it (in *The First Circle*):

it was more than flesh and blood could bear to be hopelessly caught up in impossible, grotesque, crippling schedules. You were trapped and held in a deadly grip. The system crushed you, driving you harder and faster all the time, demanding more and more, setting inhuman time-limits. This was why buildings and bridges collapsed, why crops rotted in the fields or never came up at all. . . until it dawned on someone that people were only human, there was no way out of this vicious circle for those involved, except by falling ill. . . .

On a slightly different note, Professor Tokaty of Brunel University, formerly a prominent Soviet aeronautical engineer, tells of the servile and panicky incompetence of the second level of Soviet ministers.

It was a Russian writer, Konstantin Leontiev, who, in the last years of the nineteenth century, said, 'Socialism is the feudalism of the future.' And in a significant sense the system which replaced incipient capitalism in Russia developed, or revived, what was in many respects a feudal style of economy. Developments gave the elite large-scale economic perquisites, which took the form not simply of higher incomes but also of a whole set of special privileges; the collective farms, on the other hand, formed a type of state serfdom in an almost literal sense. If we consider the collective farm system first among the economic problems of the USSR, that is because it illustrates more vividly even than the other economic distortions produced by the political culture the refusal to abandon, even modify, a rogue white elephant that has trampled the land for fifty years.

Collectivisation was, right from the start, carried out in a thoroughly irrational manner. There was no serious economic thinking: a crude administrative notion was put through simply by force. The success, too, was merely ideological, in that it reflected the almost total destruction of private ownership. The alleged economic benefits, as we know, did not accrue. Yet it is perfectly possible to put into practice the original idea, that of financing industrialisation out of the productivity of the peasantry, if the plan is handled properly. In Meiji Japan (with the disadvantage of a far smaller existing industrial base) some 60 per cent of peasant income went, via taxes and rent, to financing industrialisation—but at the same time incentive was provided which improved agricultural production, and productivity in fact doubled between 1885 and 1915, in complete contrast to the results obtained in the USSR.

To gain some idea of the extent of the transformation that has taken place in Soviet agriculture, it is useful to remember that before World War I Russia was by far the most important grain-exporting country in the world: her grain exports were well over double those of the USA and constituted nearly one-third of the total world grain market. Today Russia seems well on the way to becoming one of the world's leading importers.

Figures published by the FAO in the early seventies, when the then 'reforms' were having their greatest effect, show that one American working on the land was feeding himself and 30 others on a high-protein diet, while one Soviet citizen working on the land fed himself and 6 others on a largely starchy diet. Since then the American figure has gone up to 58 and the Soviet to 7 (the figure for Western Europe is 22). As to productivity, the USSR uses eight times as many workers as the USA to produce from 30 per cent more arable land less than 90 per cent of the US grain total for a population 20 per cent larger. American farmers were getting 1 pound of beef to every 8 to 9 pounds of feed, and in the Soviet Union the proportion was 1 pound of beef per 15 pounds of feed. The *target* for the current Five-Year Plan is to raise milk output to 3,000 kilograms per cow per year. An efficient British farm gets about 6,000 kilograms.

The complaints made by Soviet ministries, by the Central Committee, by Brezhnev in person during 1978, about agricultural failures are as bitter as ever. Even the record 1977 harvest was about 10 per cent below what the country needs to feed its population and livestock. It is still the case, indeed, that the USSR has to import not merely from the West but even from the not particularly efficient countries of the Soviet bloc itself. Yet when a Politburo member, Voronov, suggested a measure of relaxation as the only way to improvement in agriculture, he was dismissed.

As for the general economic reforms of the mid-sixties: they have not been carried out, except in such a way as largely to destroy their benefits, once again for 'ideological' reasons.

Strictly speaking, the Soviet economy is not an economy at all, in the sense that its operations are in principle governed not by economic laws but by decisions taken preponderantly on a political-ideological basis. It is, that is to say, an economy only in the sense that distribution of goods in a barrack or a prison can be so considered. This naturally raises the point that barracks and prisons are notoriously susceptible to the development of a real 'economy', in which supply sergeants and trusties are much involved. This is, of course, the case in the USSR too, and we may regard it as the lubricant without which the official economy could not work at all. Still, it is only a partial and inadequate lubricant, and the Soviet economy can only be kept going by the application, in the long run, of excessive force. Which is to say that an economy organised on Soviet principles is inconceivable without strong administrative pressures. Thus, again, the mere structure of economic organisation, determined by ideological creed, involves a command system of a very rigorous type.

Curiously enough, the economic dogma which lies so heavily on the USSR is concerned not with socialism at all but with capitalism; it avers that capitalism is characterised by 'commodity' relationships. It has been the avoidance of 'commodity' even more than any positive insistence on specific socialist method which has invariably driven the USSR away from market solutions. A decision by the highest political authority remains in all spheres the final one: if this is not enforced with the rigour of total logic, it nevertheless provides the central economic thrust of the regime.

A Balkan Communist once expressed to me his astonished admiration for Orwell. All previous Western writers of anti-Utopias had shown them to be soulless despotisms of inhuman efficiency. Orwell, in spite of having had no experience of the communist lands, intuitively found the truth that a modern despotism is a place where lifts don't work and you can't get razor blades. My acquaintance's point is a just one. He might have added that Orwell also saw the unimportance of this in the minds of the totalitarian ruling class. Their concern is not so much to solve such problems as to keep themselves in power.

The French writer, E. Todd, notes that the natural laws denied by Marxist economics, the laws of supply and demand, operate in all the interstices of Soviet society *as they did in pre-capitalist systems* — just as in feudal times in France there were also natural fluctuations in land values, salaries and prices which violated those set, supposedly immutable, by custom and law. The story of the Georgian economy in the 1970s is illustrative. Under the rule of Mzhavanadze, First Secretary of the Georgian Central Committee from 1956 to 1972, the economy worked rather well. The reason was that, partly owing to the pervasive system of clan relationships, a sort of underground capitalism operated on a major scale under the official façade. The result was that many enterprises were fulfilling or over-fulfilling their plans in what appeared to be a far more efficient way than that prevailing elsewhere in the USSR. However, the real story was roughly as follows. A director would obtain large amounts of extra raw materials on the black market, was thus enabled to produce far more than the plan envisaged, sold the bulk of the surplus on the black market, used the excess profits to pay illegally high wages under one disguise or another, and in general ran an efficient project. Unfortunately, scandals of various sorts became highly obtrusive even by Soviet standards. Mzhavanadze himself (a candidate member of the central Politburo) got involved with the wrong side in the power struggle. As a result, he was removed, under unpublished but widely reported charges of corruption, and replaced by Shevardnadze. The latter proceeded with a campaign to stamp out economic illegalities. Many directors were arrested or dismissed. The enterprises, now compelled to abandon their successful and profitable practices, at once began to fail to meet their planned targets, and Georgia was largely reduced to the general Soviet level of inefficiency.

And instances of whole Soviet republics in which corruption has reached the highest level are common (Kirghizia, 1964; Azerbaijan, 1969; Georgia, 1973—7; Uzbekistan, 1976—7), as is also the case in the great cities at a lower Party level. But only part of this bribery is economically beneficial. Most of it is in the nature of the palm-greasing to be found in the more backward countries of the non-Soviet world, as is seen in dozens of major cases, and many thousands of lesser reports of party, state and police officials taking regular bribes at established rates, but never prosecuted.

As to the economy in general, as Paul Craig Roberts has argued in his *Alienation and the Soviet Economy,* the organisation of supplies for enterprises cannot work efficiently except by informally (and often 'illegally') 'directing its activities towards overcoming problems created by its own existence', with the result that the regime has 'succeeded only in avoiding the *appearance* of commodity production', and that only by incurring enormous losses.

In general, all the attempts from the mid-sixties on to introduce a market component into the Soviet economy have failed, because the authorities have always insisted on keeping the central controls operative, even as to pricing. K. D. Karol (in the *New Statesman,* 1 January 1971) quotes a Soviet economist: 'My mistake,' he said, 'was to believe too long that our leaders supported reforms to tackle the country's economic reality. I thought they understood, from their experience, that repressive measures would never achieve results and that they were therefore ready to employ purely economic tools. Now I see there was nothing to it.'

As has often been pointed out, one of the most important instincts of a Soviet bureaucrat is to avoid any sort of personal risk. This naturally militates against innovation, since innovation, in the nature of things, is not always successful. Moreover, where central planning covers so wide a field, it is itself a strong pressure against any innovation, except those proposed centrally.

As we have noted, there is a tendency among some Western observers to assume an affinity between managers of state-owned or publicly owned enterprises in a socialist society and owner-managers in a capitalist socio-economic system, and to conclude from this assumed affinity that the former entertain the same inherent, rationally based sympathy towards political democracy as the latter. Both the assumption and the conclusion are false. In capitalist societies, as long as the state power remains relatively unobtrusive and does not challenge the central 'value-cluster' (in Bauman's phrase) on which the socio-economic equilibrium of the system is founded, the owner-managers neither owe their basic rights to the group holding political power at any moment, nor can hold it responsible for any predicament they may be in. The situation of the managers in a state-ownership system is diametrically opposed to this. In contrast to that of capitalist owner-managers, whose security is anchored outside the political sphere, their position is inherently political in nature, being founded solely and exclusively on a political equilibrium. What power they have is politically granted, politically guaranteed and politically oriented. Economic incentive is minimal.

The Soviet Union's economy is marked by a continual decline in the growth rate, so that now, generally speaking, its absolute rate of increase is considerably lower than that of the United States and some other countries, and the USSR is progressively falling behind. In Stalin's and even more in Khrushchev's time, the leadership was organising the economy with a view to 'overtaking the West'. It seems probable that the leadership then really believed that this was an aim it could achieve. Nowadays the feeling one gets in all leading Russian circles, even among the top leadership itself, is that they no longer have much, or any, faith in such an outcome.

The prospects appear to be of continued decline. In agriculture, even though enormous investment is still being poured in, things remain stagnant, and if, as many weather experts think probable, the recent run of years of favourable weather reverts to the old pattern, we may expect serious crises every three years or so. The country is also, like others, faced with the prospect of an energy crisis. Then, partly for dogmatic reasons, partly through inefficiency in productive methods, the growth of capital in the USSR much exceeds the proportionate growth of output. Moreover, in a command economy there is literally no way of testing the real cost of many items. The Russians have always had difficulty in working out how much items of foreign aid and foreign trade really cost.

The extraordinary story of the automobile works installed by Fiat in the Ukraine (the Togliatti Factory) speaks for itself. This was a prestige operation, and one conducted, moreover, under the eyes of foreigners. Yet errors and delays of every possible sort supervened. It did not start production until two years after the target date. Even now there are endless troubles, and the work force remains far larger than the Italians used. (Moreover, the total mileage of hard road in the USSR is exceeded by that of the State of Ohio).

The general decline reaches the political level as different sectors compete more and more keenly for materials and resources. To the normal tensions at the top associated with power and higher policy is added this extra instability. I would agree with Richard Pipes when he says:

> As a consequence of these divisions and patterns of conflict, the typical Soviet-type system faces its second-generation crisis with its 'new middle class' split and ridden by mutual suspicions and anxieties, with each of the contending groups fearful for the security of its own position. What is more, since a moral collapse of this class is the one thing the system cannot possibly survive, the situation is rendered much more precarious than it would otherwise be.

The argument that the Russian economy would be more efficient if it were run on different principles is, of course, a sound one. On the other hand, the present economic system is the only one compatible with the continuing power of the *apparatchik* and the special Soviet managerial class, whom one may call the economic *apparatchiks*. They could improve the Russian economy by various 'convergent' changes, but only if they altered it to something in which there would be no place for themselves.

Of course, the Politburo wants, in a sense, a more prosperous and productive Russia: Francis Bacon remarks, 'It is common with princes (saith Tacitus) to will contradictories . . . for it is the solecism of power to think to command the end, and yet not to endure the mean.' The whole point is, in fact, that the ruling class prefers to retain its position in a comparatively inefficient system rather than be out of power in a more efficient one.

The political difficulty of creating a flexible and modern economy is clear. Georg Lukács has written that economic reform is not possible without a general increase in democracy, in particular in freedom of speech. Academician Sakharov makes the same point, and he bases on the state of the Soviet economy a broad range of demands for what amounts to the elimination, on the Czechoslovak 1968 model, of the current police state. But for the Soviet leaders the opposite considerations clearly apply. If faced with the fact that economic reform is not possible without political reform, they will do without economic reform. The concessions made will be small and inadequate, economically speaking, though calculated to be sufficient to prevent real disaster, as with Stalin's grant of small private plots to the peasantry, which failed, and continues to fail, to make Soviet agriculture even moderately efficient, but manages (usually) to secure a basic ration from the farms.

It is true that all economic sense argues against the system. So does all intellectual and civic sense. But these are precisely what the system was created to contain and master.

A further consideration which makes it virtually certain that under the present regime the availability of consumer goods will not rise to match the Western level is that the USSR is now a military power capable of matching the United States simply and solely because it diverts into heavy industry and defence production an excessive proportion of its resources. If we compare it with the area of equivalent population in Western Europe (not, for the moment, considering the USA), it is clear that the combined resources of Britain, France, Germany, Italy, etc., which are more than an economic match for the USSR, would be a military match for it but for the special structure and aims of the Soviet economy.

Moreover, as Dr. Brzezinski says, 'Compartmentalisation of secret military research from the rest of the economy' has meant that much technical and scientific skill is effectively isolated from the economy as a whole. Even apart from the secrecy and isolation, this could be looked at in another way: the scientific resources of the USSR, like its economic resources, are insufficient to support its inordinately large armament and to cope with other economic problems as well.

Somewhere in this conception, too, we have to find the reasons for a well-established fact. Why is the USSR technologically backward? Its scientists, taken individually, are as capable as any in the world.

The dependence of the USSR on Western technology has been variously estimated. A careful study implies that about 15 per cent of Soviet growth in the 1968—75 period can be attributed to Western machinery. It should also be noted that as long as Western technology is ahead, a circular process constrains development, in that it is estimated that Soviet investment in Western technology returns eight to fifteen times as much (according to estimates by Green and Levine) as the same investment in domestic technology and hence tends to slow up indigenous research. On the other hand, the simple incorporation of a Western technological innovation in the Soviet economy means that the technicians concerned have not been involved in the experiences of trial and error by which their Western counterparts mastered the problem, and their expertise remains to that degree weakened.

The superiority of Western science and technology is central to the whole issue. It is not merely a matter of the freer movement of ideas in the West, and the comparatively unconstrained expression of new ones, though these play their part. It is also a result of different attitudes to the whole notion of research.

To the open culture the idea that the advance of knowledge can be clearly planned is as absurd as the idea that new social orders can be constructed. In the Soviet scheme science is beset with difficulties arising from the twin errors of, first, the conviction that the Party is in possession of a supreme philosophy empowering it to have the final say in every sphere of knowledge and, second, the assumption that 'planning' is applicable in research as in all other fields.

From these, in turn, arise what have been described as the four main defects of Soviet research: first, the interference in scientific affairs by political leaders with no understanding of science (the majority of members of the Politburo have, indeed, received technical educations, but, as has often been pointed out, they have risen not through their engineering skills but because, right from the start, they threw themselves into Komsomol and Party work at their respective institutes and universities); second, the necessity of fitting all conclusions into the Marxist-Leninist ideology; third, the conservatism and sluggishness of the economic structure, which means that (unlike the great Western firms) there is a built-in reluctance to undertake anything new and a fear of responsibility for failure; fourth, the enormously exaggerated concern about 'state secrets' which prevents the free flow of information amongst researchers. As a result of all this, the general estimate among Soviet scientists is that the *real* costs of a given programme in the USSR are anything up to four or five times as great as those incurred in the West for the same results. And we are here speaking of successful research projects, normally undertaken in areas of special interest to the Party.

In principle, scientific research is coordinated by the Academy of Science. In practice, a large number of institutes and most of the experimental laboratories are outside its jurisdiction, forming part of the networks of various other ministries and departments. Kirillin's State Committee is one of two bureaucratic machines which cut across and complicate even this already slow-grinding set of cogs, the other being the Science Department of the Central Committee of the Party.

The ministries and so forth, by Soviet custom, demand 'work plans' of their research institutions, and these plans must indicate the benefits likely to accrue from research. There are obviously large sectors of science in which planning on this sort of basis is inappropriate and in which it is anyhow impossible, or very difficult, to name the benefits. One result is that institutes are continually beset by outside officials demanding to be shown progress: another, that anything connected with military needs in particular is given support out of all proportion, as officials at every level know that while they are unlikely to be much blamed for some minor failure in genetic research, when it comes to rocket fuel the reverse is the case.

Another result, found indeed throughout the economy as well, is a tendency to resist the reorganisation of smoothly running conventional research, since this naturally involves a temporary disorganisation and slowing down and the putting in of applications for new materials which are hard to find; above all, there is reluctance to venture into untried areas, where initial production plans may prove wrong and thus damaging to all concerned. At the XXIVth Congress of the CPSU a further nuisance for scientists emerged. For Party organisations within the research institutes were then empowered to exercise control over the administration. Some examples of the difficulties produced by this double rule were reported in correspondence in *Pravda* in January 1972. For the problems caused for scientific development by bureaucracy, rigid planning and the setting of 'quotas' are freely criticised in the Soviet press, just as Soviet agricultural deficiencies are freely criticised by all concerned. But nothing ever comes of this.

Having said which, we should note that research in the West is by no means wholly exempt from paralysis induced by bureaucratic methods. John Gall in lightheartedly serious *Systemantics* notes the incorporation of a medical scientist investigating mental retardation into 'an ambitious federally funded project for a systematic attack upon the "problem" ', which results, for him and a dozen of his colleagues who make up the new staff, in a virtually complete halt to all progress. Again, he points out that systems management, often thought applicable to problem-solving, in fact can have no such function and, in all but the most pedestrian tasks, is virtually bound to fail, meanwhile tying up all the competent researchers in the field. If the problems involved are solved at all, it is by outsiders who, under our social and political order at least, cannot be actively banned from doing so. We might similarly cite an article in *Nature* (June 1978) by Dr R. Moss of the Institute of Terrestrial Ecology. His institute, with thirteen groups, forms a branch of the Natural Environment Research Council, and Dr Moss is able to demonstrate inefficiency caused entirely by centralisation and bureaucratisation (in one group, the Marine Biological Association of the United Kingdom, nearly half of a staff of 119 were administrators).

Still, while noting the errors of bureaucracy in the West, we can always be sure that in the USSR things are ten times worse.

None of this is to say that the Soviet economy is wholly 'unsuccessful'. On the contrary, it has kept up what is, in the abstract, a significant rate of advance. But this has been the result of inordinate effort and strain; above all, it has left the country lagging far behind all the other industrial nations in per capita GNP, real incomes and the whole series of indicators, while its comparative backwardness is in effect admitted by its own policies on technological imports. For the point is that it does not operate in an abstract isolation, but in a world of other powers with a different economic system, and this is continually and obsessively in the consciousness of those who rule the USSR, both as a fact intolerable to their most cherished dogmas and as an insult to their power and competence.

And yet one widely cherished illusion in the West is the idea that Soviet planning methods have something to teach the Western economies. This mistake arises partly from attributing to the words 'planned economy' in the context of the Soviet Union some transcendental meaning. Even the late Isaac Deutscher committed himself, early in the last decade, to the view that Russia would have caught up with America by the 1970s. Such delusions rise from attachment to dogma—in Deutscher's case, from the conviction that the system of centralised state planning is inherently superior.

The Soviet state naturally wishes to produce the maximum possible: it tends to accept the most sanguine estimates of the possible. As we have seen, its local agents, such as provincial Party secretaries in the USSR, strain in every way to meet requirements, even to the extent of exhausting reserves of material or turning pasturage into dust bowls in order to meet this year's plan. This leads to the constant breakdown of plans and the punishment of the officials operating them. But the system is such that the cycle repeats itself.

It was Trotsky who pointed out that only omniscience can devise a total economic plan. Every element of the economy is interrelated. Industries which depend entirely on a single crop, such as hemp, are automatically at the mercy of the weather, and so on. Their failure to achieve a given level in turn affects the 'plans' of other industries.

In fact, the Soviet Union has often operated without a long-term plan. The first Five-Year Plan was approved in April 1929, six months after it had been due to start. The second and third were approved twenty-two and fourteen months late respectively. The fourth was hardly a plan at all: it was thrown together in haste and approved only six months after its preparation had been ordered. It was only the sixth plan that was worked out and approved on time, in 1956. It was revised within a year and scrapped within two. And so it has gone on. One further weakness is that when plans are not achieved a dictatorship is tempted to conceal the fact and often does so. In agriculture, for example, it was later officially admitted that the Soviet grain crop of 1952, announced originally as 8 billion poods, had actually only been 5.6 billion. The extra was 'achieved' by the method of counting not the grain actually harvested, but the 'biological yield', that is, an estimate of the amount of grain as it stood on the stalk. For a few years, when the agricultural situation was improving under Khrushchev, the method, long prevalent elsewhere, of counting the grain actually harvested was in use. But since progress more or less ceased in the early sixties there has been a reversion to a system that is, if not quite as bad as the last one, at least something near it: that of estimating the grain as it lies, with dirt, water and so forth, in the bins of the combine harvesters and not as cleaned and dried in the barns. This is believed to exaggerate the actual figure by something over 20 per cent.

This reading of Soviet economic progress, though generally accepted by students, contrasts sharply with what a lot of people (and not necessarily Soviet sympathisers) have come to believe. An immense effort has been put into Soviet industrialisation: how is it possible that the results have been so insignificant? Part of the answer is, of course, that the constructive effort has been matched by an almost equally impressive destructive effort, economically speaking. The Revolution and the civil war drove hundreds of thousands of Russia's best qualified men into exile and left the industrial system physically as well as administratively in a state of exhaustion. When recovery had been effected, largely through natural, 'capitalist' methods, by 1930, the collectivisation campaign destroyed precisely the most efficient producers among the peasantry, at the same time reducing Russia's herds by about a half. The system then introduced was, in addition, one totally unsuited to agriculture; it amounted, as Sakharov has pointed out (in his *Progress, Coexistence and Intellectual Freedom*), to 'a profound and scarcely reversible destruction of the economy and way of life in the countryside, which, by the law of interconnected vessels, damaged industry as well.' The Great Purge of the late thirties was almost equally destructive: the new generation of engineers was in its turn considerably more than decimated for sabotage. Crash programmes resulted in the mass ruin of valuable machinery. And an already inadequate labour pool was further contracted by the removal from circulation of the millions who were executed or sent to labour camps. Economic irrationality then manifested itself in dramatic and deadly form: its principles have not been abandoned.

The official Polish economist Professor Edward Lipinski, now in retirement, in an interview in the Warsaw *Kulisy* (summarised in *East—West Digest*, Vol. 8, No. 4), notes the typical faults of a Soviet-style economy. Excessive centralisation and a monstrous bureaucracy ruin initiative and the morale of the working classes. The plan-fulfilment system leads to the hoarding of reserves and various malpractices with planned targets and raw materials. The bonus system for workers means that the main aim of work is to get the bonus rather than to do the job. Schools are judged by their pupils' marks, so they graduate uneducated people. The housing situation is a 'national disaster' which takes decades to set right. One essential reform is the end of state involvement in small services, commerce, catering, and so on.

On the face of it, it is nevertheless hard to account for the sudden feeling, widespread in the Soviet Union itself as well as in the West, that the Russian economy has suddenly got into a hopeless state. Figures for the increase in the GNP for recent years are, if not remarkable, at least respectable. It is true that they represent, as usual, the most optimistic method of estimation; that the areas in which planning has been unfulfilled, even officially, are important ones; and that the admittedly disgraceful agricultural figures are even worse than they appear, being inflated (by the crop-estimation methods described above) by some 20 per cent. Even so, there seems no immediate cause for alarm.

What appears to have penetrated, and to have caused the current troubles at the top, is the fact that once again a vigorous effort to restore the dynamic of the Soviet economy has demonstrably failed. Moreover, adequate output is only being maintained in fields which are increasingly irrelevant to a modern economy. And the failure is not a matter of accident, but is inherent in the political psychology which created, and dominates, the entire system.

CHAPTER 9

Prospects

One of the curiosities among economic theories of history is the notion, which became current in the late sixties, that since the Soviet Union and the Western countries both have heavy industry, their political and social systems are bound to 'converge'.

To accept economic determinism, even to this degree, seems very peculiar in the late twentieth century. Marx and Engels were writing in a period when the economic forces were extremely powerful and the political ones comparatively weak. Even then, Engels could remark that 'Force is itself an economic power.'

The 'economic convergence' seen in Western and Soviet-style operations appears in reality to amount to little more than the fact that certain organisational forms are, or are believed to be, particularly suitable for modern industrial production. The resemblances, even in this limited sense, are by no means as great as is sometimes supposed. But even in the broadest sense, it is difficult to see that such resemblances should automatically be regarded as having any deeper significance than, say, the fact that the old Ford mass-production methods were practised in the automobile factories of Hitlerite Germany and Stalinist Russia. One of the leading proponents of 'convergence', Professor John Kenneth Galbraith, tells us (in *The Times,* 8 October 1969) that 'the cultural shock in passing from Magnetogorsk to Pittsburgh is infinitely less than in going from either of these cities to a typical farming village (the archetypal economic form) in China or India.' The relationship between the individual and the 'industrial and public bureaucracy' is, he feels, the same.

It is true that Düsseldorf under the Nazis and Pittsburgh or Wolverhampton under our system 'resembled' each other *outwardly* and *economically* more than any of them resembled a village in the Scottish Western Isles or the Australian outback. In fact, a sleight of hand has been performed, by which economic and material resemblances are taken, almost without argument, to imply (in fact, actually to *be*) 'cultural' resemblances: obviously, there is an important sense in which this assumption is unreal.

The doctrine of convergence (that is, when the word is not merely used deceptively of various administrative resemblances or supposed resemblances) asserts amongst other things that the development of an industrial society involves both increases in wealth and social and educational changes which are bound to lead to the emergence of an open, or more or less open, society. This 'convergence', if it is to mean anything beyond the sphere of economic organisation, is always held to imply by those who argue the point a 'liberalisation' of the USSR.

'Liberal', used of the Soviet Union, is an ambiguous term, for people employ it to cover rather different things: first, the attitude of those who might be called the genuine liberalisers—those who really want to change the system, the Sakharovs, the Amalriks, even the Medvedevs; second, what might in general be termed the surviving Khrushchevite tendency within the Soviet establishment. Clearly, Khrushchev and his supporters in general wished to ease the style of Party rule. They might be distinguished from the present leadership by being called 'concessionists' as against 'repressionists'—with the most important reservation that whenever concession started to produce serious heresy, Khrushchev invariably reverted, if only for a short period, to a tightening of discipline. Tolstoy noted the same attitude among Russian 'liberal landlords': they would do everything for the peasant *except* get off his back. In fact, we must distinguish between those who would wish the *apparat* to get off Russia's back and those who merely think its rapport with the horse would be better if spur and whip were used less frequently. So even the rise of a new Khrushchevism could not necessarily be greeted as a sign of political convergence proper or of any real abandonment of the rights of the ruling class.

We must, anyhow, distinguish sharply between clear-headed and progressive ideas about the modernisation of the Soviet economy and ideas of political liberalisation. The first comparatively rational and advanced economic programme after the war was put forward by Vosnessensky, who belonged to the most radically 'leftist' of the Party factions of the time. An economic moderniser may be a political authoritarian of the most unbending type—that is, within the system. In a set-piece account of his views (*The Times,* 8 October 1969), Galbraith stated his position: 'the two systems have a broadly convergent tendency' because 'both communities are subject to the common imperatives of large-scale industrial production with advanced technology.' In no fewer than four places in this declaration he told us that we must, or might, 'assume' some point about the USSR. But assumptions drawn from preconceptions are not the best way of describing a real polity. Galbraith has also said, 'The nature of technology, the nature of the large organisations that sustain technology, and the nature of the planning that technology requires—has an imperative of its own, and this is causing a convergence in all industrial societies.' When asked, 'Are you suggesting that as the two societies converge, the communist society will necessarily introduce greater political and cultural freedom?' he replied, 'I am saying precisely that' (*New York Times,* 18 December 1966).

This argument, from the point of view of a rather crude economic determinism, would only apply in any case if there was an economic class with some political influence whose interests were bound up in such a change. And it is sometimes argued *a priori* that the Soviet managerial class supports 'reform'. Like many *a priori* arguments about the Soviet Union, this turns out to be untrue when one looks at the facts. As Dr Brzezinski has pointed out, 'the forces of reactionary resistance have included, paradoxically (and contrary to much Western speculation!), the managerial elite.' The interests of this class are, in fact, thoroughly bound up with the present system, which may not be good for society as a whole but certainly brings them both profit and prestige. With few exceptions, those who have spoken up for change are from the professional and academic classes, who would not lose by it.

It is an interesting fact that *not one* of the 738 signatories of letters protesting against the trials of dissidents in the 1960s was from the managerial group, though they did include a few engineers and technicians. Among the thousands of signatories to later protest the same analysis prevails, though a number of ordinary workers are now among the protesters.

The reason (or one reason) is that the Soviet managerial class is composed of men who can operate the present system and advance in it, who know the various bureaucratic channels and 'plans', and can fix officials and find raw materials in a black market, but who would be wholly at a loss in production designed to give their enterprise its maximum productive effect.

Galbraith argues that those who disagree with his views of 'convergence' are such people as, on the one side, 'right-wing members of the military and diplomatic bureaucracy in the United States' and, on the other, old-fashioned communist dogmatists.

By this ploy he seems to wish to say that all decent moderates and liberals everywhere must accept his line or lose their status. But the argument is a quite false one. In an exchange with Dr Ota Sik, the minister in charge of the economy during Dubček's regime in Czechoslovakia, Galbraith put the view that in capitalist countries the monopolists impose prices and create fictitious necessities by brainwashing methods, and he implied that this was not the case in the East. Sik replied that in the Communist countries centralised and bureaucratised planners had, in fact, become the greatest monopolists in history, while the citizen had no possibility at all of choosing his purchases or discussing the prices. He added that in Czechoslovakia vast quantities of goods were produced which were often quite useless and simply rotted; that the price indices were often falsified; that 65 per cent of Czech exports were made at a loss, having been produced simply to fulfil the production plans; that most machinery (tractors, for example) weighed two or three times more than elsewhere, because the execution of the plan depended on the quantity of raw materials used and not on the number of machines produced. Galbraith declared that he felt himself 'a little more Marxist' than Sik. Sik, a reformist Communist if ever there was one, said that Galbraith knew nothing of the Communist countries and had little knowledge of what Marxism meant either. (This exchange took place some years ago, at a conference held in Switzerland, of which the protocols have never been published in full owing to the veto of one or more of the participants. But Sik's book *The Third Way* offers a cooler, though revealing, critique of the Galbraith position.) Similarly, on our side of the line, the most effective demolition of Galbraithism came from that distinguished socialist thinker, the late Dr George Lichtheim, in his *A Short History of Socialism.*

It is rather as if one should say that silver miners in the Nevada of 1900 were more like the silver-mining slaves of the Laurion mines in

ancient Athens than they were like Middle Western farmers because
they were both performing the same physical and economic functions.
But even economically speaking, it is not the case that the workers or
others in a town like Sverdlovsk are living lives similar to those of citizens of Milan or Pittsburgh. The determining element seems to be the
political culture (or culture in general) that soaks into your bones
rather than the question of whether you are riding a bicycle or not.

Indeed, as against even a comparatively sophisticated version of
the 'convergence' view, I would argue that each social order and consciousness depends on deep, varied and historically based roots. If anything, the broadly political element of the Western culture may be
seen as providing the conditions for technological advance rather than
the other way about: though these advances can naturally be bor-
rowed by other cultures, such borrowing tends to wither on the vine, as
we have seen. What the whole concept of convergence ignores is that
the essence of the system Stalin created and consolidated is the power
of the leadership to ensure that political and ideological forces are
strong enough to thwart, contain and conquer the economic forces.
Who has not learnt this has learnt nothing.

In fact, there have been important examples in the Communist
countries of what might seem to be economic convergences going with,
even in a sense being responsible for, the political *contrary.* The most
obvious case is Lenin's New Economic Policy of 1921. Socialist economic authoritarianism was in a measure abandoned, the principles
of the free market reintroduced in large sectors, and so on, precisely
when such political liberties as previously existed were simultaneously
brought to an end. The Mensheviks, till then allowed a precarious
existence, were finally destroyed, and within the Communist Party
itself the Kremlin suppressed those opposition factions which had not
only persisted, but had in fact become even stronger through the
period of War Communism. (They were dealt with by a great tightening of both the system of Party discipline and the practical measures
taken to enforce it.) Indeed, Lenin's original economic organisation
of Russia was quite openly based on the German war economy of
World War I. This did not mean that Lenin was intending to converge,
or was converging, in any other sense at all with the culture, politics
or society of Imperial Germany.

In any case, whatever power one allows the economic forces, the
whole history of the Soviet Union from 1929 consists in this sense
of the imposition, by mere political force, by sheer Party willpower,

of an economic and social system which all the natural tendencies of society opposed. Stalin was able to take the economic and social forces head on and defeat them. Convergence talk flourished in the West in Khrushchev's time. His fall was, in effect, a solid vote by the apparatus against *even* those hints and appearances of such a thing which had marked his rule. Then the Soviet economic 'reforms' launched in 1965 were said to be about to prove the convergence point. In fact, they went *pari passu* with political and ideological reaction. None of the effects foreseen by the convergence theorists has emerged.

The problem is thus not an economic one. It is rather a problem of the whole civic and political culture. Indeed, when one reads theories of the natural convergence of societies more or less similar in technology, without much regard to the doctrinal and political elements in their cultures, one wonders what on earth their proponents make of several major elements in the Western historical background.

Why is it that the Jews in pre-Roman and Roman times behaved in a manner so totally different from that of any of their neighbours? It was not merely that they fought desperate wars. Rome experienced long and hard fighting in Spain and Britain and Pontus and Numidia. The Jews alone proved totally irreconcilable, to the degree of having to be dispersed before they could be subdued. Or again, another key moment in Western history: what was the motive that led the Athenians to be prepared for the migration of all of their people to the western Mediterranean rather than submit to the Great King, as Miletus, for example, had done?

Generally speaking, ideas of 'convergence' seem to be either trivial or untrue; and 'convergence' to be a metaphorical term masquerading as a scientific one.

There is, indeed, a more respectable argument which has been pursued by many scholars interested in the process by which an industrial working class, technicians and management become adjusted to the habits and attitudes necessary to the running of a modern industrial society. Some would hold that in the long run such adjustment is not truly compatible with an economic organisation which is effectively that of a feudal-type society. But 'incompatible' is a strong word if taken at its most literal. Compatibility with difficulty or with compromises is a common characteristic of the elements of all civilisations, which have always been, as Sorokin pointed out, ragbags rather than logical constructs, with disparate bits gradually rubbing each other more or less smooth. Thus in the Soviet case the system has, in fact, prevented the full evolution of a working class properly adjusted to the technical level of the economy, but not *some* evolution.

So this milder economic-social approach may appear common-sensical or at least plausible. But it contains unproved assumptions. In the first place, it too assumes that the Soviet regime is susceptible to the pressures of economics and technology in something like the same way which would be appropriate in earlier cases. It does not take into account the possibility that power, the cohesion and the momentum of the *apparat,* is of an order greater than has been the case elsewhere or previously and is directed, in effect, at policies that inhibit progress.

It has always been true that the Party and the state machine in the USSR have worked contrary to the natural movements of ideas, of society and of economics. But that is precisely what the machine was built to do. It may be eroded in a very long run, it might collapse in some unforeseen catastrophe, but while it exists, it is capable of opposing, or at least controlling, the movements which would 'quite natural-ly' change it.

Alternatively, those who put forward these views believe that the *apparat* would see that the interests of the state would be better served by the adjustments suggested. Here again there is a hidden assump-tion: that the *apparat* has a built-in common sense of a type we would regard as natural. All the evidence is to the contrary. 'Common-sense' attempts to improve the economy have always been abandoned if they have clashed, even to a moderate degree, with the power or ideology of the Party.

As Zbigniew Brzezinski has noted, 'The effort to maintain a doctrinaire dictatorship over an increasingly modern and industrial society has already contributed to a reopening of the gap that existed in pre-revolutionary Russia between the political system and society, thereby posing the threat of degeneration of the Soviet system.' Which is to say that in this field, as in all others, the dictatorship's whole intent runs counter to the living forces of society. But this is far from saying that the dictatorship shows any signs of adjusting to these pressures except to a very minimal degree.

Brzezinski urges that the transformation of the Soviet regime into a 'more pluralistic and institutionalised system', even if retaining one-party rule, is essential if political and economic degeneration is to be avoided. It will be seen that such a change (urged by Brzezinski for economic reasons) is very much the same as the minimum changes urged by Solzhenitsyn on moral--political grounds. As a programme it has everything to commend it. There is no sign whatever that the Party has any intention of undertaking it. The evidence, quite over-whelmingly, points the other way.

What can we say of the Soviet future? First of all, it is plain that the system in existence today is that created by Stalin. No changes of actual substance have taken place. The Khrushchev interlude, when, for a time, it looked as though some sort of evolution to better things was possible, may have been, as Solzhenitsyn puts it, a 'miracle', but even Khrushchev failed to institutionalise the reforms (such as they were) that he had inaugurated.

The point was clear, even then, to many Russians. When Dr Gene Sosin said to a Russian during the Khrushchev interlude that things were better, the reply was, 'Yes, but what about yesterday—and tomorrow?' Anna Akhmatova warned friends that in a system of this sort, without legal guarantees, a good Caesar might simply be followed by a bad one. Nero was overthrown and execrated, but twelve years later Domitian was on the throne. Chateaubriand, in his *Etudes histo-riques*, points out that a whole series of good emperors from Nerva to the time when 'with Marcus Aurelius, philosophy itself was placed on the throne' led to nothing, since no constitutional guarantees existed.

Khrushchev was no Marcus Aurelius. And the institutions of Stalinised Russia were far more massive, more single-minded, more narrowly traditionalist than those of imperial Rome. As we know, Khrushchev was, in fact, succeeded by a leadership which reversed his departures from traditionalism. They have not, it is true, restored the full rigours of Stalinism. But it is certainly the case that they still exhibit an extravagant suspicion and hatred of any unofficial think-ing. They have done their best (as we have seen) to minimise criticism of, or even information about, the Stalin period. In certain cases (for example, that of F. Raskolnikov) a process of complete 'de-rehabilita-tion' has taken place: the introduction to his *Memoirs* published in 1964 states flatly, 'The CC of the CPSU has completely rehabilitated him and restored him posthumously to Party membership and to Soviet citizenship.' Around the end of the decade his photographs disappeared from reference books, and editors mentioning him favour-ably were reprimanded or dismissed. Finally, in February 1969 the Party organ, *Kommunist*, categorised him as 'a deserter to the side of the enemy and a slanderer of the Party and the Soviet state'.

Nor need we be reminded of the various literary trials or of the labour camps, on a vastly smaller scale than in Stalin's time, yet still with the murderous ration scales of the 1930s, far lower than those of the notorious Japanese killer camps for prisoners of war on the River Kwai. But, above all, report after report of interrogations and investigations show the KGB men in charge arguing from exactly the same narrow and totalist viewpoint and clearly quite ready for harder action than is current now.

Ustinov's formal restatement of the Stalinist allegiance (see p. 84) merely formalised the status and attitude of the regime. More profoundly, the Soviet people are not now given even partial and general accounts of the bloodiest and most traumatic experience their country has ever undergone. The truths which Khrushchev sporadically and incompletely made public are now not referred to at all. They are simply swept under the carpet. Stalin's name has been restored almost to its former eminence and authority, with merely some rather peripheral criticism of his 'mistakes'. But enough of the crimes of the Stalin regime were made public in that interlude for its nature and his nature to be perfectly well known to every intelligent or educated citizen of the USSR.

This frightful albatross, in fact, hangs round the neck of the present regime. And it is an unceasing intellectual and moral torment to everything in Russia that represents the mind and the heart, first, that Stalin has been rehabilitated and, second, that no story, true or false, is now available from official sources about that crucial period. On the three great Moscow trials of 1936, 1937 and 1938, which were the political foci of the time for the whole Soviet public, not only is nothing said at all, but it is even the case that a number of those accused and shot in the Third Trial have been rehabilitated while others have not: but, of course, the 'confessions' were equally damning in all cases and involved all the accused equally in a single complex conspiracy. Again, in the Second Trial (that of Pyatakov and others in January 1937) one of the crimes alleged against the accused—an attempt on the life of Molotov—has long since been denounced as a falsification, but not a word has been said to restore the names of those shot for organising it. . . .

What can any Soviet citizen with an ounce of sense or feeling think? What, come to that, are we ourselves to think about the standards, the attitudes to truth and to terror, of a ruling group which for years now seems to have found such a state of affairs natural and acceptable? How is it possible not to regard the question of Stalin and the Stalin purges as a festering cancer at the heart of the ruling group? It remains, from this point of view, an oligarchy founded not simply on lies, but on stupid and universally discredited lies (by our standards: on a natural precaution by theirs).

If the Soviet present is to be cleansed of the monstrous past which still clings to it, if the Stalin terror is ever to become history rather than a parasitical component of the present day, will that mean the end of the present regime? Will it be possible for an honester, and therefore freer, style of Soviet rule to evolve?

The present Soviet leadership may feel that all it wants to do is to enjoy its power quietly and not take further risks. The question that arises is what will be the attitude of the younger generation which must eventually—long though the wait may seem—come to the top. There is nothing specifically Soviet about the fact that even if politicians are capable of learning from their own experience, generations without that experience go ahead to repeat the errors of their predecessors. Nadezhda Mandelshtam says, 'I do not believe the older generation now at the helm wants to see a new orgy of terror and killing. Knowing so well what this means they are cautious.' But, as she puts it, the new 'criminal stock' of more recent times, which has not so far managed to climb to the top, 'are young people with no memory of the terrible years, who would be capable of anything'.

Andrei Sakharov has said:

> I like this new layer of leaders coming to the top even less than its predecessors. The people of Brezhnev's generation laid the basis for their careers in the worst years of the Stalinist terror. That put the mark of Cain on them. The new generation is coming without that mark. It is more flexible . . . but there is dreadful cynicism, careerism and a complete indifference to ideals in international affairs. As far as internal matters go, they only care about the trough they swill from, and what matters is that the trough be full.

Alexander Ginzburg, asked on his arrival from the USSR (*Newsweek*, 14 May 1979) 'What about the coming generation of Soviet leaders? Do you see any liberalisation possible?', answered, 'No. None whatsoever. Absolutely not.'

Even the 'Leninist' Roy Medvedev agrees on the special dogmatism of this coming generation, the forty-five-year-olds. None of those quoted says that a new Stalinist terror is inevitable; and there are, of course, other perspectives. Nevertheless, it is a thought that we cannot dismiss too lightly that not only are the institutions of Stalinism still in existence, but the young who are recruited into the machine through (for example) the local secretariats of the Komsomol in universities or elsewhere, are precisely those most totally and narrowly devoted to a system of principle at war with all other thought and feeling among the subjects of the USSR and those of all other states.

Moreover, as Mrs Mandelshtam says in the second volume of her memoirs, the terror machine is still in being: 'Even when it is only idling, as today, it continues to function in essentially the same manner as before. At any moment, after lying dormant for a time, it could start up again at full speed.' And in general this extraordinarily clear-minded recorder of the bad past, with all her sardonicism and lack of sentimentality, shows considerable pessimism about the future.

If the crisis of the communist regime is to begin under the present leaders or their probable successors, I would expect it to come about not as the result of any of their specific policies, but rather through unforeseen catastrophes with which their methods, and indeed their personalities, are not fitted to cope. They will soon have to face, in some form or other, a major dislocation which their present small-scale economies and conservation measures will not go very far to avert. The Soviet economy is, in principle, overextended.

It will be obvious that this whole question must bedevil relations between the Soviet ideologists, military men and administrators in various fashions, even to the point of shaking the entire structure of the state.

Without elaborating the details of the forces concerned (and it should be noted that this is even more a crisis of ideas than of economics), we can at least see that we are faced by an economy and a society whose inextinguishable tendencies run counter to the political integument at present hemming them in, thus creating conditions of a classical Marxist pre-revolutionary situation. The current regime has learned one lesson from Khrushchev: that random reforms within the system have not done any good. But the *immobilisme* to which they have instead retreated equally provides no solution. It therefore appears inevitable that the pressures will continue to build up.

On the whole, one does not see the current leadership taking anything like adequate measures in time. Nor does one see any sign of potential successors who might. Although there have been occasions in the past when obsolete political systems have been transformed without serious trouble, these instances have been comparatively un-common. Moreover, such an evolution has usually been possible only when plenty of time was given for the principles of change to soak into every corner of the social mind. In the USSR today one would not expect a great deal of time to be available.

Apart from general political considerations, there is a further major obstacle to the coming into being of a 'liberal' USSR, in any sense of the word whatever. And this is that in anything recognisable as a liberalisation, even in the narrowest sense, the major non-Russian republics would almost certainly opt for independence. Even with the maintenance of communism, this would thus lead to the ending of the USSR and its replacement by a Russian republic and a number of non-Russian states. The Ukraine, the Baltic States, the countries of Trans-caucasia would attain the status of Czechoslovakia or Bulgaria. Russia would, it is true, still be the largest of the communist states outside the Chinese sphere, with a population of 134 million, but in the other countries of the bloc the populations would number 146 million. It would also lose a disproportionate amount of the former Union's economic resources; nor would it any longer be militarily or politi-cally the giant among a group of lesser beings.

It is a little schematic, moreover, to imagine that Latvia, or even the Ukraine or Georgia, would automatically remain communist in the circumstances. The point rather is that *even* making the assump-tions most favourable to communism, the development of a quite orthodox communist independence would in itself be enough virtual-ly to eliminate the great power concentration in Moscow. And so, for this reason alone, the prospect of any true relaxation by the orthodox leadership in the Kremlin becomes barely credible—so long, of course, as they actually remain in control of the course of events, which will not necessarily be the case.

Furthermore, in the national field the trend in the Moscow leader-ship is towards increasing repression. This has manifested itself in part in the purging of those Party leaders in the republics who have made concessions to local feeling. At a deeper level we find increasing stress on the development of a single 'Soviet nation'. Not merely that: there have been *ballons d'essai* in the Czechoslovak press, and from the Bulgarian leader Zhivkov, calling for an eventual merger of all the 'socialist nations'. It is quite conceivable that in the natural course of human history the nation and the nation-state will eventually give way to a world community, possibly with a common language. Over the next thousand years such a development may, indeed, seem more probable than not. And it can be argued, too, that in spite of the various cultural losses involved, this would be a good and desirable change. The CPSU, on the other hand, is not concerned merely with assisting or even gently but effectively encouraging development in that direction, but continually (one might almost say incessantly) forcing along a highly unpopular policy on grounds of dogma and control alone.

What, all the same, are the positive features, the ones favouring an evolution towards a civic order?

First, that things are *not* the same as in 1850. The 'European' element in Russia has never been effectively extirpated. The power of the great writings of the Enlightenment over the minds of thinking and feeling Russians remains considerable. The idea of the USSR as part of a more open 'European' culture persisted through the Stalin period. In his *Zima Station* Evgenii Evtushenko remarks how in 1953, on learning of the exposure of the great 'Doctors' Plot' frame-up, his uncle's first comment in deepest Siberia was. 'We are shamed before all Europe.' Many similar comments could be adduced.

The flowering of the great anti-totalitarian dissidents in the midst of the totalist culture in which they have spent their entire lives, yet which has failed to mould them, is a portent indeed. We can certainly say that all living thought in the USSR tends against the present system of ideas, just as all economic and social pressures do against the system of rule.

There is one possible amendment to be made to this. The past few years have seen a surprising spread, officially permitted or sponsored, of Russian nationalism in the cultural *apparat.* There is much talk of a fusion between this and the ruling ideology. And with all its negative aspects (as far as we are concerned), this would incorporate a vigorous and living element into official attitudes. Nor should we forget that in 1941--5, when the regime was shaken by different forces, a very considerable head was given to the older forms of patriotic, or nationalistic, *élan.*

Nevertheless, it remains true that living thought in the USSR is by and large opposed to the regime: and also that any possible rallying of Russian nationalist attitudes to the communist idea is balanced by the even more powerful (so far) rise of local nationalisms, which have manifested themselves in demonstrations all round the peripheral republics from Estonia to Tadjikistan.

Distortions of what to *us* seem the 'normal' processes of reason may give the impression that the regime's hold on the minds of the second-level intelligentsia who form its ideological and administrative force must be shaky or moribund. Such a view underestimates, as ever, the power of inertia and interest. In Anatole France's *Thais,* faced with the (to him) irrational spectacle of a pillar saint, the Roman governor's secretary says, 'There are forces, Lucius, infinitely more powerful than reason and science.' 'Which?' 'Ignorance and folly.' And the saint was an 'educated' man. Moreover, his views were to conquer. In Kipling's words:

> And they overlaid the teaching of Ionia
> And the Truth was choked at birth

. . . to rise again only a thousand years later.

In the present context one need only say that every observation shows a strong cadre of educated people at every level in Soviet affairs, even the academic, devoted to the official line or ignorant of any other. Every account of the firing of a dissident research scholar from an institute provides example after example of colleagues who denounce him for ingratitude, for favouring the West, for doubting the established truths. These supporters of the regime do not necessarily constitute a majority, but at least they form a thoroughly self-satisfied, orthodox, active centre, whose lead a more or less apathetic majority follows. And these are the 'intellectuals': when it comes to the ordinary institutions, their personnel are (or so it seems) more orthodox yet.

One does not wish to give the impression that the hold of such characters is strong enough to survive a major and wholly disorientating crisis. But nor should we underestimate the present active power, pervasiveness and persistence of the large, united and unaltered cadre of traditionalist adherents of messianic despotism, whose momentum exceeds that of the mere apathetic society as a whole.

For to speak of the alienation of the vast bulk of active thought in the USSR is not to deny either the power of dead ideas over sluggish minds and those bound by interest to the system, or the fact that none of the tendencies towards a responsive and responsible order has reached Central Committee level, at least since the time Alexander Tvardovsky was briefly a candidate member of that several-hundred-strong body. Nor is it to underestimate the absence of civic experience or attitudes among the mass of the population. It is true that there are some hopeful signs. A few years ago one would have said that the spontaneous workers' outbreaks had little connection with any general movement (though local groups of students are often reported as involved). But even that is less true today, when we have seen the beginnings of attempts to organise genuine unions. Still, though we can by no means exclude the collapse of the regime in unforeseen circumstances, we must nevertheless recognise the extent to which all the elements of power, all the components of politics, at every level and in every sphere, remain a party monopoly, as they have done for sixty years.

As far as we can tell at present, then, the probability is that political developments over the coming period are likely to be within the regime, and that it is only when pressures become so strong that concessions are made by the regime (even if not granted in good faith) that visible progress may occur. On the other hand, the resources of a tyranny in trouble being repression and concession, one fears that repression would most probably be tried first. Yet even if that is so, it seems likely that resumption of terror would solve no problems, so that eventually, under a new leadership, concession would after all have to be tried.

The justification for cautious optimism within the system may not be very cogent, but it exists. First, the agricultural system could be greatly improved, (as has been shown by certain, largely illegal, experiments)— by such things as the 'link' system, which in effect retains the title and the formal structure of the collective farm, but in practice devolves production on to family-size units. The Party mind in general has so far proved far too rigid for such a development, partly, no doubt, because of the investment of guilt in the slaughter of the peasantry on which the system was built. But these moves would, in fact, involve no relaxation of Party control. Here is an issue on which the present leadership, and probably its successors, may remain unmoveable, but which nonetheless holds an attraction for potential rulers of the future, especially if driven yet further into a hopeless corner by the economic facts. Similarly with the introduction of a genuine market element into industrial production: there is no reason, except that of dogma, to feel that this would in itself shake Party control, though in the long run it might well have some such effect. As to the beginnings of the toleration of non-communist ideas, we can at least see that even at present these are not suppressed with total rigour; in a sense, the regime is getting used to them. (The truly crucial element, a genuine court system, presents a far greater mental hurdle. . . .)

At any rate we can list the general possibilities: (a) continuation of the present system, perhaps in an increasingly tough form, with essential problems unsolved (for the time being, by far the most probable outcome); (b) catastrophic breakdown, perhaps resulting in temporary 'democratic' regimes, but unlikely to produce a stable civic or democratic order except through a further period of non-communist but semi-authoritarian tutelage; (c) a longish, yet generally peaceable, evolution of civic elements within a system remaining in principle autocratic, like that between 1860 and 1912.

It will be seen that none of these scenarios provides for the instant introduction of 'democracy' into Russia. Nor could this happen, according to a view which sees political cultures as not easily changed.

It is this point, in effect, that Solzhenitsyn has made continually: that instant democratisation produced the Leninist tyranny; that the post-1860 period of tsardom was both intrinsically preferable and more capable of evolution; that an increasingly limited autocracy could be the long road forward. It is sometimes urged that this is an unsanguine and undemocratic attitude, and that true 'liberals' like Andrei Sakharov do not share it. In fact, Sakharov both grants that the present vicious circle 'cannot be overcome in a short time' and praises the 'many fine democratic steps beginning with the reforms of Alexander the Second'.

As Solzhenitsyn notes in his *Letter to the Patriarch*, the past fifty years have been wasted, and more than wasted, in Russia. 'Half a century of the past has already been lost, and I am not talking about trying to save the present. But how are we to save the future of our country?' The greater part of the slow progress made after the 1860s has been lost. If from the present dead-end a start could be made on simply eliminating the extremes of totalitarianism, on instituting areas of legality, that would indeed be a real beginning.

In the meantime, at least, we can watch the operative factors. We should be prepared for surprises over the next decade and should not fall into the temptation of believing the *status quo* to be as stable as it may appear to the superficial glance.

The blockage in the free spread of ideas, especially into the minds of the ruling party, is unprecedentedly strong—though we should perhaps not underestimate the degree of erosion even there. But the greatest difficulty of all is a simple technical point: the machinery Stalin built is organisationally effective and ideologically disciplined to the extent that it can (in principle at least) keep the political integument in being long past the stage at which other political forms would fail. And this implies that the pressures, when they reach a critical point, will be very high indeed.

If we are to consider development of the Soviet Union away from the dead-end Party state of the present, the problem arises of how a new political class could emerge. This difficulty will present itself whether changes take place in a peaceful or a catastrophic manner.

As we have said in earlier chapters, the development of a political tradition cannot be a short and simple process. And if the half-century of civic development which had, by 1917, provided a basis for further Russian progress was then destroyed, how are we to envisage new beginnings, not in a general way, but in actual politics and political leadership?

In the constituent republics, or in some of them, a nationalist tradition has remained which might be expected to provide cohesion and a central principle of tolerable adequacy. But in Russia proper who are the politicians to be? Alexander Ginzburg pointed out, on the day that he arrived in America:

> When anybody talks to me about [democracy for Russia] I have an elementary question: whom will you elect? Everyone shrugs, because you can't elect Sakharov, or Solzhenitsyn, or Grigorenko. These aren't people suited for power. None of us is capable of running a country or even of taking part in governing it. There is no one to elect. I don't know a single such person, even among political prisoners, and I know hundreds of them. So who can talk about democracy? (*Newsweek*, 14 May 1979)

This is perhaps a trifle pessimistic: a certain feel for politics is to be found in one or two of the dissidents. Nevertheless, Ginzburg's general point remains. No doubt if the democratic struggle continues and is allowed to develop a little more broadly, something of a political element may arise.

But the fact is that all experience of administration, politics and so on has been totally monopolised by the Communist Party for two generations. So it seems on the face of it to be almost inevitable that any new class of political leader or, more generally, of politician must derive from Party circles.

It is true that all the leading cadres of the party, and all their potential successors, however young, are a virtually hopeless case. It is rather among the lower echelons, where officials have no experience of ruling the state but at least some of administration, that the potential may be found. Meanwhile, we face an embattled *apparat*.

In the context of the tenacity of Soviet dogma the international significance of the repression of dissidents has generally been understood at too shallow a level in the West.

As for the recent trials, the Soviet judiciary is not, of course, independent. Judges are in any case normally Party members, and it is a basic communist principle that Party discipline and interest transcend all others. All the same, once again, one would expect a better keeping up of appearances. For example, the transfer of two career secret police generals to the Supreme Court a few years ago might surely have been avoided. And the fact that it wasn't tells us a good deal.

Meanwhile we have seen the refusal to allow defence witnesses; the banning from the court of members of the defendant's family, of foreigners, of independent observers in general; the prejudicial *agitprop* howls of the selected audience; the fact (for example) of Orlov's being held incommunicado for over a year before his trial (and his courage in defending himself so forthrightly after this ordeal is beyond praise).

Even Stalin's great Moscow Trials made special provision for the presence of the foreign press and diplomats. These were, of course, well rehearsed frame-ups; but after World War II similar facilities were granted in the trials in the Balkans of men who refused to confess, like the agrarian leader Nikola Petkov in Bulgaria. One of the most repulsive (and, in a way, most terrifying) things about the Orlov trial was that the present Soviet authorities no longer even know how to pretend to be dispensing law or justice. The whole thing might have been designed, down to the smallest detail, by someone wishing to bring the Soviet government into maximum disrepute — again, an indication of the way the authorities think.

But there is one truly major lesson in all these trials which affects almost every Westerner, from the extreme right to the anarchists and Trotskyites, excepting only that tiny segment of the political spectrum consisting of the more pro-Soviet faction within the communist parties (plus that slightly larger and much weirder set of Soviet groupies *outside* the CP). The way the Kremlin leaders treat a Soviet citizen who wishes to propagate any unorthodox idea is a clear indication of the way they regard such ideas, wherever found. It is a declaration that if we were in their power, they would do the same to us as they have done to Orlov and to so many others. It is a denial of our right to exist. Why anyone should imagine that the Soviet attitude to foreign affairs has any different motivation is a mystery. It is in this sense that, as

President Kennedy said, 'Peace, in the last analysis, is a matter of human rights.'

From the point of view of the West, it is true, as Engels commented of an earlier time, that 'As soon as Russia has an internal development, and with that, internal party struggles, the attainment of a constitutional form under which these party struggles may be fought without violent convulsions . . . the traditional Russian policy of conquest is a thing of the past'—and that is not yet. In the meantime, various evolutions and revolutions are possible. But for the immediate future Russia is stuck with a group of rulers who are faced by a society tending in every respect away from their concepts, but who are in possession of an immensely powerful instrument for blocking social and political change. In foreign affairs we have the unpleasant problem of an inept Soviet oligarchy, with huge military resources, answerable to none and possessed of a surly hostility to all other forms of political life.

The points made here are clearly of the utmost importance to all foreign-policy decisions made in the West. There is a school of thought, or at least of speech, which continually asserts that the Soviet order has already changed in an absolutely essential fashion: that it is no longer the vehicle of an irreconcilable Leninist dogma. If this were true, it would be of great importance. To accept it as true if it were not true, on the other hand, would mean that we were basing our foreign policy on a major fallacy. One would think, therefore, that those who believe that such a change has taken place would offer evidence of some sort that this has indeed occurred.

Such evidence might include showing that the state and Party institutions which are the vehicle of the Leninist dictatorship have changed. Here we are on safe ground: no change whatever has taken place. Then it might be shown that there was a tendency to pluralism in the thought of the Soviet rulers, and hence to tolerance of other ideas: no sign of such a change has appeared, either in the conduct of the Soviet rulers towards unorthodox ideas within the Soviet Union or in their attitudes to political and other views they regard as heretical or wrong in the outside world. Finally, a tendency to reconciliation with other orders might be expected to manifest itself in the acceptance of a lower level of armament than that now in being and the avoidance of a 'forward' foreign policy in various parts of the world: this too does not sound like a very reliable description of what is actually going on.

Those who advance such a view seem to be lacking in general historical perspective and sense. It has long been a commonplace among those who can genuinely be described as historians (that is, knowledgeable not merely in a particular subject but in history in general) that political cultures and political psychologies have great intrinsic momentum and are not easily deflected. Changes may occur, but they do not occur with anything like the speed implied. It would be hard to find, throughout human history, an example of a group of oligarchs who, within a period of a few years, suddenly became democrats, or a group of adherents to a closed and totalist view of the world who rapidly changed into followers of John Stuart Mill.

The other impression one gets of the sponsors of this theory of great changes in the Soviet attitudes is that they are, politically speaking, not men of the world. They seem to be isolated either by a general 'idealism' or by the mere distancing from reality inherent in academic life. This, or other circumstances, leads them to interpret the USSR in their own terms. Soviet contacts sometimes help. Tsarism, during the extreme despotic period (under Nicholas I, for example), was represented to the outer world, and to the majority of influential visitors, through what appeared to be a highly civilised and highly Europeanised stratum. A not dissimilar situation exists today. The ambassadors, the leading officials in contact with foreigners, the hostesses of the 1830s were indeed, in a sense, Europeanised—to the degree, in fact, that French was their habitual language of conversation. Today the diplomats, the scientists who entertain Western colleagues at Academogorsk or visit them at Pugwash, are good linguists with manners and tastes adapted to the West. Some of Nicholas's similar representatives were disaffected and well disposed to democracy. Nevertheless, the bulk were loyal servants of the tsar and, in their personal capacities, were people who lived among, and benefited from, the most overt, crude and violent serfdom or slavery. . . .

Again, Walter Laqueur, Director of the Institute of Contemporary History, notes that in the West 'Soviet insistence on the continuation of the ideological struggle is all too often not taken seriously'; because the idea is alien to Western thought, people are inclined to think that Soviet pronouncements are merely a matter of lip-service to doctrine. In fact, however, 'ideological struggle is not something which concerns the philosophers. It is a synonym for political struggle, and political struggle, needless to say, means power, not only the power of ideas, but also some far more tangible things.' Laqueur adds that the notion sometimes held by Western statesmen, that Soviet policy is difficult to understand (and he quotes Chancellor Brandt directly to that effect), is only the case 'if one refuses to take seriously what Soviet leaders are saying' and if one refuses to compare their sayings with their actions.

A commonly expressed notion, especially in such periodicals as *Scientific American,* is that no 'rational' government would get into, or even risk, an atomic war. The word 'rational' here conceals assumptions repeatedly warned against in this book. To take the case of Maoist China, for example: we find a whole series of remarks by prominent officials, up to Mao himself, to the effect that even if whole countries like Italy or Czechoslovakia were destroyed, 'other peoples will remain, and imperialism will be annihilated.' Mao actually said to Nehru that in such a war, even if half the world's population were destroyed, socialism would be victorious and would soon make up the deficit.

There is nothing irrational about starting a nuclear war *if* one believes (a) that the world victory of one's system is in principle worth any expenditure of human life and material destruction; (b) that the alternative is the economic and general decline of one's system; (c) that no better opportunity of victory is likely to arise.

Of course, an expansionist nuclear power would hope not to have to use its weapons, but would aim rather to reduce its opponents to surrender by a nuclear bluff they would be too weak to call. Nevertheless, the effectiveness of the bluff depends on the real ability and determination to fight if necessary; and (as Professor Pipes has weightily shown) Soviet military doctrine firmly asserts the winnability of a nuclear war.

Admittedly, the Soviet leadership is not so un-'rational' as Mao's was. Yet we cannot grant it the full 'rationality' of the Western scientist either.

The central problem for Moscow seems to be this: the maintenance of the present political system will mean the gradual deterioration of the USSR into a second-class power. In principle, the rulers must either accept this or change their system. Neither option seems plausible. But a third possibility remains — to embark on an expansionist foreign policy. This seems to have been the choice made in the mid-sixties, with the enormous investment not so much in the strategic missile force, which could, according to certain arguments, be considered a necessary match for that of the US, but in a huge navy, whose sole role is to export Soviet influence and apply Soviet pressure in hitherto virgin territory.

The sensible choice, *from a Western point of view,* would have been to make some attempt to modernise the political and economic system, to introduce the principle of consensual pluralism. The pressures pushing the Kremlin in this direction are obviously powerful, but, as things are at present, not nearly as powerful as the built-in strength and inertia of the Party machine and the Party mind. Until the third path, that of expansion, is blocked, there is little question of even the beginnings of the evolution of the USSR into a peaceful inhabitant, in principle, of a world community.

Of course, Western civic culture is economically and humanly superior. This guarantees nothing. Barbarian conquest has sometimes been due to superior organisation and superior military technology or technique (as with the iron-weaponed and horse-borne invaders of the old empires of the Middle East and, in another sense, the Mongol conquerors of Russia). More commonly, however, it has been a matter of the barbarians mastering the techniques of their more civilised prospective victims and using them with greater energy and determination.

As I have argued in a book more specifically concerned with foreign policy (*Present Danger*), only a West equipped with adequate armament and showing adequate political will might avert danger over a long enough period to allow the evolution of the USSR into a fairly consensual and peaceable state.

The Soviet rulers are by no means sure of themselves. Their development of an expansionist policy has been undertaken very tentatively and has only gathered momentum because of the absence of credible opposition to them from, in particular, the United States.

In such circumstances the only diplomacy is that of hard bargaining. The idea that the granting of concessions out of sheer good will may induce a change of heart and comparable concessions on the other side stems from ignorance of the motivation of the other culture. All attempts to apply to the USSR concepts derived from totally different societies, with different histories, cultures, governmental systems and ideologies, are labour-saving devices which do not really save labour.

The evolution of the Soviet state into something approaching true civic culture is not a short-term prospect. But, let us repeat, if the West pursues the correct policies, it should be the single direction which lies open. And we should recall that such an evolution is essential in the long run if world peace is to be maintained and a cooperative world order is to be created.

Above all, the representatives of the Western consensual culture must constantly bear in mind that it is impossible to conduct a sensible foreign policy if one makes baseless assumptions about the most profound motivations of the other political cultures and psychologies which at present share the globe with our own. And such misunderstandings are endemic in circles in the West concerned with international politics or with instructing the public mind about their nature. This is a situation which it is hardly enough to call unsatisfactory: it is potentially disastrous. Alexander Herzen wrote over a century ago: 'Let Europe know her neighbour. So far she only fears him. Let her find out what it is she fears.'

PART THREE

The Mechanisms of Misunderstanding

CHAPTER 10

Systematisation Fallacies

The general characteristics and the opposing principles of the despotic and consensual cultures seem clear enough. One would expect that they would be understood on both sides. In our own sphere that would imply a general agreement, in particular among the educated classes, not only about the facts, but also about the sort of policies appropriate to them.

It need hardly be said that the real picture is very different. Misunderstandings about both our own and the despotic cultures, and about the nature and possibilities of politics in general, are widespread *especially* among the educated classes. So we are bound to consider, as a major element in the relationship between these cultures, both the nature of and the reasons for such misunderstandings.

I shall later argue that political attitudes are very much a matter of temperament. Meanwhile, one motivation of great importance seems to be a wish for, and so an assertion of, certainty in fields where it cannot be attained: Bryan Magee tells us, speaking of the psychological effects of the undermining of 'certainty': 'Popper's arguments that we can know of no meaning in history other than that invested in it by human beings have a psychologically disturbing, because disorienting, effect on some people who feel themselves placed in some sort of existentialist void by them.' The Israelites complained of being led out of the house of bondage. And the intellectual serfdom of supposed rationality and certitude retains its attraction.

It is something of a paradox that the shallowest and most pretentious expressions of this notion should huddle under the protection of sociology. For the founding fathers, such as Weber (and, in his different way, Durkheim), marked out a new area of the study of society precisely in opposition to the idea that institutions are simply intellectual creations and can be formed at will and that the individual in society can so deracinate himself as truly to stand outside it, judge it and specify its replacement. They equally saw that there could be no such thing as a society without a certain moral consensus, together with ritual and sacred subjects which imply a deeper level of solidarity than mere conscious acceptance, and that any society that abandoned these would disintegrate.

Moreover, far from its being the case that an air of objectivity can be genuine, it is perfectly plain that in most cases the social and political scientist, like anyone else, has his prejudices and preconceptions and misrepresents them by this sort of concealment. I have argued elsewhere that open admission of views tends to force the historian towards the practical limits of objectivity as regards evidence, and that it is an error to suppose the contrary. The more rigour is claimed where it is unobtainable, the more pervasive the tacit assumptions and prejudices appear to be.

The key word in modern studies of politics is 'model'. With its overtones of something that works in the same way as its original, like a model steam engine, it is highly inappropriate. A modest and realistic word like 'sketch' would be more suitable, in not giving the impression that the model-maker has, at least in essentials, mastered the workings of his original. He never has. Polities are *sui generis*. And though they may be conveniently treated under general categories for many purposes, the description of the elements involved must not be pressed beyond what is possible and appropriate, in this or in any other field where rigour is inapplicable.

The contrary tradition of Aristotle, which normally proceeds from the actual state of affairs, seems preferable. As he remarks:

> In studying this subject we must be content if we attain as high a degree of certainty as the matter of it admits. . .Such being the nature of our subject and such our way of arguing in our discussions of it, we must be satisfied with a rough outline of the truth, and for the same reason we must be content with broad conclusions.

The open society is, in fact, the result of the absence of a belief in rigorous political science. As Nicola Chiaromonte has put it, it is the most perverse of all modern ideas (though similar notions go back a long way) that 'the course of things must have a single meaning, or that events can be contained in a single system'. Judgments in political matters may be made in simple terms and be none the worse for that. Churchill understood the Nazis better than Chamberlain did, not because he had a vast vocabulary of political science terms to analyse it by, but because he had some knowledge of history and of evil. Again, I remember after the Hungarian Revolution that the distinguished scholar Professor Peter Wiles, who had chanced to be in Budapest at the time, was interviewed on television. Asked what, in his view, were the causes of that revolution, he answered simply, 'They were fed up with telling lies.'

'*Die Politik ist keine exakte Wissenschaft*', as Bismarck told the Prussian Chamber in 1863. It was only at about this time that such a remark was evidently beginning to be necessary. German academics who had, as they thought, systematised most other fields of knowledge, were now treating history and politics as though these too could be constrained by a set of formulae, developing a tradition which had only recently become dominant, though going back to such aberrations, two hundred years previously, as Leibnitz's extraordinary 'mathematical proof' that the Count Palatine of Neuburg must win the Polish throne (*Specimen demonstrationum politicarum pro eligendo rege Polonorum*, 1664).

It has been one of the marks of our time that the prestige of the physical and other genuine sciences has been so great that other studies have wished to share it. Unfortunately, it is not as easy to introduce scientific rigour into areas in which the quantity of available information cannot as yet support such structures. As a result, in psychology, sociology, linguistics, literary criticism and so forth inflated theorisings have been treated as though they were established doctrine. The position is roughly that of phrenology in the last century. A complicated and, on the face of it, sophisticated methodology was used to study phenomena which appeared to be directly related to the subject, but from which in practice absolutely no useful information could really be extracted. Physiognomy was also developed as a 'science' by Lavater: Norman Douglas in his *Siren Land* effectively ridicules the attempts by its practitioners to deduce many contradictory characteristics from a bust of Tiberius—one which, as it happened, was probably not of Tiberius at all.

Yet the academic mind cannot be kept from premature theory. Behaviourism, systems analysis (and soon, no doubt, catastrophe theory) arise elsewhere and are applied one by one to politics.

As Dr Ida R. Hoos points out, the word 'system' is so general a term that it can be used in any field from nuclear weaponry to elementary education and thus leads to the assumption that the ideas of design, engineering and analysis suitable to one can be applied to others. She comments (in *Systems Analysis in Social Policy*):

> In the real world there appears to be about as much justification for committing society's sundry malfunctioning systems to the care of a systems analyst whose sole claim to expertise is technical as to call a hydraulic engineer to cure an ailing heart because his speciality is pumping systems. Although the term 'system' can be applied to both space hardware and social problems, the inputs are vastly different, as are the controls and objectives. In the engineered system, the components are tangible, the variables controlled, and the outputs identifiable. In the social sphere, the crucial elements often defy definition and control and do not behave according to a set of rules. There is no quality control of a social system; the test of its effectiveness is to a large extent a reflection of values and it is certainly not amenable to mathematical measurement.

Resemblances of form rather than of intent or actual activity tend to mislead. A wolf bears a very close resemblance, physiologically speaking, to a basset hound. Its reaction to a pat on the head, however, is different. A death camp is 'structured', both physically and operationally, very much like a holiday camp. Two identical cars may present different dangers if one is driven by an alcoholic psychopath. The Roman Empire had the same structure under Nero and under Vespasian, under Gallienus and under Aurelian.

The same objection applies to *all* premature systematising. The success of conceptual and mathematical rigour in the fields in which it can be applied (for example, in the engineering triumphs which go into the *Apollo* spacecraft) must be distinguished from the failure of such applications in areas where rigour is, in fact, inapplicable. The failure of scientific sociologists in putting vast sums of money into poverty programmes which have done nothing to alleviate destress, except to some degree among the bureaucracy, is matched by the failure of MacNamara's military academics and their computerised science of war, with its escalations and responses.

And this disaster, in 1966, was little more than a repeat of 1916, when the entire Western European culture was severely shaken, if not nearly destroyed. Then the arch-villain was Field Marshal von Falkenhayn, the most 'scientific general' ever to ruin his country, as Liddell Hart remarked, who put into effect a 'calculated' method of winning the war for Germany. The arts of strategy were forgotten, the uncertainties of the battlefield dismissed. The French army was to be destroyed not by attempting a breakthrough, but by attacking a position which the French were obliged to defend at all costs and where they would 'bleed to death' whether the objective, Verdun, was captured or not. This was to be done simply by a concentration of weaponry which could not be matched within the narrow French salient. The result was the great ten-month battle of 1916, with its 700,000 dead or missing on a sixteen-kilometre front. It is true that the French army was never the same again, but nor was the German. The only net German gain in exchange for one-third of a million dead was 'the acquisition of a piece of raddled land little larger in area than the combined Royal Parks in London'.

Generally speaking, attempts by the new schools of political sciences to introduce rigour into the subject are comparably fallacious, and hence dangerous if taken seriously (and, if not, a notable waste of money). There have been reports of an attempt to analyse problems of international detente by feeding twelve hundred factors into a computer. Such readily numericised factors do not exist: at best there are numbers of infinite variables and of unknowns.

The notion that everything can be reduced to mathematical manipulation is in any case basically mistaken. We do not even have a general mathematical solution to the three-body problem, which can only be solved by progressive approximation. Again, as we all know, it has long since been proved by Gödel that some problems are in principle insoluble, mathematically speaking. But, more generally, we should consider the fact that it is impossible, even in principle, to design a computer that could cover all the potentialities of a chess game. For it can be shown that such a computer would need more units than there are particles in the entire universe. And chess has rules in the sense that international politics does not.

In most areas of historical and anthropological investigation genuine scholars have progressively abandoned theories of linear development and the older attempts to attain generality by the selection and inflation of often superficial similarities as 'essential'. On the other hand, at a certain theoretical level worthless generalisation is still rampant — nowhere more than in 'political science'. It is for the most part evident to serious students that (except in a very short-range sense) predictability in the political and social fields is both in principle and in practice unattainable, at any rate with the aid of the weak and fallible general theories at present in existence. The urge to promote premature and inadequately supported generality, far from being a higher development, is a sure sign of primitivism.

Sorokin remarks of some of his fellow sociologists that their 'speech disorders' include the 'blind transference of terms from the rational sciences', the 'ponderously obscure description of platitudes' and 'neologisms which hinder precise communication'.

In the scientific journals proper all the more interesting papers are those which seek to test a theory by finding exceptions or apparent exceptions to its operation. 'An Anomalous Case of . . .' is a typical paper title in such a journal. In the quasi-sciences the opposite is generally true. The concern there is only too often to prove what is already believed. Nor, in most cases, are there factual or experimental data which the propounder of the theory would admit as casting doubt on belief if they went one way rather than another. It is true that the adherents of rival theories reject each other's proofs, but the methods they use are seldom those of the sciences.

Insofar as they do retain the element of intellectual rigour which makes them liable to refutation on empirical and evidential grounds, these proofs are invariably so refuted. Insofar as they are irrefutable, it is precisely because they are so general and flexible as to convey no real information. In that case, why do they emerge? We are plainly in the presence not of an intellectual but of a psychological phenomenon.

How did such delusions, which so frequently falsify views of our politics and those of international politics, ever arise? It is, at any rate, an astonishing tribute to the power and persistence of the desire for tidiness and certitude.

Even stranger is the influence of that elastic systematisation 'Marxism', if no longer in Eastern Europe or even in France, at least in a section of Western thought. Marx tells us that his ideas came from three main sources: German philosophy, French socialism and English economics. He started off, of course, with the first of these in its portentous, though otherwise not very impressive, Hegelian form. Hegel was above all one of those philosophers who, rather than directly applying themselves to the genuine problems raised by Hume and Kant, erected a vast mechanism of interlocking concepts, vague enough to be applicable to almost any situation.

One notes of Hegel, a true heir of the Sophists and similar philosophers, as Gibbon noted of the neo-Platonists, that 'This freedom of interpretation. . .exposed the vanity of their art. . .the solemn trifling and the impenetrable obscurity of these sages who professed to reveal the system of the universe. As they translated an arbitrary cipher they could extract. . .any sense that was adapted to their favourite system.' When Kant showed that it was possible, by pure ratiocination, to prove the validity of two opposite propositions, his aim was to convey that pure reason was inadequate to the understanding of a transcendent order in the universe, not that some new rationality could be developed according to which both contradictions were correct. But such was the conclusion Hegel drew. His work, at once extreme and pettifogging, was of sufficient bulk to impress the 'wise fools'.

The Sophists two millennia previously had exaggerated the power of pure ratiocination and had thus produced a rootless antinomianism. Hegel took the dead-end of pure reason and deduced from it a form of 'rationality' in which self-contradiction was admitted and elevated to a principle of thought. His successors, the Marxists, used Hegelianism to give a novel air to the old mechanistic rationalism of the eighteenth and previous centuries and to provide it with a means, as in a conjuring trick, of escaping the consequences of refutation.

A formula that explains all formulae must also logically have an explanation for itself, thus becoming a member of the 'class of classes', which early in our century was shown to lead to paradox. This the Hegelians, and the Marxists after them, happily evaded.

But the main concept from Hegel which really meant something to Marxism was its simple notion that everything proceeds by the mutual reaction of 'opposites', in 'contradictions'. Hegel, thinking of the world as Idea, intended this to be the equivalent of seeking the truth by debate, and the word 'dialectics' is a term of intellectual controversy, not of material happenings. But Marx found it possible to apply it in a material sense. He had already noted from French writers (though the notion goes back to Classical times) that one of

the most striking phenomena of the history of society, at least sometimes, is what is describable as a class struggle. Socialism he got
from the French Utopians like Fourier and Saint-Simon and worked
it in as the last of the various social orders produced by the series
of class struggles he saw in history. English economics, with its
Labour Theory of Value, enabled him to invent the Theory of
Surplus Value, giving 'scientific' validity to the notion of the
irreconcilability of class interests he saw in modern industrial
society.

Marxism specifically distinguished itself from all other ap-
proaches to socialism on the grounds that it alone was 'scientific'.
Marx uses the word 'science' in a special Hegelian sense, true, but
still as indicating a single theory of universal development: indeed,
Hegel had in effect constructed a non-theistic theology. But it is
also the case that he (like Marx, indeed), felt himself empowered
on this basis to intervene in the sciences proper, as when, in the
very year in which the discovery of Ceres was announced, he
published a dissertation proving that the existence of a planet
between Mars and Jupiter was impossible, thus anticipating the
prophetic skill, in the social field, of his pupil.

The fundamental point of Marxism was, of course, that the
development of the means of production was the sole motive power
of historical change; but, as has been pointed out, such a theory
cannot explain why the means of production developed at all.

What remains today of Marxism, once a large and ambitious
structure, is little more than the basic dogma that our society (and
all others) is driven by unappeasable strife, in which one con-
testant must inevitably destroy the other. It was back in the 1840s
that Marx announced this discovery, though the search for the
supposed evidence for it took another forty years. Marx stated
flatly that all history was the history of class struggles. His great
point was that people had previously made all sorts of political,
philosophical and other moves without realising that their motive
was class struggle, but that at last the truth was out.

The Marxian attitude to this was odd. It might be thought that
when unconscious causes of strife are brought to light the natural
thing would be to subject them to conscious control and abate them.
When Christianity identified Original Sin as a source of trouble,
it did not say, 'Well, now we know what's wrong, go ahead and indulge
it.' Marx, on the other hand, sought none of the benefits of his

supposed new knowledge: he merely urged the side he put his money on to do its worst.

Of course, his formula was in any case inadequate. There have been many clashes in history between social groups or economic classes: to name them the 'essential' is merest metaphysics. The century was full of one-track pseudo-sciences of the phrenology type. The fact that yet another *Herr Doktor* had discovered the mainspring of history did not much affect real historians. They tended to stick to the view that the complexities of reality are to be treated as such. But Marx went ahead to justify his notion. Considerable, if misapplied, inventiveness was needed—and that was Marx's real talent.

Marxism (and in this important point successive Soviet governments have been consistently orthodox) holds that consciousness is determined by the mode of production. Marx derived all the evils resulting from capitalism—alienation, exploitation, crises, etc.—from 'commodity' production, that is, from the market system. In fact, the whole history of the USSR testifies to a refusal to face the fact that a complex modern economy cannot operate without a market mechanism. Why (even leaving aside economic common sense) Marx thought that a bureaucrat's decision was less alienating than the 'unplanned' play of market forces is not clear. In any case, 'commodity' became the Marxist shibboleth.

To direct people's consciousness into decent, cooperative channels, the non-commodity system must be established: in this, at least, Lenin and Stalin and Brezhnev are good Marxists. Unfortunately, the results, as we have seen, are (a) that the non-market economy does not flourish, and indeed only survives at all through the existence, usually winked at, of large-scale market lubrication of its grinding gear wheels; (b) that the resulting shortages produce an extreme personal economic motivation among the populace; (c) that Marxist faith in the consciousness of the 'worker' is shown to fail once he gets a job with power to it, as Bakunin predicted. And, as Solzhenitsyn's hero points out in *Cancer Ward,* the conception of 'class origins' is in effect racist:

'. . . All right, maybe I *am* the son of a merchant, third class, but I've sweated blood all my life. Here, look at the calluses on my hands! So what am I? Am I bourgeois? Did my father give me a different sort of red or white corpuscle in my blood? That's why

I tell you yours isn't a class attitude but a racial attitude. You're a racist!. . .'

'It makes no difference if you had ten proletarian grand-fathers, if you're not a worker yourself you're no proletarian,' boomed Kostoglotov. 'He's not a proletarian, he's a son of a bitch. The only thing he's after is a special pension, I heard him say so himself.'

Marx (like others facing a fresh social phenomenon) came to his conclusion about the mystic historical nature of the new proletarian class before he had even seen an actual proletarian — as, indeed, was true of Lenin in the 1880s. But, come to that, Marx seems to have had a very odd idea of the bourgeoisie. Who can read without laughter those paragraphs of the *Communist Manifesto,* which are solemnly printed year after year, about bourgeois sex life in Victorian times?

The Communists have no need to introduce community of women; it has existed almost from time immemorial.

Our bourgeois, not content with having the wives and daughters of their proletarians at their disposal, not to speak of common prostitutes, take the greatest pleasure in seducing each other's wives.

Bourgeois marriage is in reality a system of wives in common. . . .

Even apart from the notion of the Victorian bourgeoisie sharing each other's wives on this grand scale, there is something a little unreal, is there not, about the idea of the factory owner passing around the slums which house his employees, debauching a wife here, a daughter there? Particularly, perhaps, during the period of which Marx was writing. It is true that Marx himself seduced, and had a child by, his maid—who might perhaps be regarded in this context as a proletarian employee. . . .

Marx's dogmatism about the nature of 'classes', by the merest verbalism, confined them to groups defined by 'ownership' or other-wise narrowed the issues; it still does for many, whose minds resemble, on a more abstract plane, the products of those societies in which infants' heads are bound with wooden constraints which force them into unnatural and unsuitable shapes.

It is a curious fact that Marxism does not have, and does not even pretend to have, any mechanism to explain the internal development of the social system it describes as 'Asiatic'. In these areas of traditionalist despotism, under which the larger part of the world's population lived for thousands of years, Marx quite explicitly and admittedly found no class conflict, in the absence of opposing groups categorisable as economic classes. Change only came, as he puts it, when Western culture burst in on them: an unconscious illustration of Marx's Eurocentrism. But this is an extraordinary state of things. There is no law of geography which dictates that it would be impossible for all the inhabitable areas of the earth to lie in latitudes, and be subject to physical conditions, of the type that produced the Asiatic empires. But a theory of history which even pretends to be comprehensive becomes absurd once such a point is admitted. (Indeed, how can any 'rigorous' theory account for Britain's being an island, a fact which has certainly contributed most importantly to the world's social and political development. Its insulation was the merest accident on any rational time scale, dating from some ten thousand years ago, a geological instant.)

It is another point highly destructive of the Marxist scheme that no serious student, even among those who incline on the whole to the Marxist view, accepts that all institutional and economic developments in the various countries of the world can meaningfully be ascribed to the four or five Marxist categories. Their variety is now far more striking than the points they have in common, as is the case with any study when particulars become more widely known. A whale may be called a fish only by an inadequately informed categorizer.

It may be remarked that Marx and Engels wrote at a time when economic forces were unprecedentedly powerful and political ones very weak, at least in the countries they were chiefly concerned with. Since then political mechanisms more powerful than the social forces have been invented, and the wills of new dictatorships have been enforced against all the real wishes of society and in opposition to the needs of the economy. The epoch of Stalin, Mao and Hitler is the very last one to which a materialist conception of history, as the product of economic trends, could possibly be applied.

It is true that among the half-educated, a general vocabulary of social orders has become Marxised. Feudalism, socialism, capitalism: these are the words used to describe states all around the world. In some ways more of a nuisance still, they are taken to be *the* categories of history and to imply that a Marxist, or near-Marxist, evolution is what is actually happening, a view not likely to be shared by many historians.

(But even at a lower level, the self-christenings of the extreme left are often accepted or left unchallenged. One American Senator was even found to express his regret, during the troubles in Angola, that the United States had not for once found itself on the side of a 'national liberation movement': the picayune American involvement extended, in fact, to the support of two guerrilla groups which had fought the Portuguese continuously for many years and on a bigger scale than the movement so labelled. The only qualification they lacked was that they were not anti-Western, or at least not pro-totalitarian.)

Another fault of Marxism, and generally of all theories stressing conflict as the centre of historical development, is that its proponents distort history by inflating anything resembling a riot or revolt into the central event of the period. Prof Torn Haga, mentioning a few peasant risings in eighteenth-century Japan, was asked why they hardly entered into his general account of the period. He replied that they were peripheral and atypical and were only widely bruited at present because of a doctrinally motivated Marxist search for events suited to that theory. The same, of course, could be said of English history. To read some writers, one would think that the nineteenth century consisted largely of the Peterloo Massacre, the Tolpuddle Martyrs and Bloody Sunday. All were exceptional rather than typical events, and even if they were not, they would contrast pretty markedly with experience in, for example, France. Six were killed in the Peterloo rioting; none of the Tolpuddle Martyrs, though they were all disgracefully victimised and 'transported', was actually martyred in the normal sense; while Bloody Sunday produced precisely one death, an accidental one. Indeed, the use of such a term for such an event shows a remarkable scraping of the barrel by those determined to find British parallels to Continental shenanigans. In fact, the total death toll in civil disturbances in Britain over a century and a half can hardly be as much as one hundred, or, to put it another way, the equivalent of a single busy afternoon on a Paris barricade. This search for, and exaltation of, armed clashes is really no more than a mirror image of that patriotic romanticism about battles so much sneered at by people perfectly happy with this left-wing equivalent.

Arthur Koestler tells in his autobiography of a talk he was giving in London during the 1940 Blitz. A man was saying that here in England, we had long been free from violence. At this point the windows blew in. But the man went on, over the roar of the anti-aircraft guns and the crash of the bombs, with the line of his argument. From Koestler's point of view, this was a fantastic paradox. But, of course, it was not: we distinguish completely between the principles of civil society and the principles of war. Anyone who argued that as British troops were fighting elsewhere, it was all right to be violent in the civic context would have been thought to rave.

The basic Marxist theory that social orders eventually become barriers to the expansion of production was applied by him to what he regarded as the capitalist social order. His work made specific deductions; in *Das Kapital* he speaks of having discovered the 'Natural Laws' of Capitalist Production, adding that 'these laws worked things out with iron necessity towards inevitable results.' And Marx's Marxism was indeed a scientific theory, in the sense that it made predictions which were falsifiable. (Most of these have long since been falsified.) In particular, of course, the industrial proletariat was inevitably to get poorer and poorer, ownership was to become more and more concentrated and, above all, the capitalist mode of production would be incapable of expansion and innovation. It should be noted that these predictions of Marx's were not random suggestions, but were rigorously deduced from his whole analysis of the workings of the capitalist system.

The Marxian Theory of Value is not an abstraction. He seriously urged on many occasions that price fluctuated round 'value' as determined by labour theory. For Marx, in the end, presented himself above all as an economist. Nowadays nothing whatever is left of his economic views, ponderously, lengthily elaborated. Yet he himself would have conceded that without the supposedly 'objective' support of his economic researches, his social theories would have lacked all verification and intellectual respectability and would have been mere rhetoric. He proved, to his own satisfaction, that the class rift in modern times is rooted in the fact that all profit is extracted (as 'surplus value') from the workers. This again is purest metaphysics. No evidence was presented. Profit might equally well be entirely the fruit of capital alone, or of a combination — of capital and labour.

He drew several conclusions: that as the proportion of capital to labour in production increased, profit must (obviously) fall and wages decrease; that capitalism would operate as a constraint on production; that the industrial countries must become increasingly polarised between a small group of capitalists and a huge and increasingly improverished proletariat; and that the latter must overthrow the former in a revolution.

The erroneous Ptolemaic system in astronomy triumphed for intellectually reputable reasons: it was because the genius of evidence and analysis deployed on its side was greater than that on the side of the truth. It was also, of course, more complex. This might be thought a point against its acceptance. But complexity itself impresses many people, while simplicity seems to be lacking in richness. Marx is not really up to Ptolemy. He produced, it is true, and in the same way, a big book with big claims. But its actual predictions were refuted fairly early, and the equivalent of the multiplication of epicycles has, in this case, not been very impressive.

There is nothing necessarily disastrous about the existence of erroneous political and social theory. People might, indeed, argue that the avoidance of a comprehensive theory until a successful one is found is a bad thing, that sciences have progressed through erroneous general theories. But Phlogiston Theory (let us say) did no one any harm. If Marxism were simply academic, albeit erroneous, there could be no complaint. It is its impact on society, its attempt to force social orders to follow a system that does not in fact apply, that results in terror and regression.

Marxism fails as a 'science' on the grounds that it is not predictive, but also because its internal logical coherence is inadequate. Of course, what now passes for Marxism has abandoned the essentials of Marx's own analysis (or has added special amendments which, in fact, reverse the meaning). Thus it has become at best no more than a very vague and general theory, postulating that capitalism causes certain troubles; that the class struggle within it is the decisive phenomenon; and that this will eventually replace it by 'socialism'.

Before his death in 1883 Marx himself already saw that some of his predictions were not working out. By the early 1900s it was clear that the whole conception was a mass of error. The German Social Democrat Eduard Bernstein noted that the Western working classes were everywhere better off and unalienated, and that a juster society could be achieved by cooperation and compromise, so that Marx needed 'revising'—a polite way of saying 'writing off'. Except as rhetoric and piety, classical Marxism was dead, killed by facts.

In his way, among the revolution-addicted intelligentsia of backward Russia, Lenin saw this. His conclusion was different. History was not moving as Marx predicted. It must, by sheer willpower and organisation, be *made* to go the way Marx had said it naturally would. It was as though, after the refutation of phrenology, a devotee had affirmed that if a man hadn't got the right bumps he could bloody well be hit on the head till he developed them. The working class was failing in its allotted role; its duties were taken over by a party of professional revolutionaries. Lenin's was in effect not a class struggle at all, but a struggle against all other elites in favour of his own. His identifying himself with 'the workers' was a mere verbal and mystical justification, used even in those times when he admitted that the real workers were sick of him and his rule. It is, of course, in its Leninist form that Marxism survives, reduced to a theory of social war and terrorist dictatorship, a poison in all decent societies, to justify the violent and encourage the power maniac.

The Marxist revolutionary believes it to be in the nature of things that dictatorship and terror are needed if the good of humanity is to be served, just as the Aztec priests believed themselves to be entirely justified in ripping the hearts out of thousands of victims, since, had they not done so, the sun would have gone out, a far worse catastrophe for mankind. In either case the means are acceptable, being inevitable —that is, *if* the theory is correct. . . .

As for economic views of the Marxist sort (though not only of the Marxist sort), why they became 'popular' is well explained by Hugh Gaitskell in his contribution to *What Everybody Wants to Know about Money.* Such views

> are frequently vague or complicated and not as a rule expressed in the clearest possible manner. How is it that, in spite of this, they achieve such fame and popularity? . . . vagueness and complexity are not really limitations, but, on the contrary, advantages. For they make the task of criticism tedious and difficult and enable the heretic to say with perfect truth that his views have never been refuted. At the same time the support of the plain man is not in any way forfeited. For the most part he will not bother his head with the complicated details. He will be content to accept the broad conclusions largely on irrational grounds.

Major Marxist doctrines, in fact, seem to have been formulated with the idea of giving the rank-and-file follower the idea that some simple semi-instinctive attitude is supported by 'science' and erudition. The Theory of 'Surplus Value' has no logical basis and no deducible economic meaning. It is simply a rather grand way of saying 'the capitalists rob the workers'. As I have noted elsewhere, there was an attempt to debate this theory in the Italian Communist Party in the late twenties.

Palmiro Togliatti could not be persuaded to show any interest: the theory was, he said, not for the economists but for the masses (Ignazio Silone in *Dissent*, September–October 1970).

Something similar can be said about Lenin's Theory of Imperialism, which asserted that capitalism had temporarily evaded the long-overdue doom predicted for it by Marx through the export of capital to backward countries, 'where profits are usually high, for capital is scarce, the price of land is relatively low, wages are low, raw materials are cheap'.

In fact, capital was not exported to the colonial countries on any great scale. British foreign investment involved virtually no net outflow. The French colonies exported more than they imported. And the 'super-profits', as Lenin put it, allegedly arising from the colonies were a myth. Even the Rand mines gave an average annual return of just over 4 per cent.

Again, Lenin was concerned to show that 'finance' capital now controlled 'industrial' capital. But in Britain, for example, there was no important degree of merger, let alone control. His theory also insisted that finance capital should be the mainspring of imperial expansion: in fact, the big five German banks argued strongly against German expansion in Africa. Thus Lenin's Theory of Imperialism, too, was simply a way of rallying the pomp and circumstance of 'science' in support of the simple idea 'capitalists rob colonies'. (That wars for the control of this or that region in fact long preceded capitalism is obvious; it is also clear that wars launched by post-capitalist Marxist states, with the aim of acquiring just such control, persist.)

Sometimes Marxist attitudes are thought to be rational at their own level. This is far from being the full story. On the contrary, possession of, or by, the idea that one has final answers to all the problems of history and of society seems inevitably to lead to 'final answer' dogmas in other fields.

It must be symptomatic that (as we have noted) there is a strong tendency among Marxists to accept pseudo-sciences in other fields. The mechanism involved seems to be related to the desire for complete solutions — which are, of course, more commonly found in the pseudo-sciences than in the sciences proper, just as Marxism's own claim to a definitive theory of society, history, philosophy and so on contrasts so markedly with the views of most serious historians and philosophers.

Wilhelm Liebknecht, one of Marx's most trusted followers after

Engels himself, tells in his memoirs that Marx examined his skull with his fingers on their first meeting. Though not 'as zealous a devotee' of phrenology as revolutionaries like Gustav Struve, 'he believed in it to some extent', even having 'the phrenologist of the party' (that is, of the Communist League), Karl Pfaender, give him a further and more professional check later. Fortunately, Pfaender did not find 'anything which would have prevented my admission' into the League. Again, in 1866 Marx became enthusiastic about the theories of the adventurer Pierre Trémaux, who held that the distinctions between the races were attributable to the different soils on which they lived.

We have already touched on the extraordinary array of pseudo-sciences which attended triumphant Marxism in the USSR. But this sort of thing is not merely a Russian excess. For example, in the early sixties the Maoists reverted to various ancient but implausible devices, such as the swallowing of tadpoles as a means of contraception. Acupuncture, the ancient Chinese 'medical' system of sticking needles into various parts of the body to cure a variety of disorders, became accepted, and during the Maoist Cultural Revolution 'bourgeois' acupuncture specialists were driven out in favour of inexperienced enthusiasts. A team of these used previously 'forbidden points' for sticking the needles in so effectively that a high proportion of deaf-mutes treated by this method were heard to shout 'Long Live Chairman Mao!' (New China News Agency, 3 November 1968).

Not all Marxists would have been capable of such powerful idiocy. But to some degree Marxism itself can certainly be blamed. First of all, the principle of accommodating science to a particular metaphysic rather than leaving it to act autonomously seems bound to produce distortion. Secondly, the notion that Marxism is a basic universal science leads to the condition in which many people professing it feel that they are already fully educated and, in effect, capable of judging any subsidiary studies without adequate humility or effort. Hence, perhaps, its attraction for a certain type of Westerner.

More important, perhaps, these notions tend to show that those who seek cure-all formulae for reconstructing society are temperamentally inclined towards 'unorthodox' fads in other fields. This in turn may tend to cast doubt on the validity of their political-economic analyses. At least, there is some implication that the attraction of Marxism is not grounded on its rational persuasiveness, a point we shall return to as crucial.

CHAPTER 11

Verbalisation Fallacies

There is no clear-cut distinction between the fallacies of systematisation and those of mere verbal fetishism. Extreme systematisation seeks a complexity of 'rigorous', even mathematical, interconnections. The more flexible varieties, like Marxism, provide a ramshackle framework, which can be spread and stretched to cover all phenomena. At a lower level still, we get a job lot of weasel words, between which the connection is even less formalised and which are often little more than a set of reflexes: instead of a real world, they mark a sphere inhabited by crude categories, an array, a collection of verbalisms too lax to be thought of as amounting to a system, even a fallacious one.

Over twenty years ago Albert Camus wrote:

> Conformism today, it must be admitted, has fastened on the Left. It is true that the Right is not brilliant. But the Left is in full decadence, a prisoner of words, bogged down in its vocabulary, capable of no other than stereotyped answers, failing consistently to measure up to the reality from which it asserts nevertheless that it derives its laws. The Left is schizophrenic and should undergo treatment, by pitiless criticism, by using the heart, by sound reasoning, and by a little modesty.

'Bogged down in its vocabulary', in particular in 'democracy', 'socialism', 'revolution', 'capitalism', each leading vaguely to the others and returning back to itself in a roundabout, self-reflexive pattern.

Revolution

In her memoirs, entitled *Hope Against Hope* and published in 1971, the widow of the great Russian poet Osip Mandelshtam (who died in a Stalinist labour camp in 1938) quotes her brother as saying that the decisive part in the communists' subjugation of the intelligentsia was played not by terror and bribery but by the word 'revolution' which none of them could bear to give up. It is a word, he added, to which whole nations have succumbed. And still we find, as a commonly propagated notion, the conviction that always and everywhere throughout the world a Social Revolution is a Good Thing: a new variant of the simple *1066 and All That* approach to history.

'Revolution' (as used by the extreme left) is a specialised term implying in principle, first, that radical alteration of the social as well as the political structure takes place; second, that such change is beneficial; third (often at least), that it is inevitable; and fourth, that no other solution to social and other difficulties is practicable. The term testifies, in fact, to an abject trust in unproven, or disproven, political theory.

Sanguine attitudes to 'revolution' have existed mainly among comfortably situated intellectuals, who resent their own societies but suffer little from them. The modern 'liberal', rejoicing in the scandals about the Establishment, may remind one of the shock given to the old regime in France by the affair of the Cardinal's Necklace. Fréteau de Saint-Just, quite typically, of course exulted: 'What a triumph for Liberal ideas! A Cardinal a thief! The Queen implicated! Mud on the crosier and the sceptre!' He was himself of course to go to the guillotine before ten years were up.

But as Camus points out, 'none of the evils which totalitarianism claims to remedy is...worse than totalitarianism itself.' He might have added that, on the record, it does not even remedy those evils against which it particularly declaims — except, sometimes, in a purely superficial sense. That is, it may cure unemployment, as in Russia in the thirties. However, it is not unemployment as such but the hunger and misery it may cause which is the objection to it; and the Russians substituted for the temporary mass unemployment of the West the far greater misery and hunger of the more enduring and more heavily populated labour-camp system.

Meanwhile even a fairly unsatisfactory political arrangement, imperfect by the standards of all verbal tests, is preferable to any self-perpetuating regime, however tolerable at first, for it is invariable experience that the latter degenerates. But even 'liberals' who are not deceived, or not exactly deceived, on this particular point are often trapped by what on the face of it is a more substantial affinity. For both they and the revolutionary appear to be (in a sense, in fact, are) supporters of compulsory state action for what seems to be the common good. Nor is the difference between the two an absolutely clear-cut one, though, as de Tocqueville remarked about the differences between the moderate constitutional monarchies and the more left-wing republics even of his day, the revolutionary regime 'promises more but gives less'. Those who preach that the faults of our society can be cured by certain formulae, to be put into effect by an elite, should be required to show that they have studied the history of previous experiments on the same lines.

The logical errors of the simple-minded 'revolutionary' view are as obvious as the actual results. Bryan Magee notes that the idea that nothing can be changed until everything is changed is self-contradictory. We are, as it were, in a ship at sea. Improvements can be made in its structure, but an attempt to change it all at once would be absurd. He adds:

> The fact is, of course, that nearly all of us require the most important aspects of the social order to continue functioning through any reconstruction: people must continue to be fed and clothed and housed and kept warm; children, if they are not to be intolerably victimised, must continue to be cared for and educated; transport, medical, police and fire services must continue to operate. And in a modern society these things depend on large-scale organisation. To sweep it all away at once would be to create, literally, a chaos; and to believe that somehow out of *that* an ideal society would emerge borders on the mad, as does even the belief that a society merely better than the one we have now is more likely to emerge from chaos than from the society we have now.

Moreover, we have surely had enough of optimism about each new revolutionary regime. Its inevitable evolution into non-benevolent despotism ought to be established adequately by now. It is partly for this reason, instinctively or commonsensically understood, that radical perfectionism was found to have little appeal to the masses of the people in the Western world.

Yet a point accepted even by non-revolutionary 'liberals' is the idea that the first necessity in all countries with imperfections is a radical change in class relations or class structure. It is, of course, true that the economic hierarchy of all countries in the world is in some sense unjust from an egalitarian point of view. And if a guaranteed method of correcting one injustice without creating another were known, there would be something to say for urging such change. What is not clear is why it is thought that these radical changes, supported by revolutionaries in all countries and by 'liberals' in countries other than their own, should be regarded as the *only* method rather than the most difficult and the one most destructive of the economy and most productive of bloodshed and further injustice. It would be difficult to show that countries which go in for revolution have benefited, even in the sense indicated, as compared with countries that have not.

One of the most vulgar of errors, not at all incidentally, is the notion that violence proves seriousness. The contrary is usually true. In most cases violence proves superficiality of thought.

Above all the whole 'revolutionary' attitude ignores both organisational and human possibilities. Its notion of a perfect or perfectible revolutionary rule contradicts all experience. As Jefferson remarked, 'In every government on earth is some trace of human weakness, some germ of corruption and degeneracy, which cunning will discover, and wickedness insensibly open, cultivate and improve. Every government degenerates when trusted to the rulers of the people alone.'

And if the rulers are corruptible by power, it is equally the case that the revolutionary regimes are committed to attempting the impossible. Aristotle said, 'Two things we must keep constantly in view — what can be done and what should be done . . . both things possible and things proper.' But, for the revolutionary, if a thing is 'proper', its achievement can be secured by adequate willpower, violence and all the rest.

In fact, for this reason Western society is the only one containing a serious possibility of evolution; or rather, the others can only evolve, eventually, through the equivalent of attaining the Western political level. In the West the potential exists for a just society (which, whether in a form describable as socialism or not, might meet the criteria put forward by socialists).

Freedom; democracy

We have heard much adolescent-style debate on freedom. Of course, there is a sense in which it is a limitation on my 'freedom' that I cannot, or cannot yet, copulate in Piccadilly Circus or hit the Mayor of New York on the head with a baseball bat. But the conclusion to be drawn, by anyone except a maniac for verbalisms, is that terms should not be used in this way.

Such confusions exist even about the question of 'democracy' within the institutions of an open society. At any serious (as against verbal) level, it is fairly obvious that in conditions of the greatest civic and political liberty, there are areas in which an authoritarian element, with considerable subordination, is necessary. As John Paul Jones sensibly put it in 1775, 'True as may be the political principles for which we are now contending . . . the ships themselves must be ruled under a system of absolute despotism.'

The navy, indeed, is an extreme case. And in our time, even the navy has to some degree softened the 'absoluteness' of the despotism. This is a matter of expediency and compromise, but no democratisation in any real degree makes sense, any more than it does in, let us say, a university, at the other end of the spectrum.

'Democratisation' of un-democratisable institutions is sometimes, doubtless, the expression of a genuine Utopian ideal, as when the Jacobins by these means destroyed the French navy. But more often it is (in the minds of the leading activists at least) a conscious attempt to ruin the institutions in question, as when the Bolsheviks used the idea to destroy the old Russian army. When this (among other things) enabled them to take power themselves they were, of course, the first to insist on a discipline even more rigorous than before.

When the Provisional Government took over in March 1917 the country had been run by fairly efficient political and administrative machinery, and the discipline in the army was satisfactory. (It is a myth that 'war weariness' was among the causes of the 'February' Revolution: it was, on the contrary, carried out with the idea that the tsar and his milieu were insufficiently committed to the fight against Germany, and the programme of the new government, at first enthusiastically accepted by the soldiery, was designed to make the war a more national one.)

But the liberals who now took over in the capital and the localities changed all this. In the name of 'freedom' they destroyed the local administrative machinery and replaced it with amateurs; they destroyed the police force and replaced it with nothing. And in the army they permitted 'democratic rights' incompatible with discipline. So, generally speaking, what the liberals and right-wing socialists achieved

as a result of putting their democratic principles into effect in a dogmatic fashion was the virtual destruction of democratic state power,
to the degree that a petty *putsch* was able to overthrow it.

But even in less critical circumstances a democratic or consensual
order inevitably involves some restrictions on liberty: that is the
price for not being Robinson Crusoe. As John Jay says in the second
Federalist Paper, 'Nothing is more certain than the indispensable
necessity of Government, and it is equally undeniable, that whenever
and however it is instituted, the people must cede to it some of their
natural rights, in order to vest it with requisite powers.'

As to the argument that the use of 'force' by the state automatically warrants violence by its opponents, one is reminded of John
Selden's comment on this sort of debating point—that it has 'As much
Logic as the Boy that would have lain with his Grandmother, used to
his Father; You lay with my Mother, why should not I lie with yours?'

Paradoxically, many of those who wish to undermine functions
essential to the mere exercise of government, such as defence and
security, also want a great extension of state power and intervention
in areas which are by no means a central or necessary part of government as such.

This is seen as the fulfilment of egalitarian or 'democratic' aims.
Yet in practice it seems to be an invariable rule that the more the state
is used and the broader the sphere in which it intervenes, the greater
the extent to which small groups of elite policy-makers dominate the
whole process, whatever façades of mass agreement are maintained.

In Britain this emerges with great clarity as early as the original
Fabians. The authoritarian, we-know-best tone of the Webbs and Shaw
(and even Wells) is truly remarkable. The two last, indeed, were ideas
men rather than directly concerned with power, but all of the Webbs'
work, immensely influential in the Labour movement, shows enormous concern for the 'right' ordering of society and virtually none for
the opinions of the people, except as a tedious formality necessary for
historical reasons under our system. Hence, without doubt, the attraction of the Soviet Union for these two, precisely at the time when it
was entering the period of the most total Stalinism, which resulted in
their huge book *Soviet Communism: A New Civilization?*, from which,
in the second edition, they removed the question mark. One has only
to read Richard Crossman's diaries to see how this authoritarian tone
was maintained. As Aristotle remarked (in the *Politics*), 'Many
steps, apparently democratic, may be taken that lead to the fall of a

democracy. . . .'

Thus we are told that countries should always be allowed to decide their future by 'free elections'. But an election is not free if one of the potential winners is never going to give the population a chance to change its mind. A free election presupposes later free elections. Under the present rules, as formulated in many a left-wing paper, a country could peacefully vote in a communist government: until a communist regime anywhere has allowed itself to be voted out, however, this is not a reasonable notion.

Capitalism; Socialism; Class

Among the simple verbalisms of our time, 'capitalism': and 'socialism' rank high. As commonly presented, the contrast between them is a false one. 'Capitalism' is an economic term and can only be used to describe a whole social or political order on the tacit assumption that such orders are thoroughly determined by their economic structures, as they are not. Similarly, the 'capitalist' motivations are the economic, not the moral or legal ones. But this is not to say that, except among embezzlers and psychopaths, the individual 'capitalist' is ever motivated solely by 'capitalist' considerations. On the social plane, one might compare economic competitiveness with military aggressiveness in war. In a total war no moral or other controls operate. In wars as fought by the West there have always been, even in medieval times, certain moral limits. 'Total' economics (that is, capitalism pure and simple) have similarly failed to prevail in Western economies.

The 'free market', for some reason, conveys an image of economic anarchy. But, as we have said, it has never been free in the sense of not being bound by laws—laws against fraud and forgery, laws enforcing contracts—for such laws form the necessary framework of a properly operating market economy. It is a condition of the free market that trust must prevail between those engaged in commerce: they cannot be 'cut-throat' in any usual sense.

In fact, the really exploitive element in market capitalism emerges under two conditions. The first is when there is no law at all, as in trade with savage areas. The risk is then so great that profits are both high and unreliable and the inducements to improve the margin by any means soon make trade barely distinguishable from piracy. The second is the situation in which capitalism is over-regulated, where the state is able to divert the natural benefits of the market to its own monopolist nominees or even into its own pockets. Again, the margin is minimal and the inducement to fraud is greater. In the extreme case where capitalism is actively illegal, as in the Soviet Union, so that no mechanism exists to regulate (as against destroy) the market, trade is inevitably beset with bribery and blackmail.

In Czechoslovakia, in the 'Prague Spring' of 1968, censorship relaxed to such a degree that an article could be published by a Bata executive to the effect that under capitalism the great shoe factory had kept some of its profit for the owners, while under socialism a far greater share of it went to an enormously increased 'managerial' staff — and, moreover, the shoes had become much worse.

Again, the social power of economic fact, as against governmental ruling, has been pointed out by Simone Leys in connection with bride-purchase in China. In both mainland China and Taiwan it has been illegal for a long time. It persists on the mainland, but has been unknown for about twenty years in Taiwan, not for any reason of political purity or efficacy, but because peasants at the edge of subsistence had no choice, while the development of industry, with well-paid jobs for girls, has changed the economic imperatives in Taiwan.

Among the myths which have no real basis outside developments in Marxist phrase-making sixty or seventy years ago are those connected with 'monopoly' capitalism: the generalisation is quite frequently heard that the big firms control the market and no new ones can emerge. Quite apart from the fact that the endless technological advances associated with capitalism continually produce new processes through which small, new firms become giants within a decade or two (Xerox, for instance), it is not in the least rare for a small firm with an improved product to break into the markets of established giants — as with Polaroid taking on Kodak, or Wilkinson in the razor market. Meanwhile the phrase 'monopoly capitalism' is usually a term of abuse without serious content.

If capitalism is preferable to some other economic forms, it is not because it is just, but because the injustices inherent in any real system are, in its case, understood to be such; that the exercisers of economic power never win anyone's blind trust. When the economic rulers are nominees of 'the people' and claim to be seen not as bureaucrats but as democracy incarnate, who can query them? One might thus add a fourth to Montesquieu's desirable division of powers. For it is apparent that economic power unconnected with state power is thereby more vulnerable to social regulation.

Britain has to some slight extent managed to combine public owner-ship with a certain independence from the state by means of public corporations, though it would hardly be said that these have not given trouble in various ways. And the degree to which the capitalist and socialist concepts have lost their value is clear enough in the various allegations made by communist states against each other, and by other left-wingers against all of them, to the effect that certain states have 'degenerated' into capitalism — though they often have no private ownership and not even a market relationship among the publicly owned and planned enterprises. Indeed, the combination of public ownership, a market economy (as, to some degree, in Yugo-slavia) and various other permutations are all possible, and the identification of a particular combination as pure 'socialism' is mere laziness of mind.

But let us insist: there is no such thing as a socialist economy. There are market economies and command economies and various combinations of the two. What is usually spoken of as a socialist eco-nomy is merely a command economy. This sort of economy is not really an economy at all: any more, as we have noted, than one can really describe an army's methods of organising its supply and issue of rations in economic terms, unless by straining the word economic beyond its natural usage. Except at subsistence level, economics is a matter of supply and demand, of markets. And, insofar as the systems of the Soviet bloc work at all in any sphere but the organi-sation and production of weapons, it is, as we have said, because of the existence of the illegal or semi-legal 'second economy' which provides the channels for the true economic forces.

The command economy got confused with the idea of a just and democratic social and economic order to a large degree by accident, when the idea of the 'nationalisation of the means of production, dis-tribution and exchange' was adopted as the official aim of the Labour Party in England (and, in principle, of other socialist parties); while different ideas about providing social control — such as guild social-ism or syndicalism — became unfashionable. It should by now have been realised that nationalisation is quite compatible with private ownership of the state itself, by a single entrepreneur (e.g. Stalin) or a small board of directors (Brezhnev and Co.). And, indeed, all the many countries which have destroyed 'capitalism', far from devising juster or more democratic social orders, or giving the public or the workers more control, have regressed even as far as that is concerned. A (very partial) exception was precisely the limited and (as to all essentials) temporary experiment with workers' councils and a form of market economy in Yugoslavia.

A non-capitalist organisation of production has been conceived in various ways. Basically, there are two main positions: that of control by worker's cooperatives and that of state-controlled nationalisation. The merits of each have often been debated in rather abstract terms. It is interesting to note what really happened when in Russia in 1918 (and, to a considerable extent, in parts of Spain in 1936) the capitalists fled. In both these cases the initial, spontaneous reaction was for workers' committees to organise production. But it very soon emerged that the great defect of the whole conception was the ignorance and incompetence of the new regimes in the financial sphere, so that the normal resources of credit failed. The result was that successful enterprises — that is, not simply those which were better run, but also those which combined efficient management with good luck, in that they were able to rely on regularly obtainable supplies of raw material and so forth — became strongholds of the principle of continuing workers' control. Those which were failures demanded state intervention: and the state was ready.

One result of this *étatisme* is that in almost all countries with large state sectors, communist, Western or Third World, a 'new class' (in Djilas's phrase) has emerged, whose contribution to the economy is the provision of worthless services, much better provided by the usual movement of the economy, for which they receive remuneration which becomes increasingly taken for granted (as with other useless classes in the past) as deserved.

In the communist countries the case is clear. With no genuine legal economy, a slow-moving but privileged bureaucracy must serve instead. It has been plausibly argued that in Italy the communists, with the ignorant connivance of other parties, have already built up these cadres (a large 'intellectual', 'cultural' etc. class of employees) even before coming to power, and that this will be the class interest on which it can reliably depend in enforcing its will. But in the countries of the West without such communist threat a similar social layer has consolidated. It is true that many of the members of this class are of no more real use than the openers of toll bridges in the early nineteenth century. But this is not their fault. Edward Heath has appealed on their behalf of the grounds that they too are human and not to be blamed if misled and misused. True, but after all this applies to all those whose jobs are obsolete or useless; nor can we take it out on those who falsely encourage the proliferation of this 'new class'.

It may be argued that there is so much vigour in the American economy, at any rate, that it can cope with an old man of the sea in the form of the Washington bureaucracy. I will not here develop a theory of the total dead weight even the most dynamic entrepreneurs and engineers can carry. But at least it seems possible that in the other Western countries the limits have been reached, and we are now obliged to attempt to reverse the trend; alternatively, that we (in Britain notably) are too far down the slope to prevent the emergence of a society of rights and no riches, which will deteriorate on something like the communist pattern but without the ability of the communist states to keep down—at least to a large degree—the complaining consumer-but-non-producer.

In the Third World (with a number of very effective exceptions) we have the added difficulty that the idea of the bureaucrat, rather than the economic activist, as the central figure in economic matters is part of the scheme of things. Where there is no other centre of allegiance an educated class of mixed ethnic background, but existing as the cadre of the new state, becomes, even more than elsewhere, the 'new class' for which the country exists.

In certain cases this turns into the kleptocracy of which Professor Peter Bauer has written. A lot has been said lately about bribery by international corporations. The first thing to note is that it is usually governments and officials who have been bribed. One may, indeed, distinguish between graft and corruption. Graft, in one Latin American country, is defined as paying a bribe to get the driver's licence to which you are anyway entitled but which you are unlikely to obtain over a very long time without this bribe. Corruption consists of giving an official money for a driver's licence for which you are not qualified, through having failed the sight test, for example. In the first case the bribe does not reflect very badly on the briber, and perhaps not really very terribly on the bribed either, but rather on the political order in which he is embedded.

A link which may be suggested between Adam Smith's principles of economics and those of political liberty is the parallel between his ideas of competition between producers, with the best winning, and that between purveyors of alleged truths, with (in the long run) the truer prevailing. At any rate, there seems to be a real parallel between socialist notions of having achieved the final answer in economic, political and social matters, and the fact that all 'socialist' countries suppress unorthodox opinion.

Another idea of Adam Smith's, that the more the energy invested privately in the economy, the less the strength left over for political violence, is more plausible every year. Except in the 'future' (the one imagined by various proponents of every type of social theory, when production is to be so great that there will be a vast surplus of everything) all economies seek that ideal condition in which the balance of real goods available finds its own 'natural' exchange rate exactly suited to the supply and the demand of all concerned. This applies equally to a 'planned' economy, in which the 'planning' has this as part at any rate of its theoretical aim. Given adequate control of the money supply, one can at least assert that a market economy seeks to approach the sound barter principle as closely as possible, while a planned economy seeks to replace it by 'expert' estimates of what it might be supposed to be. Or such, in principle, are the two poles. As an *economic* development, the phenomenon normally generalised as capitalism marked the release of productive and exchange capacities hitherto unrealised, as Marx himself pointed out. And Trotsky argues that the coming of capitalism, which 'in a certain sense realised the universality and permanence of man's development' for the first time prevented a repetition, in Vico's terms, of the historical cycles to be found in earlier history.

The attack on capitalism nowadays is largely moral and aesthetic. But if it were admitted that the motives of the capitalist are selfish rather than social, ugly rather than pretty, and those of the revolutionary idealist both selfless and beautiful, the point is mainly, one would have thought, of psychological interest. For what happens, after all, is that the capitalist goes on being a capitalist, but the idealist becomes a commissar. If capitalism provides workers with higher standards; if the alternative is, by most criteria, worse in practice; if capitalism is surrounded by a plural society capable of controlling and regulating it; and if it is less conservative, more susceptible to change for the better than other systems, then the aesthetic type of judgment must be seen as a contemptible piece of self-indulgence.

One has even heard it said that capitalism is inimical to art — as if the great flowering of the Renaissance had not been in the merchant cities of Italy and the Low Countries; as if the Medici had become great patrons by the use of feudal or socialist funds. Come to that, it was mercantile Athens which, above all, created the greatest treasures of the Classical world. Then, we are given a largely mythical history of the horrors of industrial capitalism in its early stages. The historical question has been widely discussed — and by modern criteria the conditions of the people at the time of the Industrial Revolution were bad. But they were better than they had been (and far better than the miserable conditions of the Soviet people in their own industrialisation period). Between 1800 and 1900 the British population increased from 10.5 to 38 million; the birth rate in fact declined, but the death rate declined far more rapidly, from 36 per 1000 in the 1730s to 21 per 1000 between 1810 and 1819 and 14 per 1000 by World War I. Similar figures are available for all the newly 'capitalist' countries, and their significance cannot be ignored.

But it is anyhow obvious that there are worse things than capitalists, that it is possible to destroy capitalism and preserve or reintroduce far worse horrors. Stalin did not permit the private ownership of the means of production. There were no 'wage slaves' working for individuals—except, indeed, for the private owner of the entire state. But Stalin introduced social forms which even Marx had regarded as worse than capitalist labour. On the one hand, slavery: there was about the same proportion of slaves in the whole population of Russia in 1940 as there had been in the United States before the Civil War, and they were being treated very much worse. On the other, serfdom: half the population, having enjoyed the brief interim of land reform with which communists conventionally attract or neutralise the peasant while power is being consolidated, were herded (an exact word in this context) into the collective farms, and the internal passport system which Lenin had denounced was restored. It is true that the slaves and serfs were the property not of private owners but of the state. So had many of the serfs been in the old Russia, and so had many of the slaves been in the ancient world (for example, the Roman *servi publici*).

Again, while America is today more 'capitalist' than Russia, it is also more 'socialist', if socialism has anything to do with popular control of the economy. For on any argument there is at least some element of such control in the United States and none in the Soviet Union.

So capitalism is hardly the point. As we have said, capitalism is an economic system, not a political or social one. It is compatible, at least up to a point, with a variety of political systems. Of course, it is true that the economic structure of a country powerfully affects the social attitudes of its citizens. That it is the decisive factor is a Victorian superstition.

Capitalism cannot solve social problems: which is only to say that we have an economic system which has solved the problems of productivity and is beginning to cope with those of economic stability, but which has no pretensions to do more. The problems of the very poor and of racial minorities are not to be solved by economic means. But, equally, capitalism was not responsible for Auschwitz or for Kolyma. Auschwitz was not a profit-making concern run by gold speculators interested in extracting the stoppings from the dead in the gas chambers, but was run by idealistic bureaucrats.

In his *Without Marx or Jesus* Jean-Francois Revel, as a left-wing European, makes the point that in the context of most of the present social concerns of the left the United States is 'in advance' of Europe. By this he means all the political, moral and aesthetic elements of the 'counter-culture', the growth of an anti-'utilitarian' mood and the almost unlimited tolerance of these things by the state. One may, on the contrary, feel that the greater part of this is fashionable nonsense, which the United States economy is powerful enough to indulge as a sort of parasite. Nevertheless, among all the nonsense one may certainly detect a genuine wish to broaden and enrich the social order; the mass of rubbish may well be blown away by later fashions, leaving a genuine residuum, to the benefit of the community. At any rate, Revel concludes: 'Henceforth — and the process has already begun in the United States — individuals, on the basis of their affinities, will regroup to create cultures which will no longer be wholly conditioned by a system of production.'

At least it will hardly be denied that the Western system shows, and has long shown, a capacity for improvement. Those socialists who see nothing particularly odd in accepting a regime of terror as more or less justified, since it will supposedly lead to the just society, should perhaps grit their teeth and consider the possibility of accepting capitalism, whatever their temperamental objections to it, as at least an equally likely basis for such a development. For if a good society can emerge from Terror, that is from an admitted evil, then why should it not emerge from Greed? Indeed, Greed seems rather more amenable to control from outside than Terror does.

Lenin accepted that nine out of ten revolutionaries were knaves or fools. But if good results are supposed to emerge from bad motives in the case of the revolutionary, the same principle can hardly be denied to the non-revolutionary. And it cannot be asserted that because the profit motive is in itself selfish, its social results are automatically bad. It is not only a question of Pope's

> What his hard heart denies
> His charitable vanity supplies.

It might even be the case that 'What his Warm heart promises and fails to deliver through total misunderstanding of the whole problem, his charitable selfishness comes through with.'

Of course, the old drives of greed and power exist but naturally a political order designed to restrict them—and, in a sense, to use them—also exists, at any rate in all advanced societies. Let us remember, too, that it was precisely the non-capitalist ruling element in tsarist Russia which, from the eighteenth century on, was involved in the extra oppression and exploitation of the industrial workers; and that it was precisely the non-capitalist terror bureaucracy which did the same in the same country in the post-Revolutionary period.

More generally, the comments of the Czechoslovak liberal communist Economic Minister of the Dubček period should be strongly heeded. Sik writes:

> When the basic market principles are able to make themselves felt operations tending towards an optimum in relation to capital costs will be signalled by growth in profit, while firms deviating from the optimum will register a decline. Hence, not simply capitalist 'greed', but far deeper causes make the accumulation of profits an indispensable feature of economic life which will be with us for a long time yet.

As for socialism, the value, or at least the attraction, of the socialist idea for Western societies initially was that it provided the necessary moral or spiritual critique of the failure of the old liberal state to 'satisfy the yearnings for political community', as Irving Kristol puts it, in that the concentration on individual rights

> ultimately deprived men of those virtues which could only exist in a *political community* which is something other than a society. Among these virtues are a sense of distributive justice, a fund of shared moral values, and a common vision of the

good life sufficiently attractive and powerful to transcend the knowledge that each individual's life ends only in death. Capitalist society itself — as projected, say, in the writings of John Locke and Adam Smith — was negligent of such virtues. It did not reject them and in no way scorned them, but simply assumed that the individual would be able to cope with this matter as he did with his other 'private' affairs.

The sense of belonging to a community has greatly weakened in the modern world, and many yearn for a social order which would restore it. Socialism claims to do just that. This claim, it is true, is hopeful fantasy. While the Utopian socialism of the kibbutzes and communes has occasionally created oases of community for a time, the 'scientific' socialism of the communists (and even that of the social democrats) has but brought on a further alienation. We should not for that reason treat the urge to community which follows these will-o'-the-wisps as unreal or weak in itself, let alone despise it.

In fact, the situation resembles that of Karl Marx faced with the (to him) delusive existence of religion. Believing it to be false, he yet wrote movingly (unlike Lenin, who snarled viciously at all religious belief) that 'Religion is the sigh of the oppressed creature, the heart of a heartless world, the spirit of soulless stagnation. It is the opium of the people.' While denouncing religion itself, he respected the feeling behind it; and so may we expose and refute socialism as a fantasy solution to our problems, but not ignore the aspirations which have turned to it for hope of community.

Of course, as we have said, capitalism — even that capitalism called *laissez-faire* — in no way implies the absence of law, order and mutual trust. On the contrary, the market could not operate at all if profitable activities like forgery, banditry and fraud were not suppressed. Its development involved, in fact, the 'King's Peace' on the one hand and, on the other, the ability to trust others which is behind all the old credit systems. It needed both legal and moral restriction. Which is one reason (among others) why the current nonsense among Young Conservatives to the effect that if you want a free market, you must not have laws which restrict other freedoms is so vacuous. Free Trade, at its peak, never implied free trade in pornography or poison.

Capitalism is thus not by any means without legal or moral implications. But these have not been enough in themselves to create or maintain a sense of community. The socialists, it is true, have equally failed to create such a sense, producing instead the antinomianism of the permissive society and the social atomisation of an egalitarianism in which individuals are manipulated only as puppets in vast cold-blooded organisations. (But the conservatism which itself accepts *etatisme* and itself manipulates the citizenry in this way represents something worse than socialism—is little more, in fact, than socialism deprived of its remaining moral content.)

This half-conscious, or inadequately formulated, feeling for community results in fantasy futures — and fantasy pasts too. Chesterton writes:

> We shall not wake with ballad strings
> The good time of the smaller things,
> We shall not see the holy kings
> Ride down by Severn side. . . .

'The good time of the smaller things' evokes the 'real' community in much the same way as, say, the words of the Marxist William Morris, in *News from Nowhere.* A typical modern left-wing intellectual (E. P. Thompson) similarly writes of his ideal:

> some men and women might choose to live in unified communities, sited, like Cistercian monasteries [note the nostalgia], in centres of great natural beauty, where agricultural, industrial, and intellectual pursuits might be combined. Others might prefer the variety and pace of an urban life which rediscovers some of the qualities of the city state. Others will prefer a life of seclusion. . . .

Leszek Kolakowski comments on this, 'This is a very good sample of socialist writing. It amounts to saying that the world should be good, and not bad.' Kolakowski adds that when it comes to the distortions of money values and so on, Thompson's 'superiority consists in that you know exactly how to get rid of all this and I do not'. He continues:

> the experiences of the 'new alternative society' have shown very convincingly that the only universal medicine these people have for social evils — state ownership of the means of production — is not only perfectly compatible with all disasters of the capitalist world, with exploitation, imperialism, pollution, misery, economic waste, national hatred and national oppression, but

that it adds to them a series of disasters of its own: inefficiency, lack of economic incentives, and above all, the unrestricted role of the omnipotent bureaucracy, a concentration of power never known before in human history.

The early socialists thought of their system quite simply as a blueprint for a social order and had no special views about who would carry out the necessary reorganisation. Saint-Simon hoped to get Louis XVIII to do it. Robert Owen, too, at first looked to converting the authorities to his views. It was only when this was seen to be a chimera that socialist thinkers (not only Marx, but also Proudhon, Bakunin and others opposed to Marx's methods) turned to the new industrial working class—and so the vast verbal fetishism of the 'proletariat', the 'workers' and so forth was born. Socialism, in fact, came first and the idea that the working class should carry it out came second. But for over a century most socialists have regarded 'class' as the only recourse, at least in principle. Naturally, a considerable number of elitist elements exist within the socialist movement, but support, and particularly electoral and insurrectionary support, has to come from somewhere, and in modern industrial societies the working class has come to constitute the majority of the population (at any rate, it does not enjoy the greatest wealth, power and prestige and so is ripe for rousing against the possessors).

The modern socialist parties of the West are in part derived from the representation of the genuine, untheoretical interests of the working class in modern society: the element of Utopianism, the principle on which the working class will be used to overthrow the present system and enable the socialist leaders to create a new one, has played a rather lesser role. It should be asserted again that the traditional connection of abstract socialism with the working-class movement is accidental and habitual rather than theoretically essential. The true revolutionary socialists of our period use a 'proletarian' phraseology but have simply gained organisational control of working-class movements, or sections of them, and have used them to put an elitist, despotic, self-perpetuating party leadership into power which has then transformed the economy and society—to the disadvantage certainly of the old ruling classes, but also to the disadvantage of the working class. Indeed, in some cases (for example, China and Cuba) power has been obtained without much in the way of the participation, or even the existence, of an

industrial working class, though the phraseology has remained orthodox. All in all, and at best, it seems reasonable to say that the
whole process is one in which Utopian revolutionaries have turned
to the proletariat as an instrument or symbol largely for want of any
other.

For when a population will not listen to reason then (it is held)
coercion must be used against workers and others alike. The popu-
larity of certain high-minded dictatorships, if not at home, at
least in some Western intellectual circles, is based on extraordinary delusion. It took forty years effectively to destroy the Soviet
myth, in spite of the hearty cooperation of the Soviet authorities
in providing endless proof of its falsehood. Shangri-la was then
transferred to China, to Cuba, to that fairly exact carbon copy of
Stalin's Russia, Communist Vietnam, even to Mozambique: all of
them 'socialist'.

The fault of the simply 'rational' man is to regard his system
of symbols and their manipulation as more important than empirical
data, to treat verbal labels as things. This is particularly so when it
comes to the general words like socialism, which carry an emotional
charge. For example Professor G. D. H. Cole attached more importance to the formal resemblances and similar ideological origins
of Western social democracy and Soviet communism than to their
rather obvious differences, as one might say, 'Goneril is Cordelia's
sister, so it is absurd to say they have nothing in common.'

One of the victories of Stalinism was the imposition, on many
in the world concerned with social progress, of this idea that dictatorship is to be preferred to democracy if it pursues certain policies.
In the old days, when dictatorship was accepted as suitable to fairly
backward countries, it was on the assumption that further progress
would lead them to the higher political system which democracy was
then universally assumed to be. After Stalin it came to be assumed
that social progress could be made more swiftly under dictatorship.
But one of the most significant things, from one point of view, is that
many in the West who argued for the ethical, social and other advantages of 'proletarian' dictatorship were also prepared to speak of the
USSR as more 'democratic' than the West. This was often associated,
as it still is, with talk about Soviet concern with 'economic democracy',
conceived of as more essential and necessary than 'formal' political
democracy, though in the context the phrase is, of course, totally
meaningless.

Even now, judgment of regimes not by their political maturity but by alleged or hoped-for 'socialisation' is not uncommon. What should have been learnt from Stalinism and Maoism, etc., is that ideologically motivated elites are liable to cause worse economic failure and injustice than popularly elected regimes. The sacrifice of liberty to economic ends is dubious doctrine at any time; in fact, the ends are not attained.

Bryan Magee points out, in his book on Popper, that the idea that these sacrifices (and many worse ones) should be necessary to the creation of a better future is, in any case, a logical error.

> One set of events close in time . . . are referred to as the 'means', followed by another more distant set of events which are called the 'end'. But . . . there can be no serious defence for privileges claimed for what is merely the second set of events in an endless series. What is more, the first set of events, being closer in time, are more likely to materialise than the second. . . Rewards promised by the latter are less sure than sacrifices made for them in the former.

And so it has always turned out.

Yet it remains common, even among those who regard themselves, in one sense or another, as moderates, to think the Good Society can be produced through an intervening period of terror and, in general, large-scale suffering. But the Good Society always fails to appear, because of the crudity of both the political ideas and the economic theories involved. Economically, the system is always impossibly rigid and unadapted to its purpose; it can only work at all with a certain amount of underground and unadmitted lubrication by the market forces so that corruption is endemic. This lubrication is nevertheless inadequate, so the machinery can only be got to work at all by the application of quite disproportionate force, like a man keeping a rusty old bicycle going by sheer muscle power. And this is to say that to get directives obeyed at all requires constant and extreme authoritarianism, supported by the severest possible sanctions from the top down: to put it another way, economic laws are such that a true socialist economy is incompatible with any political arrangement other than the despotic.

Let us nevertheless recall that another of the troubles caused by the socialist idea is that the great majority of critics of modern society have tended to frame their criticism in socialist terms. This is true to the degree that once socialism is shown to be delusive, the impression is given that valid criticism of modern society has been refuted. That is obviously not the case. And were the critics of our society to confine themselves to the negative task of pointing out its faults rather than becoming devotees of a seamless alternative, their arguments might last better. However, it is certainly true (as Michael Novak has argued) that the socialist attitude has led to a great oversimplification of any theoretical basis for improving existing institutions, and that we must return to a general approach of a modest but more realistic kind, abandoning the *naivetés* of 'schemes of equal outcome and homogenized results' and, in particular, of national planning, 'an incoherent attempt to pretend that politics, with its interests and conflicts, can be transcended by the decisions of non-democratic experts'.

When Milton said that he valued 'the liberty to know, to utter and to argue freely according to conscience' above all liberties he was making the great point against the impossible perfect society. Any society that considers itself flawless, and any movement which aims for such a society, is in principle opposed to the society Milton advocates, a society that, acknowledging its imperfections, hears, considers and reforms grievances.

It is at any rate clear that the actual sufferings inflicted on the British, American and similar populations by their system and their rulers are simply not remotely on the same scale as those produced by the 'temporary' dictatorships allegedly constructing socialism. We all know the intellectual or quasi-intellectual process by which this construction (and its attendant suffering) occurs:

Step One: There is much injustice around.
Step Two: Socialism will remove this injustice.
Step Three: Therefore, anything that helps to bring socialism about is to be supported —
Step Four: — including much worse, and less easily tackled, injustice.

Supposed democratic socialists convince themselves, moreover, that there is a different calculus, under which socialism (or a claim or approach to it), regardless of the despotic form of the state, may be considered more *advanced* than a democratic community. This is a total fallacy. Higher levels of social justice have not been, and cannot be, achieved under political primitivism.

It is at least to E. P. Thompson's credit that he is prepared to talk about the future. For socialists seldom are, except in vague terms and usually in a negative fashion ('alienation' will disappear, etc., etc.). They sometimes envisage a future without conflict, of which Lewis Mumford has written:

> If the goal of human history is a uniform type of man, reproducing at a uniform rate, in a uniform environment, kept at constant temperature, pressure, and humidity, living a uniformly lifeless existence, with his uniform physical needs satisfied by uniform goods, all inner waywardness brought into conformity by hypnotics and sedatives, or by surgical extirpation, a creature under constant mechanical pressure from incubator to incinerator, most of the problems of human development would disappear. Only one problem would remain: Why should anyone, even a machine, bother to keep this kind of creature alive?

Such would be the result, in T. S. Eliot's words (in *The Rock*), of seeking 'systems so perfect that no man could ever be good'.

And among these happy Eloi we are also to have an efflorescence of 'creativity'. Why, it is hard to say, except on the principle that the Good Society must have everything. As we know, genius is often, perhaps always, the product of tensions and struggles. Yet one is often told in this sort of literature that once cleansed from the pressures of class society, every man may be a Shakespeare or a Beethoven. But giant originality is one of the characteristics of Beethoven and Shakespeare. How can there be several billion ways of being gigantically original? And these results are supposed to emerge from extreme centralisation!

The excessive intrusions of state power found nowadays throughout the West are to some degree the product of the consciously bureaucratic attitude of the Webbs and the other early Fabians, who gave British socialism its direction as 'state socialism' and upheld it in opposition to 'guild socialism' which, as we saw, at least offered a more humanly attractive mirage. It is indicative of the true bias of most socialists of that time that they opted not for the more libertarian and cooperative style, but for the one by which the imposition of their own views would be more easily effected. When it came to the point they showed that their true love was power rather than communal amity. Orwell remarks, 'I notice people always say "under Socialism". They look forward to being on top—with all the others underneath, being told what is good for them.'

There are, indeed, admirable and experienced thinkers who are trying to retrieve from the socialist current all the good it might contain. Leszek Kolakowski writes:

> When I say 'Socialism', I do not mean a state of perfection but rather a movement trying to satisfy demands for equality, freedom and efficiency, a movement that is worth trouble only as far as it is aware not only of the complexity of problems hidden in each of these values separately, but also of the fact that they limit each other and can be implemented only through compromises. . . Attempts to consider any of these three values as absolute and to implement it at all costs not only are bound to destroy the two others, but they are self-defeating. . . .

With socialism in this sense no non-fanatic could have much quarrel. And Kolakowski is, of course, quite clear that such balances are attainable in the civic, and not in the despotic, cultures. Yet until such voices as his are heard, and the vast stratum of the lumpenintelligentsia is weaned from the simple set of verbal reflexes which now possess them, genuine progress, genuine improvement in the human economic and political condition remain at risk. And genuine understanding of the modern world scene continues to be dangerously imperfect.

CHAPTER 12

The Credulity Caste

An intellectual (one of them has recently confessed) is a man who is 'excited by ideas': that is, not one who is concerned, but one who is thrilled. He is not an intellectual at all, properly speaking, but an 'emotional'.

One might sometimes think that everyone was an intellectual now. The whole middle class has been through the universities in the United States already and in England soon will have been. There, though in many departments education as such is no longer being provided, they will have picked up at least the reflexes of the intellectual.

The uneducated man is at worst just ignorant about foreign countries. The educated man, or what we now call the educated man, knows a vast amount which is not so. In his defence it can perhaps be argued that people have to be half-baked before they can be fully baked. All the same, when one thinks that it took fifty years to rumble Russia, a dreary task lies ahead for those people (and I take my hat off to them) who will, by the year 2,000, have hammered the reality of North Korea or Mozambique into the heads of the intelligentsia and — who know? — ten years later even the reality about Cuba. But one only hopes that by that time some other socialist Shangri-la will not have emerged (in Burundi perhaps, or Bhutan, or maybe on Mars), that the process of delusion transfer proves not to be an unending one.

The brief making of a debating point, the one-shot logic-chop, is nowadays commoner than ever, but the true development of argument is at one of its lowest ebbs. Coleridge noted a bad period in the 1820s (though, naturally, it was nothing like as bad) and compared it unfavourably with the epoch of 'Charles I and the Cromwellate'. At *that* time (he remarks) 'the premisses are frequently wrong, but the deductions are almost always legitimate; whereas, in the writings of the present day the premisses are commonly sound, but the conclusions false.' (We are nowadays in a worse position still, as the premisses are usually false to start with, as well as the method of argument.)

Kipling complained of such things fifty years ago:

> ...brittle intellectuals
> Who crack beneath a strain —
> John Bunyan met that helpful set
> In Charles the Second's reign.

He also thought that people should remember lessons taught eight generations earlier. In our day it is a matter of inviting people to strain their memories to recall what was said (and more aptly and concretely) half a generation ago, by George Orwell and others. To declare what one thinks to be right without fear or favour is doubtless a virtue. But it would surely be a much greater one if accompanied by some sign of having acquainted oneself with relevant facts and of examining what one says for consistency or accuracy. One should not only say what one thinks; one should also think what one says. As a character says in *Waiting for Lefty,* 'For all their education, they don't know from nothing.'

In the country of the illiterate, the intellectual is king. Indeed, it may be taken as one of the defining signs of a backward society that students and so on are politically important in it. Anyhow, formerly this was not the case in the Western democracies, but only in what were then thought of as the more backward capitals of Latin America or the Middle East.

One major reason why the intellectuals, and not the mass of the people, are usually wrong is that while the latter generally rely on unformulated feelings and attitudes (or formulated only at a very broad level) the former by their nature cannot manage, as we have noted, without conceptualisation and verbalisation. And it is precisely the *vocabulary* of public life and of politics which has decayed. Worse: the words and concepts in general use at this debating level are mainly those of the enemies of political civilisation.

This shallow attitude is particularly noticeable in sociological-political teaching. An abstract attitude (and abstract not in the sense that generalisations hard won from the great body of intractable raw material are abstract, but in the manner of hack generalities) is what emerges. And certainty is obtained — at a cost.

It is common experience that all political positions can be shown to contain logical contradictions, from pure pacifism, to support on humanitarian grounds for 'liberation' tommy-gunners and so on, through to the extreme right. This does not mean that no political position is tenable. It means that logic is a very tricky instrument. It is a couple of centuries since Kant demonstrated its deficiencies in Section 2 of his chapter on the 'Antinomy of a Pure Reason', where in parallel columns he proves a series of contradictory proposals (indeed, his third antinomy on the conflict between strict causality and freedom of will cannot be said ever to have been resolved, while remaining of absolutely basic importance). Carnap noted the extreme difficulty of conducting even the most rigorous and unprejudiced philosophical deduction without unconsciously shifting the meaning of terms (even if only slightly) enough to distort and destroy the whole argument unless checked and tested at every move by an empirical reference.

In any case, as is often pointed out, no verbal structure as such can cover the whole reality, let alone the potentiality, of the infinities and intricacies of the real world. Partly for this reason, attachment to non-open societies is, as we have seen, productive of endless verbalisations.

Similarly, there are two sorts of philosopher: the clear enquirer into what appear to be the paradoxes and problems associated with our understanding of the universe, and the portentous systemiser who provides a vast verbal structure to fit anything. The latter is, of course, the philosopher of the caricaturist, the 'sage' who will unravel all our problems: he is, in fact, the philosopher the lumpen-intelligentsia want.

I was particularly struck in Washington recently, as I was listening to a paper on the decline of fertility in seventeenth-century France presented by Professor Vander Veile of Leuwen University and commented on by M. Philippe Aries, to find that when questioned by the audience, both of these very learned and expert men agreed that they were unable to account for the main fact which had emerged from their and other recent studies — that mass contraception evidently came into use in France a century or so earlier than anywhere else. They were unable even to advance a plausible hypothesis (but were able to show that all plausible hypotheses would be untenable).

Of course, and particularly in social and political studies, the highest scholarship often resides in the admission of ignorance. In this case what was particularly striking was that very important social phenomena with important results had their causes hidden somewhere amidst the 'cultural' determination of attitudes.

In the old days people may have taken things on trust, but they usually did so from established experience or from long-term students of the field in question. The present situation is quite fantastic. It seems, for example, that a high proportion of the more or less educated classes believe that Thor Heyerdahl's *Kon-Tiki* has proved the South American origin of the Polynesians, although scholarly opinion is practically unanimous in its dismissal of this proposition. I remember some years ago the *Evening Standard*'s correspondent in Washington advancing, in successive weeks, a ludicrous defence of the entirely crackpot Velikovsky theories of the solar system and (a very significant concatenation) an equally baseless and, indeed, internally contradictory run-over of the Rosenberg Case.

Nowadays we are continually being told that 'researchers' employed by a paper or a television company have proved something or other. A television company, rebutted on a major point about the sinking of the *Lusitania* by an officer who was actually on watch on deck when she was struck by the torpedo, vigorously defended not their presentation of the facts but simply their faith in their researchers. As Joshua Reynolds remarked: 'A provision of endless apparatus, a bustle of infinite enquiry and research, may be employed to evade and shuffle off real labour — the real labour of thinking.'

There is nothing sinister or surprising about the fact that a large proportion of those who go into these 'investigative' media are of 'progressive' tendencies. Generally speaking, those who leave the universities after study, or non-study, of the less rigorous of the 'humanities' are those who seek careers neither in the professions, nor in the technical areas, nor in commerce, nor in administration. No doubt most, or many, commentators holding such views nevertheless make every effort to be fair. All the same, it is very much a doctrine of the left, or of an important section of the left, that the cause comes before such judiciousness. And this at least implies that in some cases objectivity in news presentation might be rated low by many. At least, even if we assume that right-wingers or moderates would be equally prejudiced, the fact remains that there are very few of them in the media. And bias on these matters is inevitably rather more pro-IRA (for example) than could be normal elsewhere. The imposition of some control on such things is denounced as 'censorship': but an in-built bias, if not corrected, is itself a form of censorship, because it unfairly underemphasises one side of the story.

At any rate, active falsification should not occur: as when Mr Felix Greene, a veteran apologist for Maoism, was simply presented on TV as a well-known expert; or when a South African communist (that is, a member of one of the few Western communist parties which supported Russia over the Czechoslovakia crisis) was called a 'liberal'. In this latter case no blame attached to the communist, but the BBC might seem to deserve censure.

Academics themselves have often shown unexampled idiocy in their interventions in public affairs of which they know nothing. One is reminded of Bibbon's rebuke to the great chemist Priestley when the latter criticised Gibbon's historical and theological position:

> I declined the challenge in a letter exhorting my opponent to enlighten the world by his philosophical discoveries and to re-member that the merit of his predecessor Servetus is now reduced to a single passage, which indicates the smaller circulation of the blood through the lungs from and to the heart.

When an academic, particularly a scientific one, tells one about his trained mind and his habit of using words precisely, one can be almost sure that a lot of drivel of an extremely vague nature is likely to emerge. And one is reminded of Orwell's much quoted remark.

> I have heard it confidently stated, for instance, that American troops had been brought to Europe not to fight the Germans but to crush an English revolution. One has to belong to the intelligentsia to believe things like that: no ordinary man could be such a fool.

The constant exchange of self-congratulation among 'progressive' sages is also comic. One can hardly read a work about any of these people without being told how sincere, how courageous, how concerned they are. It has never been made clear in what way they are supposed to be superior in these fields to their critics and opponents. In fact, one can take it as a good rough test of the merits of two professors or politicians of whom one has never heard that if one is described *ad nauseam* as sincere or courageous, the other is the better man.

Any compliments left over are, of course, poured on the young:

> In semi-literate countries
> Demagogues pay
> Court to teenagers, (W. H. Auden)

The young and 'ardent' are, in fact, the usual storm troops of extreme movements. *Giovinezza! Giovinezza!* (Youth! Youth!) was the anthem of Italian Fascism. It was the *Hitlerjugend* leader, Baldur von Schirach, who asserted, 'In a higher sense, the young are always right.' This cant is remarkably prevalent, to one degree or another, over a wide range of Western thought — or rather talk.

But the young are precisely those who, even in a civic society, have little or no experience of real politics. As Aristotle remarks in the *Ethics*:

> Every man is a good judge of what he understands; in special subjects the specialist, over the whole field of knowledge the man of general culture. This is the reason why political science is not a proper study for the young. The young man is not versed in the practical business of life from which politics draws its premisses and its data.

This proposition has, on the whole, been accepted in most societies. It is not even the case that the early Bolsheviks attached any transcendental value to youth, though their membership and most of their leaders were, in fact, young and they were the heirs of the student revolutionaries of the previous century. (Trotsky was twenty-eight in 1905, just as Saint-Just was twenty-four in 1793: but neither of them made anything of that!)

The recent cult of young idealism, particularly in America, has two unfortunate aspects. First, the young are encouraged to take their own primitive enthusiasms as generally true, without the normal abrasion of adult comment. Worse still, the adults who encourage them are consciously abdicating the achievements of experience and are procuring a general reversion to intellectual childhood. And the attempt has been made, in 'educational' institutions in particular, to use the young as cannon fodder in the struggle against the system.

George Dennison, who has himself been described as an 'educational romantic' (as a consequence of his admirable work at the First Street School in New York, on children whom the public schools had given up) quotes a horrible example of an American run-of-the-mill progressive school he visited:

> The problem at this school was that the director regarded staff and students less as people than as events in his own protracted struggle against middle-class America. The faculty, too, consisted of True Believers, and I had never before seen such a listless, resentful bunch, or heard the words 'creativity' and 'spontaneity' bandied about quite so often.

When one hears 'progressives' speaking in these terms one's first reaction is surprise that they do not know that the pantomime has all been gone through before. Have they not read *The Possessed,* and in particular the progression from 'liberal' father to totally destructive son? Solzhenitsyn sees that parallel:

> Young people, at an age when the only experience they have is sexual, at an age when they have no years of personal suffering and personal comprehension to draw on, young people are enthusiastically repeating the discredited platitudes of our Russian nineteenth century, and they think they have come up with something novel.

In particular, he refers to the cult of revolutionary violence.

It is notably patronising to excuse student activism on the usual 'progressive' grounds. 'He is having tantrums, but then he's only a baby' is something that even the most uncontrolled character might hardly relish. And the student who thinks of himself as better qualified than most other people to make rational decisions should be the last to claim such special treatment.

I never find any difficulty in treating students as rational adults. They may not be as well informed as I am about certain subjects, but that is what the condition of the student implies. And neither have they lived through world political situations which we remember as immediate but to them are history; yet they are not incapable of grasping the past unless prevented by essentially obscurantist theories which decry the lessons of history—particularly when it comes to what happens in revolutions (let alone in the pop dramas of the paperbacks).

Thus the reason why no one with knowledge of real history could take the recent 'rebel' students seriously was because they had no notion whatever of the actual established results of authoritarian revolution. I see Senator Hayakawa found that, alone among the arts students, it was his *historians* who did not provide recruits for the revolt which brought him to prominence. And, indeed, the tendency in certain 'political science' and similar faculties to reduce these matters to conceptual frameworks divorced from their historical background and the actual processes of development amounts to a training in ignorance.

Universities are not, in any case, real educators in politics, for obvious reasons. William Lamb (later, as Lord Melbourne, Prime Minister of the United Kingdom), whose family was in close touch with the real politics of the time, wrote from the University of Glasgow about the vanity and self-importance of some fellow students who

> asked, with a supercilious sort of doubt, whether Pitt is really a good orator, or Fox has much political knowledge. This will all wear off in time; though, to be sure, one of them is three and twenty. . . . You cannot have both the advantages of study and of the world together. The way is to let neither of them get too fast a hold of you, and this is done by nothing so well as by frequent changes of place, of persons and of companions.

And what do these young learn that Plato did not already see in the epoch of the Sophists?

> When those who are all unworthy of instruction draw near and hold intercourse with her beyond their deserts, how must we describe the character of those notions and opinions which are the issue of such a connection? May they not be called, with the utmost propriety, sophisms—a spurious brood, without one trace of genuine insight?

This system of self-education through innate illumination reminds one of the fruits of self-education in general:

Consider one of the most voracious and highly motivated self-learners of the last generation, Adolf Hitler. He read widely, and thought intensely about what he read. But being his own judge of what he wanted to learn and how well he wanted to learn it, he was, at best, 'loosely educated', in the splendid phrase of Sir Winston Churchill.

(Samuel McCracken, 'Quackery in the Classroom', *Commentary,* June 1970)

Students who wonder at the attitude of some critical adults towards their enthusiasms should read, above all, Gibbon's *Autobiography,* where he deals with his own adolescent admirations with amused indulgence rather than hostility. He had written to his father announcing his conversion to the then scarcely legal Roman Catholicism 'with all the pomp, the dignity and self-satisfaction of a martyr'. But, he adds, 'I am proud of an honest sacrifice of interest to conscience' and consoles himself, too, with the thought that he had been won over by the 'noble hand' of Bossuet, certainly a grander figure than some modern gurus. But (in another connection) he applauds more generally the way in which 'the belief and knowledge of the child are superseded by the more rational ignorance of the man'.

Meanwhile the young do not know (or are distracted from) the feel, the roots, the habits, in fact, of their culture, though an outside observer could probably deduce their background even from their own critical attitudes. For most of them this latent knowledge will come back as experience and grow as the relations between grand abstract words and real possibilities shake down. The minority only will have effectively cut these roots and sunk into the bitter void of fanaticism.

After the Napoleonic Wars a society of student radicals, the *Burschenschaft,* was formed in the German universities. Among its teachings was the idea that the righteous man recognises no external law. When he is convinced that he is right he unconditionally carries out the dictates of reason as revealed to him. This was known simply as 'the Principle', and (since Jesus rather than Allende was then regarded in such circumstances as the typical 'martyr to conviction') they had a slogan: 'A Christ thou shalt become.' When one of these students, Karl Sand, assassinated the writer Kotzebue (having concluded that he was an enemy of the German people) he left a paper by the side of his victim with 'A Christ thou shalt become' written on it—referring, of course, not to Kotzebue but to himself.

When the young are going through their period of questioning everything they often find 'sophisticated' mentors who can provide them with arguments which their non-intellectual parents are not equipped to counter. They go on to develop from this the idea that they, and left-wingers in general, are uniquely equipped intellectually and that they are capable of winning arguments against any representative of 'reactionary' views. It would of course, in reality, have been pathetic to see one of these dogma-drunk kids arguing with a truly sophisticated apologist even for Fascism—Benedetto Croce, for instance.

To enthuse uncritically over the virtues of youth, as youth, is, of course, essentially an insulting way of patronising young people. It is all very well for the politician to speak in this way occasionally when working the constituency of the young, just as he might, in a different speech, extol the virtues of turnip farmers or copper miners — that is, as a conventional compliment well understood as such by both sides.

We are now, in both the UK and the USA (and elsewhere too), perhaps the first society in which the adolescent, far from having to undergo any testing disciplines or discomforts, is fed, physically and emotionally, like a prize pig.

It is, of course, bad for anybody to be told constantly how wonderful he is: for the young this constant adulation, against which they have no natural defences, is particularly deleterious. What they need is massive criticism, cold water on their hot air. They need to be continuously told that their ideas are not original, hardly even serious, and that in all other times and places they have inevitably led to disaster. They should be told that they cannot even be regarded as worth talking to until they have learnt some history: that until they have read, understood and coped with the views of major critics of Utopianism, they are still wet behind the ears.

More generally, the qualities needed to cope with the intensely complex and dangerous problems of the modern world are not anyhow those usually associated with youth, or at any rate not with youth as it is now defined. Vision, enthusiasm, yes; one-sidedness, simple faith, fanaticism, no.

But, as we have said, it is less the young themselves than their admirers who cause a decline in intellect and morality. The cult of youth, at least in the form in which it is usually presented to us, is in effect an attempt by adults to make enthusiasm and inexperience the main political criteria. This is not to say either that enthusiasm is valueless, or that inexperience cannot be cured. There are many people who at the age of twenty or so have retained sufficient contact and communication with their culture, or have sufficiently studied history at least to be vicariously experienced in the sense in which we use the word. But those of their elders who maintain ungrown-up standards of debate, or of arriving at policies, have already lowered themselves to the level of teenagers or (more probably) have never advanced beyond it. Naturally, they must accept children as equals, regard their voices as of particular value; they must not remind them, above all, of the pernickety and irritating insistence on sense or proof to be found in older speakers.

Aristotle continues his remarks on the ineptness of the young in politics:

> Hence the young man is not a fit student of Moral Philosophy, for he has no experience in the actions of life, while all that is said presupposes and is concerned with these: and in the next place, since he is apt to follow the impulses of his passions, he will hear as though he heard not, and to no profit. . . .

But he concludes with the devastating coda:

> And I draw no distinction between young in years and youthful in temper and disposition, the defect to which I allude being no direct result of time, but of living at the beck and call of passion, and following each object as it rises. For to them that are such the knowledge comes to be unprofitable, as to those of imperfect self-control. . . .

Solzhenitsyn also notes the youth-creepers among the old: 'They try to ingratiate themselves with the young—anything so as not to look "conservative". And this is yet another Russian phenomenon of nineteenth-century origin: Dostoyevsky called it "being in bondage to advanced notions".' And the writer too may be infected: 'If his young compatriots blithely proclaim depravity's superiority to modest toil, if they succumb to drugs or seize hostages, then the stench of it mingles with the writer's breath.'

But the most devastating analysis of the young-at-head is perhaps that of a Czech student refugee from the Soviet take-over of 1968, who found in many Western intellectual circles an astonishing absence of sense, and diagnosed it as due to insufficient contact with reality. He wrote:

Western socialism, especially in its radical form, took me completely by surprise. It seemed so completely unreal, something from a different planet or a different era. You have completely dissociated theory and practice. The men I met are all properly repelled by the realities of authoritarian rule, but they keep on preaching the same weary Utopian ideologies that can lead to nothing else. They live in a romantic dream-world in which their dear radical rhetoric is perfectly consistent with their apparently sincere faith in freedom and justice. But do they really think they could apply their radical Utopia in a real world and still respect their libertarian commitments? Do they really think their Utopias could be benign if their revolutions were not comic-opera coups on indulgent campuses but real ventures in the exercise of power?

I met a few hard-headed colleagues, but most of the men who clamoured for attention were three-semester intellectuals, pampered children of your permissive, affluent society, throwing tantrums because Father gave them only education, security and freedom—but not Utopia. They bitterly resent society because it does not treat them as the fulcrum of the universe: though from what they told me about themselves it seemed that their families did treat them that way. I can't take them seriously. They seem to have no idea of the cost or the value of the privileges they receive abundantly and *gratis*. They dismiss them as 'bourgeois'—in Czechoslovakia we are struggling for just a fraction of what they dismiss. I suppose their histrionics do have some individual cathartic value, like the old duelling fraternities, but socially they seem infinitely irrelevant. Can you imagine one of them in Czechoslovakia?

What surprises me most is not that they take themselves seriously—students always do, and we are no exception—but that their elders take them seriously. In the West it seems possible to grow quite old without having to grow up—you have so much slack, so much room, so much padding between yourselves and reality. You can afford a great deal: we can't. For instance, can you imagine reading Sarre's *Les communistes et la paix* here in 1952? That was just at the time of the Slansky trials. Or reading Marcuse on repressive tolerance, in Prague at the time of the Writers' Union Congress? It was not until I started visiting the West that I began to understand that a Sartre or a Marcuse can simply afford a great deal of illusion. You all live in a different era—you still believe in Utopia. You simply haven't faced up to the fact that you can't build a Utopia without terror, and that before long, terror is all that's left. You have little stomach for terror—after twenty years, we have even less. But you like your radical illusions too well. We've had our fill of Utopia. (*Survey*, January/February 1969)

For criticism of the young, on the grounds that they are cut off from much contemporary and even more past reality, also applies to many adults in the West. They, too, have contrived to remain uninformed about the realities of communist political culture and even more unprepared for the imaginative effort of considering that there may be styles of political and other life beyond their cushioned experience.

And what do they and their youth auxiliaries pick up? Let us look at a few examples: one may certainly say that young persons could scarcely commit themselves, without incitement, to propositions at once so fanatical and so absurd.

On 1 May 1971 we find reports of an attempt by students at York University to exclude the Monday Club (a right-wing Conservative organisation) from the allocation of Students' Union funds available to all other groups, including Anarchists, Trotskyites and Women's Lib: 'The students also felt than on political grounds the Monday Club should not be tolerated in any liberal society.' The use of the word 'liberal' is the interesting point here.

During the student elections at the University of Southern California in the same period a student conservative newspaper, *Free Trojan* was banned from the campus by the student government on the grounds that it might affect these elections. The way they put it was: 'To say that free speech is more important than a fair and free election is to transpose the means and the ends.'

A British professor tells of presenting a paper before a group of American university teachers: 'Afterwards, a young woman of advanced "liberal" views approached me and said in all seriousness: "You're advocating censorship; you shouldn't be allowed to publish it"' (*The Trousered Ape* by Duncan Williams).

Parochialism, we have suggested earlier, leads to the inappropriate

applying of one's own local criteria in spheres where the result is totally misleading. But it also has another effect. Party or sectional
hatreds become so great, or are worked up to such a degree, that people
start to say—then to *think*—that the despotic states must be good
really because their own local opponents attack them so strongly; or,
by a similar process of thought, that the despotisms criticise faults
in the democracies, so must themselves be no more than the
representatives of reforming ideas. Besides, one's own grievances,
however small, always appear larger than worse ones far away, unless
one makes the effort required for any responsible comment. As
Tennyson said in his *To One Who Ran Down The English*:

> You make our faults too gross, and thence maintain
> Our darker future. May your fears be vain!
> At times the small black fly upon the pane
> May seem the black ox of the distant plain.

This seems to be a tribal, temperamental partisanship, not a matter
of thought proper. The key remark (by Leslie Fiedler) applies, though
not only in America: 'How desperately they wish in each case that
the Hiss, the Lattimore who speaks their language might be telling
the truth; that the hyper-patriot who combines the most shameless
stock phrases of nationalism with behind-the-scenes deals, who dis-
trusts literature and art and intelligence itself, might be lying.' And
so does Camus' complaint that the French leftists do not really love
Russia so much as that they 'heartily detest part of the French'.
Orwell similarly notes:

> The majority of pacifists either belong to obscure religious sects or
> are simply humanitarians who object to taking life and prefer not
> to follow their thoughts beyond that point. But there is a minority
> of intellectual pacifists whose real though unadmitted motive is a
> hatred of Western democracy and admiration for totalitarian-
> ism. . . All pacifist propaganda of this type avoids mention of
> Russia and China.

Hence, too, the bias or blindness noted by Solzhenitsyn in Western
appraisals:

> According to one scale, a month's imprisonment, or banishment
> to the country, or to a so-called 'punishment cell' where they feed
> you white bread, rolls and milk, shocks the imagination and fills the

columns of the newspapers with anger. According to another scale, people find acceptable and forgivable prison sentences of twenty-five years, dungeons where there is ice on the wall but where they strip you to your underwear. . . .

For the blockage against facts in these minds is extreme, and those thwarted and irritated by the mediocrities of current Western life resent and reject learning how much more intolerable are the extremities they theoretically prefer.

The so-called Establishment has now long been self-questioning, even to an exaggerated and almost masochistic degree. The time has now come surely for opponents of the Establishment to lose their own self-righteousness and submit themselves to a comparable self-criticism. For, in fact, the political judgment of the politically excitable 'intellectual' is the worst of all. Orwell writes in his 'Such, Such Were the Joys' of how, when he was ten years old, he knew more facts about sex than when he was six, but that his true knowledge was smaller, since he had forgotten the most important thing, that sex is enjoyable. In the same way, the 'politically informed' intellectual is often able to forget that totalitarianism is not enjoyable. That fact is, of course, known to the less well-informed, ordinary man.

Rationalisation is a perennial custom. What is so striking about fashionable rationalisation is its extraordinarily low level. Marxism is, or can be made, a moderately sophisticated ideology. The same can be said of existentialism and its derivatives. The level at which these things are now treated, in published works, by teachers and so on, is merely despicable. During the Vietnam War a number of senior members of universities took a whole-page advertisement in *The Times* to voice the demand that the British Government take a neutral position over the war, on the grounds that only thus could it fulfil its function as co-chairman of the Geneva Conference. Whatever the rights and wrongs of the war, this particular formulation was quite undisguisedly silly: the other co-chairman was the USSR, and if logic rather than enthusiasm had played any part in the drafting of this appeal, it must have allowed that Britain, in order to preserve the balance, should provide as much support to the Allies as the Russians did to the North. (If the point had had any validity at all, which, of course, it hadn't.)

Again, a group of several hundred American economists signed a letter some years ago saying that to their knowledge Andrea Papandreou was not a conspirator. Does it really need to be said that their ignorance of the matter was compatible with both his innocence and his guilt? When the millionaire Italian publisher Feltrinelli was found dead in suspicious circumstances (with a bundle of explosives by a pylon) a large group of Italian academics *instantly* signed a manifesto declaring his innocence. In 1964 a large number of American 'qualified' psychiatrists signed what purported to be a professional analysis of Senator Goldwater as a clinically unbalanced character. I remember the anger of a friend of mine, a professor of psychology at an American university and himself a strong opponent of Goldwater's, at this extraordinary breach of professional ethics and of scientific principle. (Goldwater eventually received heavy damages from them in a court action.) What one notes most (in varying degrees) is the lack of shame due to narrow conviction or factious fanaticism, which alone have the power to exempt men from this feeling.

Indeed, the 'intellectual' is often not evil, just foolish, the prey of forces too strong for him. It is also the case that many of those temporarily alienated from our own society by trendy propaganda are often then counter-alienated right back again by trendy idiocy. But we should not underestimate the sloppy appeal of the *idée reçue*. As T. S. Eliot put it:

> The ideas which flatter a current tendency or emotional attitude will go farthest; and some others will be distorted to fit in with what is already accepted. The residuum in the public mind is hardly likely to be a distillation of the best and wisest: it is more likely to represent the common prejudices of the majority of editors and reviewers. In this way are formed the *idées reçues*—more precisely the *mots reçus*—which, because of their emotional influence upon that part of the public which is influenced by printed matter, have to be taken into account by the professional politician, and treated with respect in his public utterances. It is unnecessary, for the simultaneous reception of these 'ideas', that they should be consistent among themselves; and, however they contradict each other, the practical politician must handle them with as much deference as if they were the constructions of informed sagacity, the intuitions of genius, or the accumulated wisdom of ages. He has not, as a rule, inhaled any fragrance they may have had when they were fresh; he only noses them when they have already begun to stink.

'Him new, him good' was the motto of the tribe which died of
cultural shock while its more insular neighbours survived. . . .

On the other hand, it is true that, as Whitehead once remarked,
'almost all really new ideas have a certain aspect of foolishness when
they are first produced.' At a lower level, it could similarly be said,
for example, that the first appearance of men's fashions in clothing is
on exhibitionists, popinjays, change-mad freaks or self-conscious
'petty bourgeois revolutionaries'. Even brown shoes were once thought
a vile and vicious innovation, and only through the efforts of otherwise not very laudable characters did it become possible for us to wear
them: and who cannot be grateful to those imperfect beings who managed to get rid of the hard collar? And so it is quite reasonable to suppose
that many of the customs which now appear to most people to be de-
plorable on account of those who practise them may in the longer run
be assimilated in a broader and saner way. Mr Poul Anderson, the
sane and imaginative science fiction writer, hypothesises in one of
his books a society with a very large component of differently motivated communes. But these are, in Anderson's future, fully aware of
their dependence on a rich and highly technological economy, and the
exclusive self-righteousness and propagandist 'life-style' attitudes associated with that sort of thing as it exists at present have evaporated.

One may perhaps say that in a society in which they are effectively prevented from obtaining or affecting political power and setting
up their own styles of theocracy, Utopians may play a fertilising
role, just as strychnine in its pure state is fatal but suitably diluted
becomes a weapon of therapeutic medicine.

Of course, a great many innovations lack such justification and
will not survive, just as many of the innovations in the clothing of the
post-bloomer period have not proved viable (there is an overlap here,
certainly; see Orwell's description of the horrible clothes worn at
socialist summer schools). Among fairly recent trends, it always
seemed unlikely that the customs of one lot of the 'radical' young,
to look as ugly as possible and smell nasty (on the grounds that the
bourgeois don't like this), would ever dominate any more or less civilised society, for the bourgeois dislike some things because they are
human beings and not because they are bourgeois.

Not every opinion of this sort is worthless in itself. The trouble is,
rather, that having accepted a given view, these 'progressives' are
totally without a sense of proportion when it comes to putting their
opinions into practice. The legalisation of abortion becomes not the

best, on balance, in the equitable regulation of a horrible problem, but a crusade for a wonderful liberty.

Naturally, no one of any sense would hold that the ideas most commonly held, or those at any given moment constituting the highest fashion, are likely to be the right ones. Historically speaking, innumerable instances could be cited to show that in the long run it has *always* been the critic of such ideas who has had more of the truth in him than his opponents—a notion which ought to appeal particularly to those who believe in endless progress. For it should be (though it is not) especially difficult for them to believe that the history of thought has suddenly reached its final conclusion. But the temperamental pleasure to be had in it is not to be blocked. As A. E. Housman put it:

> This is the felicity of the house of bondage, and of the soul which is so fast in prison that it cannot get forth; which commands no outlook upon the past or the future, but believes that the fashion of the present, unlike all fashions heretofore, will endure perpetually and that its own flimsy tabernacle of second-hand opinions is a habitation for everlasting.

The great flaw in a conformist culture is the lack of discrimination. It is also the great flaw in the extreme anti-conformist protest.

As Greek culture declined, the manifestations included highly systematic Alexandrian criticism, comparable with, (though, of course, better than) our own, together with a verse of superficial sophistication based upon it. At the same time, at a lower level, lunatic sects emerged. Ophites and their like have a good deal in common with such degenerate phenomena as scientology, flying saucer lore, Reichian psychology and all the other fads of the hippy and post-hippy culture. In the meantime, generations of at least equal intelligence have gone wild over absurd theological fads, schemes for millenarian political Utopias, aethetic crazes and pseudo-sciences. In this, as in many other ways, the teaching of real history might be of benefit. At least it would make it a little more difficult, perhaps, to maintain the unique rightness and irrefutability of some lunatic positions.

The medieval Arab historian Ibn Khaldoun remarks (too sanguinely), 'The wise and the ignorant are unanimous in their appreciation of history, since in its external aspect it is no more than a series of anecdotes which tell us how external circumstances upset human affairs, while in its interior aspect it implies a just perception of the causes and origins of phenomena.' But history is the last thing this temperament wants to hear of. It is too complex, too detailed, too un-idealistic—unless passed through the chopper of a simple ideological sausage-machine. At present even people emerging from the universities lack the perspective of history, even recent history. The little history they are taught has now become so sociologised that politics itself appears as little more than an epiphenomenon. It is right, indeed, that the social forces which were to some degree neglected in history as it was written up to about two hundred years ago should be given their proper place. But the effect of this method of teaching is damaging for two reasons. First, it removes the framework of the merely factual, the dates and reigns and battles and so forth. These are now regarded as inessentials. But even if inessential, in the absence of knowledge about them the 'social' aspect sinks into an amorphous jelly of generalised forces. The second and more powerful objection is that it is precisely in the political (and military) struggle that history has actually worked itself out, that the will and judgment of individuals or classes have found leverage and expression, as we might think was obvious in the epoch of Stalin and Mao and Hitler.

Jefferson urged that education of the members of a modern democratic community in particular should be 'chiefly historical'. History,

> by apprising them of the past, will enable them to judge of the future; it will avail them of the experience of *other times and other nations*; it will qualify them as judges of the actions and designs of men; it will enable them to know ambition under every disguise it may assume; and knowing it, to defeat its views. In every government on earth is some trace of human weakness, some germ of corruption and degeneracy, which cunning will discover, and wickedness insensibly open, cultivate and improve. Every government degenerates when trusted to the rulers of the people alone. The people themselves therefore are its only safe depositories. And to render even them safe, their minds must be improved to a certain degree. This indeed is not all that is necessary, though it be essentially necessary.

In the study of history itself there has been an unfortunate search for 'methodology', which is to say that an attempt has been made to impose on the writing of history a set of mechanical rules guaranteed to produce adequate results. But, as Jacques Barzun points out, even the 'factual' side of history, the process of verification, is 'conducted on many planes, and its technique is not fixed, it relies on attention to detail, on common sense, reasoning, on a developed "feel" for history and chronology and familiarity with human behaviour, and with ever enlarging stores of information'. He adds that the sort of judgment which is in the end the crux of the historian's equipment is in all essentials the same as that needed in matters of everyday life, where error and falsehood equally have to be coped with.

These difficulties, natural to any serious enterprise, make it possible for hostile minds to insist that the 'facts' are dubious. And, indeed, it is difficult to establish beyond cavil even many of the important data of history. Many of the true facts are so extraordinary that a natural, if sometimes unconscious, bias against accepting them sometimes comes to be established. Richard Whatley, in a paper written a few years after the Battle of Waterloo, argued that the evidence for the career of Napoleon was so extraordinary that it would certainly not have been accepted if attributed to some Israelite or other king in ancient times. He was also able to show that contradictory accounts existed of most of the major events of the Napoleonic period. And he concluded ironically that there was no reason to believe in the Emperor's existence. . . .

It is, indeed, the case that where history, and particularly recent history, is concerned we are often in a position where a great many important facts (possibly most of them) are, taken individually, very hard to substantiate beyond reasonable doubt. Nevertheless, paradoxically it remains true that from an assembly of facts, few of them absolutely certain, a clear account of a full series of events, defective only in a certain fuzziness at the edges, can yet be established.

If the facts are dubious in this sense, the anti-historian can also urge that historians have held opinions and that this invalidates them (while validating the particular historicist the anti-historian fancies). A British historian (John Morris) has written:

> All great historians, from Thucydides, Tacitus and Bede to Gibbon, have preached their own beliefs; they are great because they recognise their purpose and make it plain to their readers, and because they found their argument on a careful assessment of their own sources, distinguishing between knowledge and report. If we reject their conclusions, we do so on the basis of their own evidence, interpreting it differently. We need a sharper criticism of more pedestrian writers, ancient or modern, who are less aware of their own bias, who are content to endorse a conclusion because it is

'generally accepted', and we must be especially wary of the man who claims to set down objective truth free from bias, for the closer he comes to his ideal, the more he is enslaved to the passing prejudice of his own day, uncritically reading present assumptions into the experience of the past.

We are all products of the world we live in, and we cannot hope to escape from its present assumptions. We can try to recognise them, to discount what is not valid for the past.

This is the point, quite misunderstood by truly partisan exploiters of history, which is central to all true knowledged.

Meanwhile, let me give an example of partisan historicising, still accepted though long ago exposed. The late Isaac Deutscher, a guru of the modern 'new left', writes in his last collection of essays, 'It was only after the Communists had been ejected from the French and Italian governments that Stalin began to eject the anti-Communists from the Eastern European governments.' In fact, it was in January 1945 that Vyshinsky's ultimatum secured the expulsion of Maniu and the democratic parties from the Romanian government. Petkov and the Bulgarian equivalents were out by that summer. In East Germany the Social Democrats were destroyed in April 1946; Mikolajczyk and his Peasant Party had been excluded from the Polish government by February 1947; and in the same month the Smallholder leadership in Hungary had been accused of conspiracy and their secretary-general arrested. It was in May 1947 that the communist ministers left the governments of Italy and France.

If mere facts of this type are so treated, we can imagine what happens to broader realities. In effect, history—if attended to at all—is regimented into false perspectives, just as contemporary reality is.

The emotions behind misunderstanding are often respectable in isolation. But some abstract desire for 'peace and progress' is no substitute for policy based on thought. Nor is instinctive hostility to the centres of political and military power in one's own country a good excuse for supporting, in effect, the much nastier (on any grounds) establishments of our enemies. Thus we get, for example, the argument advanced by Graham Greene and others in favour of Castro that he is better than Batista. One has met this argument before: 'One must support Rakosi because Horthy's dictatorship was so unpleasant.' The logical fallacy is plain enough. The political organisation of states is not limited to various forms of dictatorship. There is also

—democracy.

Nor is the present Castro dictatorship a successor to Batista's. It is the successor of the anti-Batista coalition which Castro himself headed before betraying it. The communists collaborated with Batista for many years. Many of those who opposed him, including original Castroites, are now in jail or exiled. (And while Castro served a short prison sentence for an armed attack on a barracks, one of his own commanders, Major Matos, served a twenty-year sentence simply for a political disagreement.) Whether Batista or Castro was worse will doubtless be established eventually to the satisfaction of history: we now know that Rakosi was far worse than Horthy. Either way, it is particularly distasteful to find foreigners, themselves living in a democracy, justifying the sufferings of the many unfortunate Boxers, on the grounds that the local Napoleon is better than Mr Jones. Moreover, a distinction can surely be made in foreign policy. The Castro regime is aggressive and, in effect, expansionist. The Batista regime was not. This is not a moral judgment, but the point is one that we can hardly be expected not to take into consideration. But one may feel that one of the actual attractions of the Castro regime is precisely its hostility to the West. Such, at least is the extreme attitude.

Then there is the 'moderate' with his mediocre political philistinism, his conviction that the truth probably lies somewhere between two 'extreme' views and that any problem can be settled by well-meaning representatives on all sides sitting down and chewing the rag. The first of these principles was what led similar circles to feel, in the thirties, that it was as difficult to believe that Stalin was framing Old Bolsheviks as it was to believe that the Old Bolsheviks were trying to assassinate Stalin, and that the truth probably lay somewhere between — the charges were doubtless exaggerated but contained an element of truth. In fact, the truth was entirely one-sided. In the present international situation the principle of the give-and-take compromise settlement, the attempt to stop what might be an unpleasant scene by a bit of committee work, is like Chamberlain's application of Birmingham City Council methods to negotiations with Adolf Hitler.

The motivation of this sort of 'moderate' is simply a dislike of trouble, a wish that everything could be settled somehow. Doubtless, we all have this wish. But what it amounts to is a gradual drift from 'Oh, if only both sides would be reasonable!' to 'Oh, if only our side would be reasonable!' This is compounded by defects in the dissemination of information. Over Vietnam, for example, sensitives who usually manage to keep insulated had selections from a real war pushed in their faces. Anything that takes place in front of a Western journalist and then appears in the daily papers or on TV in London and New York is disturbing. Here the totalitarians score. The torture chambers and the labour camps are humanely kept out of the sight of Western journalists — apart from the wholly exceptional occasion on which a number of these were taken round the AVH cellars in Budapest during the brief breakdown of 1956.

Such argument (and other similar ones which it would be tedious to repeat) must be part of the experience of every reader. They reflect something more general: that a false picture of most alien situations has been built up in many minds. How did this happen? The question is not one involving expertise (about Vietnam, for example): it is one involving knowledge of how false political impressions are created. I recall the fighting in Greece in 1944. British troops were brought in to thwart the seizure of power by the communist-controlled EAM. The British Government, including its large Labour Party contingent, solidly backed this action. A large section of 'public opinion' was horrified. Most of the press, as far as the right-centre, took the view that the EAM, consisting 'largely' of non-communists, was not under communist control; that, as an anti-Nazi resistance movement, it represented the aspirations of the Greek people; that all the British were doing was to impose an unpopular, right-wing, reactionary regime by brute force upon an unwilling people.

Free elections held not long after the Greek fighting should have put paid to that sort of feeling. But the incident was simply forgotten: the wrongheaded and ill-informed circles had learnt nothing and forgotten nothing and here they still are, thirty-five years later.

The misinformation in this case seems to have become pervasive for several reasons. First, several of the reporters who, from behind the British lines, were sending back inept commentary, were fellow-travellers or (in one case) the possessor of a Greek communist mistress. This is not necessarily, perhaps not at all, to question their sincerity, but it clearly affected the slant of their stories. Secondly, many journalists are arrogant and sceptical (as is fair enough) about official handouts, but credulous about anything that can be presented to them as fresh and first-hand stuff. In Greece EAMites (and even men on the anti-EAM side who nourished personal hostility to their own country's leaders), were particularly industrious in their efforts to gain a journalistic ear. Thirdly, at home in Britain there were partisans of the enemy, or liberals who did not wish to see the necessity for action, or general critics of the Government, who could easily, almost unconsciously, provide from a large range of real facts a picture accumulatively based on a biased selection. The reader could feel (as with 'A Vietnamese Prisoner is Tortured', 'A Village is Burned by Napalm', 'A Buddhist Monk Speaks Out', etc., etc.) that he had objectively formed a full view when he had not, in fact, done so. Your student rebel — and, alas, your academic rebel — was particularly susceptible to this sort of thing, because apart from the bias of what was presented to him, he had a built-in bias for accepting the good on one side and the bad on the other, as with the totally fictitious 'bombing of the dykes'.

This results in something like hysterical blindness, in the medical sense. Malcolm Muggeridge, recounting his experience as a correspondent in Moscow, has mentioned the extraordinary sight of Westerners not merely uncritically accepting what they were told, but even letting their enthusiasm override the evidence of their senses: 'town planners looking up in awe at gimcrack buildings which were beginning to fall down before they were completed'.

This basic lack of seriousness in all pro-totalitarian attitudes is quite remarkable. It goes back a long way. One of the more curious points is that Westerners who thought in terms of the 'progressive' nature of Lenin's regime could ignore the extent to which it was repudiated after 1917 not only by the broadest possible spectrum of the left-wing and socialist political elements in Russia, but also by artists, writers, academics and so forth. It might have been possible to remain uninformed about those who, for a hundred natural reasons, remained in Russia, preserving a reluctant silence, or those (in the more optimistic cases) who hoped for the best and sought to accommodate themselves to the *fait accompli* and, over a shorter or longer period, were disillusioned or shot. But the sheer bulk of the emigration of both political liberalism and non-political creativity was on a scale which had never before been seen. The experience has been repeated a dozen times since. Yet, after a few years, it seems to fade from the 'Progressive' memory.

Nor have the communists ever had any difficulty in rounding up a bunch of Western scientists and others to authenticate the most improbable lies. In particular, they never have any difficulty in rounding up clergymen or 'democratic' socialists. But any socialist who is not just defending a case for debating reasons must admit that he would prefer to live under a conservative government than a communist one. With all its faults, the former at least does not ban the

208 The Mechanisms of Misunderstanding

socialist parties and put their leaders in jail or before the firing squad. No amount of abstract or economic theorising can alter this point.

Typically, G.D.H. Cole (in his *Communism and Social Democracy 1914-1931*) based himself on a fetishism of the formal economic structure, with the accompanying thesis that communism, though in many ways reprehensible, is a sort of socialism. He saw that the Soviet 'centralist bureaucracy' was 'destructive of personal liberty and freedom of thought and action'. But he largely discounted this on the grounds of the brutalising social and economic repression of capitalism. (Whether for this or some other reason, his book is full of errors and omissions, almost all of them tending to make things look a little better.)

There is a case for orthodox communism. It is put by Gletkin in Arthur Koestler's *Darkness at Noon*: that a vast amount of terror and general unpleasantness is necessary to create better things. In my view, the case has actually been disproved by the experience (most recently of the Soviet Union) which shows that you can have the terror and not get the better things. But at least the case can be argued on its merits. The 'progressive' or 'democratic' pro-communist line simply has no contact with reality at any point.

Lenin said that every cook must learn to rule the state. On the Western left, one sometimes feels, the slogan has been taken over with one important amendment: the substitution of 'k' for 'c'.

Even a deep and genuine study and knowledge in detail may be compatible with quite crazy general assumptions. Lord Kingborough's immensely learned nine-volume *Antiquities of Mexico* was nevertheless compatible with a belief that the ancient Mexicans were the lost tribes of Israel. Sir Bernard Pares, a long-established academic and expert on all things Russian, with fifty years' experience, went to the USSR in 1935 and was instantly taken in by normal duping procedures, with the result that later editions of his previously scholarly *A History of Russia* contain remarks about the fake Moscow Trials which it is hard to credit even now and which continued to appear in an edition put out in 1962 *after* the then Soviet leaders had themselves repudiated some of them! Pares's work had all the authority of the most respectable academician: we could tell it was all right by the mere prestige of the author. . . . These things remind one of a remark made by one of Peter de Vries's characters about another: that he is only profound on the surface; deep down he is superficial.

No doubt, or at least perhaps, the academic world is in some sense the repository of a general wisdom. Nevertheless, it is old experience that those academics who engage in practical politics are inclined to aberration.

When one thinks of the countries which are, or have lately been, ruled by intellectuals, one shudders. Take the rough working test of a doctor's degree: Dr Verwoerd (in succession to Dr Malan), Dr Castro, Dr Jagan, Dr Salazar, Dr Sukarno and old Doc Duvalier and all—something there for everyone. I am reminded of a reply made to an American intellectual who was maintaining that soldiers (presumably he meant General Eisenhower) are worse political leaders than intellectuals are. It was shortly after de Gaulle came to power, and I was able to enquire which alternative he was putting forward, Professor Bidault or Professor Soustelle.

When one sees them getting involved in real politics, one recalls similar things that happened in the seventeenth century, not always with good results, as John Selden tells us in his *Table Talk*:

> He that comes from the University to govern the State, before he is acquainted with the Men and Manners of the Place, does just as if he should come into the presence Chamber all Dirty, with his Boots on, his riding Coat, and his hat all daubed. They may serve him well enough in the Way, but when he comes to Court, he must conform to the Place.

Even in a sphere in which pretty well all the knowledge is available, the ability to act on it may depend upon indefinable skills. A professor of ballistics does not necessarily make a good baseball pitcher. But nor is it entirely clear that a good baseball pitcher who applies himself to the science thereby becomes noticeably better at his trade. In our context, at any rate, academic arrogance has increased in proportion to the decline in academic standards and is largely to be found among those who most actively undermine those standards. Of course, one is speaking only of the most 'activist'—and usually the least academically impressive—of this caste. One can look back on many similar periods of delusion. Koestler, in his autobiography, reminds us of the time when London was full of 'the thousands of painters and writers and doctors and lawyers and debutantes chanting a diluted version of the Stalinist line'. But the irresponsibility of even truly intelligent intellectuals, when it comes to supporting a regime on to which they have projected some sort of hope, is quite astonishing, worse than the attitude of the *philosophes* to the Russia of

Catherine the Great. The Iron Curtain is only effective to a limited extent in cutting off information about communist realities. It only achieves its full objective when supplemented by the Bone Curtain compounded of ideology, anti-patriotism and egocentricity which already surrounds the minds of certain Westerners.

After Gomulka had come to power, at the Polish Central Committee plenum of October 1956 a speaker remarked that the whole city knew that people were being murdered. The whole city knew that there were cells in which people were kept for three weeks standing in excrement, etc. The whole city, that is, except visiting Western progressives: one of these (Mr John Freeman) had filled several pages of the *New Statesman* a few months earlier with a report on Poland denying the existence of terror. Mr Anthony Hartley later met one of his informants, who remarked, 'What would you have expected me to have said to him?' (A few years later we got *The Times* printing an article on Albania which not only asserted the intense loyalty to the leadership of everybody there, but added that this was a fine trait.)

Surely we do not need lessons in the gullibility of high-minded leftists when it comes to Communist 'evidence'? To take a single instance: the germ-warfare hoax run by the Maoists during the Korean War. The Dean of Canterbury told the Britain-China Friendship Association, 'The facts about germ warfare are conclusive and irrefutable.' He had, in fact, seen the evidence, a test-tube full of insects which his hosts told him were infected with disease germs.

An 'international scientific commission', on which the British representative was Dr Joseph Needham, FRS, published a document of which the length and objectivity were similar to those of the reams we later got about Vietnam — over six hundred pages. The Maoist spokesman formally charged on several occasions that insects, rats, shellfish and chicken feathers impregnated with germs had been dropped by the Americans in China as well as North Korean territory. Needham commented, 'We accepted the word of the Chinese scientists.' In fact, to put it charitably, the whole thing was an exercise in credulity. Finally, there was the third 'Congress of Peoples for Peace'. Its platform abounded with Brecht, Sartre, Bernal and the others, and it formally condemned American germ warfare.

It used to be a matter of educated dupes or dupers angling or selecting facts to suit their dogmas. The present, or second, generation seems to consist very largely of uneducated dupers simply getting the facts wrong or suppressing them entirely. *The Internationale,* anthem of the left, did not in its original form tell us:

Cant in revolt now thunders
And at last ends the age of reason.

George Orwell, that Briton to whom all men of sense must regularly appeal, comments that the big public 'are at once too sane and too stupid to acquire the totalitarian outlook. The direct, conscious attack on intellectual decency comes from the intellectuals themselves.' What is missing in Western intellectuals, and in a most extraordinary fashion, is the feeling of what totalitarianism is about. They have not experienced it. And for some reason they seem unwilling to make the imaginative effort which is the only substitute. But the effort is an intellectual and an ethical duty, and it can be made. Orwell, who had no experience of totalitarianism, had an extraordinary insight into it.

Perfectionists, those keen on the *mieux* which is the enemy of the *bien,* will naturally find as much to condemn in any society, particularly in one not disposing of a government monopoly of information. But the rule of the saints has always proved a bad alternative even to the very worst in democratic corruption. No dictatorship ever stayed benevolent for long, for the obvious reason: the most ruthless addicts of power fight their way to the top.

Yet let us say again that except in a few cases, in which the personalities concerned seem to have become wholly desocialised — in fact to be no more than political psychopaths — a residue of the traditions and the values of our society seems to remain, even among many people who have persuaded themselves that they are radically and revolutionarily opposed to our system. Orwell somewhere speaks of the 'solemn farce' of British Marxist professors writing letters to the papers about this or that departure from the high standards of British justice. But though there may be a paradoxical, even a funny side to it, it is also heartening to find that roots are not easily cut.

Popper suggests, in the addendum to the later editions of *The Open Society and Its Enemies,* that the myths provided by religion and tradition have indeed been replaced by relativism, nihilism and intellectual despair, and that the intellectuals (Hayek's 'second-hand dealers in ideas') are responsible. Popper urges, however, that the positive power of the intellect and of intellectuals should be put to good use: that the intellectual fallacies of fashionable nihilism can be refuted and it is up to them to refute it. This is to argue, in effect, that the old clerisy having virtually disappeared, the intelligentsia in a general sense can be persuaded by the rational and general arguments destructive of sophism that are advanced by Popper, historians and others. And that then they may repair the damage.

Perhaps in certain cases. As Orwell points out, the reason why the intellectual's greatest efforts of thought do not succeed in eliminating, or even recognising, his prejudices is that what is required is an effort which is not merely intellectual, but also moral.

All the same, we must hope that minds may clear, or enough of them may, while there is yet time. We cannot afford to have the public, or any important section of it, misled on the major issues before us.

PART FOUR

Motivations and Perspectives

CHAPTER 13

Matters of Temperament

What, then, are the sources of political attitudes? It is not easy to get into another man's skin, let alone that of another culture. The great Condé once remarked to the Cardinal de Retz that the reason why historians got things wrong was because

> *Ces coquins nous font parler et agir comme*
> *ils auroient fait eux-mêmes à notre place.*

He noted, in fact, that intellectuals of his own culture would not, or at any rate had not, made the effort adequately.

It is not even as if Condé himself was an intellectually musclebound thug of a professional soldier. Those who delighted to frequent his chateau when he was in disgrace — Molière, Racine, Boileau, La Fontaine, Bossuet — make almost a roll call of the genius of the Grande Epoque. . . . But if academics fail to understand the temperaments of the generals of their own culture, they are all the more unlikely to grasp the temperaments producing and produced by other traditions. Similarly, Napoleon was able to tell an Austrian negotiator (during the 1813 truce) that others had difficulty in understanding a man like him, to whom the death of a million men meant nothing.

And this is of individuals of different psychology within a single culture. When it comes to alien cultures, the immodesty of some anthropologists and social historians, who believe that they have got into the essence of a society, is a constant trap. Louis MacNeice, the poet, who was also a professor of Greek and deeply versed in ancient Athens, could nevertheless write:

> And how one can imagine oneself among them
> I do not know.
> It was all so unimaginably different,
> And all so long ago.

And this is Athens! Incomparably closer to us, in many ways, than most of the other ancient cultures and many modern ones.

And yet the effort must be made. And when it comes to modern alien cultures, no understanding, and so no policy, will be worth anything until academics, statesmen and all others concerned make that effort, to the degree that unreal assumptions are driven even from their almost unconscious first thoughts on affairs. After that they need, it may be suggested, to master the idea that these deep-set forces of motivation are not merely very strange to us, but cannot easily be changed by argument or manipulation.

As has often been said, the true criticism of Chamberlain is that he could not really imagine a man like Hitler or a party like the Nazis. 'He's a good fellow and t'will all be well', whatever may be said of it as theology, is a parochial and limited attitude when it comes to foreign politics. It is not only on the left — and, of course, many on the left are exempt — that one finds this inability to grasp the totalist mentality imaginatively. The notion that people who raised the alarm in the 1930s were being immoderate and unreasonable was found in *The Times* and at All Souls, in all the blinkered and complacent crannies of the Establishment. The idea of a quite different set of motivations, based on a different political psychology, was absent.

We are faced with the absolutely crucial problem of making the intellectual and imaginative effort *not* to project our ideas of common sense or natural motivation on to the products of a totally different culture. For the central point is not so much that people misunderstand other people, or that cultures misunderstand other cultures, but that they have no notion that this may be the case. They assume that the light of their own parochial common sense is enough. And they frame policies based on illusions. Yet how profound is this difference between political psychologies and between the motivations of different political traditions, and how deep-set and how persistent these attitudes are!

Political opinion seems largely a matter of temperament. Strikingly enough, this is implicitly admitted by Marx himself in that passage in the *Communist Manifesto* in which, having insisted that in general people act according to their class economic interest, he makes an exception for — Marxist intellectuals! 'A portion of the bourgeoisie goes over to the proletariat, and, in particular, a portion of the bourgeois ideologists, who have raised themselves to the level of comprehending theoretically the historical movement as a whole.' As we know, most Marxist and communist leaders have been of bourgeois origin. Marx is here admitting that their motivations are not those normally provided for by Marxism. What are they, then? Marx himself would have been the last to say that any of his followers were the intellectual superiors of Darwin or Clerk Maxwell, nor is it likely that a communist in this century would claim that Molotov was the intellectual superior of Ivan Pavlov or Anton Chekhov; or Louis Aragon of Louis de Broglie, or Albert Camus. But if not intellect or interest, we are left with temperament.

Even the philosopher, William James remarks, is really much motivated by temperament:

> Temperament is no conventionally recognised reason; so he urges impersonal reasons for his conclusions. Yet his temperament really gives him a stronger bias than any of his more strictly objective premises... Wanting a universe that suits it, he believes any representation of the universe that does suit it.

In his *Utopia and Revolution* Melvin J. Lasky quotes a letter of Pavel Axelrod, then one of the leaders of the Russian revolutionary Marxists in the struggle against Eduard Bernstein and 'revisionism'. Axelrod remarks (privately, to be sure) that 'the whole thing is a matter of temperament,' adding that the real objection to peaceful evolution, whatever its advantages, is that it 'would be exceedingly boring'. Similarly Simone de Beauvoir, in a revealing passage in *The Prime of Life,* says that she and Sartre were 'temperamentally opposed to the idea of reform'.

In an examination of the relationship between the particularly egotistical and the idea of a quick and radical change of his opponent (society) Eric Hoffer, in his *The True Believer,* remarks:

> The inordinately selfish are particularly susceptible to frustration. The more selfish a person, the more poignant his disappointments. It is the inordinately selfish, therefore, who are likely to

be the most persuasive champions of selflessness.

The fiercest fanatics are often selfish people who were forced, by innate shortcomings or external circumstances, to lose faith in their own selves. They separate the excellent instrument of their selfishness from their ineffectual selves and attach it to the service of some holy cause. And though it be a faith of love and humility they adopt, they can be neither loving nor humble.

This supports the view that part of the motivation of the doctrinaire revolutionary is weakness in the face of the unpredictable chaos of reality on to which he projects immutable law, thus turning the universe, at least notionally, into something safe and comprehensible.

Dostoyevsky also points out, in *The Possessed,* that causes are attractive for another reason, because they provide an excuse for behaving badly, giving 'the right to dishonour', which, as he puts it, is endlessly fascinating. One of the things which gave Stalinism its prestige in the West, even (or especially) among those who recognised that its methods were immensely ruthless, was the abstract, Utopian notion that there was a certain horrible grandeur in what was going on. Men of ideas, who had profoundly considered the laws of history, were creating a new society and taking upon themselves the guilt of the necessary merciless action. Such an attitude is to be seen even in the interrogators in Arthur Koestler's *Darkness at Noon:* and Koestler has recorded that a young Frenchman once wrote to tell him that he had become converted to communism by that very book.

Rauschning tells us (revealingly, in the context of temperament) that Hitler had said that he could always make a Nazi out of a communist, but could not do this with a Social Democrat. And the affinity of left-wing and right-wing radicalism, of communism and Nazism, is, of course, shown with particular clarity in Hitler's *Table Talk,* recorded during the War. He is full of remarks such as:

I don't blame the small man for turning communist... When one thinks of that riff-raff of bourgeoisie, even today, one sees red... I find our communists a thousand times more sympathetic than Stahremberg [the Austrian right-wing leader], say. They were sturdy fellows.

He criticised Franco.

Later on, the Reds we had beaten up became our best supporters.

[In 1934 the British ambassador noted the fact that former communists were the smartest units of the Berlin SA.] When the Falange imprisons its opponents, it's committing the gravest of faults. Wasn't my party, at the time of which I'm speaking, composed 90 per cent of left-wing elements? I needed men who could fight. I had no use for the sort of timid doctrinaires who whisper subversive plans in your ear.

Even earlier he had said:

In our movement the two extremes come together: the communists from the left and the officers and the students from the right. These two have always been the most active elements, and it was the greatest crime that they used to oppose each other in street fights. The communists were the idealists of socialism.

When the totalitarian parties had eventually settled down into their final shapes they gave the impression of having maintained a long and formal mutual hostility. It is more to the point to remember that Laval's early career was as one of the few anti-war pro-Lenin socialists of France in 1914-18; that Jacques Doriot changed from being a leader of the French Communist Party to heading the most pro-Nazi of all French organisations, and so on. Or, on another tack, that Gramsci, for example, was one of Mussolini's closest comrades, right into the latter's 'defencist' phase. Both Lenin and Trotsky are quoted as privately expressing great regret that Mussolini, held by both to be the one man would could have brought about a revolution in Italy, had diverged into Fascism. And, in fact, the earliest leaders of the Fascists were almost entirely from the left, though this started to change fairly rapidly.

Indeed, in Mussolini's last phase too — the 'Salo Republic' of 1943--45 — he instituted a rule which on all the usual criteria was the most 'radical' in all Europe. Like Mussolini, the Nazis — in both cases rightly — felt at this time that they had been endangered by 'reactionary' elements: after the attempted coup of 20 July 1944, I remember hearing their radios raving against 'the blue-blooded swine'.

Unlike Mussolini, Hitler did not himself emerge from the leading ranks of left-wing socialism; but he did emerge from the general 'radical' ambiance of semi-intellectual café discussion. Indeed, we should remember that 'nationalism' (its modern version) has the same roots, as does 'eugenics', which was fashionable even with Fabians, with its racialist implications. But the main element was precisely the 'radical', extremist attitude, with its assumption of the total destruction not merely of the present order, but also of all its principles, moral, social, religious.

In such a context Professor Hugh Seton-Watson notes that Hitler's Nazis were 'fanatics with an *ersatz* religion', who rejected not only Christianity but also traditional morality as such. Nazism's central feature was 'moral nihilism'. Seton-Watson adds, 'Moral nihilism is not only the central feature of National Socialism, but also the common factor between it and Bolshevism.' This is not to deny the other resemblances, in particular the roles of ideology and the Party. But it goes deeper. And 'ideology' itself seems thus to be a psychological mechanism, by which a man starting with fairly normal social inhibitions can short-circuit them and turn himself, for many purposes, into a psychopath.

On the other hand, the modern messianic totalist uses a rational-sounding political *vocabulary,* one not very different from that of the 'liberal' academic. The latter tends to feel not only that discussion, debate, 'dialogue' can take place, but also that here, too, is a rational man with sympathetic aims.

It is hardly possible to exaggerate the mistakes that arise from what would appear to be so simple and easily corrigible a misconception. I know of the daughter of a prominent Eastern European Communist politician who had, at one time, been arrested, tortured and barely escaped execution during the purges which affected his country. His family, as a result, became completely disenchanted with the whole system. When he was released and regained a high position his daughter imagined that he, too, would have been chastened by his experiences. There was absolutely no sign of this. He was delighted to be back and full of pleasure at the prospect of inflicting on his countrymen, and on his former comrades where possible, any form of terror that might prove suitable. The view he seemed to take was that the rules of the game were tough, and he was not in the least surprised that when he was on the losing side he would suffer by it. The notion that there might be something wrong with the whole system had simply not occurred to him at all; his thinking was limited to 'It's my turn now.'

W. H. Auden writes (in *Vespers*) of the difference between an 'Arcadian' and a 'Utopian' temperament.

When lights burn late in the Citadel, I (who have never seen the inside of a police station) am shocked and think: 'Were the city as free as they say, after sundown all her bureaus would be huge black stones.'

He (who has been beaten up several times) is not shocked at all but thinks: 'One fine night our boys will be working up there.'

George Orwell notes Bernard Shaw's attitude to the Russian Revolution. His bloodless rationalism could only see in Lenin and his subordinates people conducting a reasonable experiment, and he accused Churchill of falsely characterising them as devils when they were no more than rational human beings at work. Orwell comments that whether one regards them as angels or devils, one thing certain is that they were not reasonable men.

While particular individuals may be particularly prone to accepting the despotic-revolutionary idea, it is also the case that this acceptance, and the merger of the individual into the organisation devoted to imposing that idea further, changes that individual — and for the worse. Richard Wright, the black American writer who was for a short time a member of the American Communist Party, says in his *American Hunger*:

An hour's listening disclosed the fanatical intolerance of minds sealed against new ideas, new facts, new feelings, new attitudes, new hints at ways to live. They denounced books they had never read, people they had never known, ideas they could never understand, and doctrines they could not pronounce. Communism, instead of making them leap forward with fire in their hearts . . . had frozen them at an even lower level of ignorance than had been theirs before they met Communism.

For, as Norman Cohn has remarked (in his *Warrant for Genocide*),

There exists a subterranean world, where pathological fantasies disguised as ideas are churned out by crooks and half-educated fanatics for the benefit of the ignorant and superstitious. There are times when that underworld emerges from the depths and suddenly fascinates, captures, and dominates multitudes of usually sane and responsible people. . . . And it occasionally happens that this subterranean world becomes a political power and changes the course of history.

We had a good example of 'progressive' misunderstanding of this temperament in 1978, when the Reverend James Jones and his supporters committed mass suicide in Guyana, and he turned out to have been well regarded by various *bien pensant* left-wingers in the United States. Jones had had himself appointed to important posts in both Indianapolis and, more lately, San Francisco. He had letters of appreciation from dozens of political figures, from the Vice-President down. As a result, some attempt has been made to conceal, or blur, how much he and his community were devoted to a Marxist, communist vision of the world and of their own aspirations. The pathetic letters found in their files are mostly from members of the community confessing to insufficient devotion to 'Marxism-Leninism, to 'socialism', to 'communism', rather like the 'self-criti cism of orthodox communist parties, with essays by school children about the hope of Carter being rightly executed by Red Brigades, and so on. Jones continually worried about CIA persecution, a common sign of this type of aberration. He transferred his commune to Marxist Guyana, where it was well received. He tried to transfer to the USSR, holding several meetings with Soviet diplomats to this end, and after the *débâcle* left trusted henchmen with instructions to take the considerable wealth of the community and hand it over to the Russians. . . .

A respected American columnist, Meg Greenfield, dismissed the political issue here as superficial, since mere attachment to racial and other equality does not imply the Jonesian apocalypse. But in attributing it to mere cultism, as though to an odd religion, she is wrong. None of Jones's later writings have a trace of any but a political appeal.

Yet the fact that the language of the 'rational progressive' is used by him and by others who, after further experience, turn out differently is no new discovery. Moderate 'leftists', liberals and all, have long been taken in by the fact that last-things lunatics use the same words—even, in an abstract way, think the same thoughts. At the deeper level the difference is not between ideas, but between temperaments—one might say between souls. Not that this has usually been of much service to the liberals, socialists and so on facing the firing squads of the Marxists they had thought of themselves as understanding and cooperating with.

Moreover, it is a little strange to say that the Jonesites were unpolitical, in the sense that they went a bit far. The death rate was, proportionately, lower in Cambodia (and unfortunately did not, as with the Jonesites, include the leaders). But it was well within 'cultist' notions. So, in another sense, was Stalin's super-massacre of his supporters: different in scale, not so very different in attitude to human life. As Jones put it, his aim was 'revolutionary collective suicide to save our skins from the Fascist Americans'. (And orthodox Marxists had long ago justified the suicide of Marx's son-in-law, Paul Lafargue, on the grounds that it was rational if he could no longer serve the cause.)

A remarkable dramatisation of the results of reasonable men misunderstanding unreasonable men who used the same terminology is provided by the French Revolution. La Harpe, the only eventual survivor, tells a story of a dinner held at the beginning of 1788, at which all the guests were leading intellectuals opposed to Church and State and longing for the reorganisation of society in the 'revolution' which would bring in 'the rule of reason'. One of those present, Cazotte, an adept of the Illuminati, claimed to have the gift of prophecy. He told them that the revolution was, indeed, almost on them. They jokingly asked what would happen to them under the new regime. Condorcet, Cazotte replied, would die in prison of poison he had taken to cheat the executioner. 'What has that to do with philosophy and the reign of reason?' 'It is just what I told you, it is in the name of philosophy, of humanity, and liberty. It is under the reign of reason that you will come to such an end.' Chamfort, Cazotte went on, would cut his veins with twenty-two slashes of the razor, but would fail to die for some months; Vicq-d'Azyr, on the other hand, would succeed in a similar act. De Nicolai would die on the scaffold, Bailly too, and de Malesherbes, and Roucher. . . .

> 'Then we will be subjugated by the Turks and the Tartars?'
> 'Not at all . . . I have told you: those who will treat you thus will all be philosophers, and will have at every moment on their lips all the same phrases that you have been using for an hour, and will be repeating all your maxims.'

By the time six years had passed, every word had been fulfilled and Cazotte himself had become both hero and victim of one of the most pitiful events of the Revolution.

Many intellectuals, or socialists who consider themselves to be intellectuals, seem to be misled by a sort of temperamental solidarity with 'left' totalitarianism. I remember Dr Czeslaw Milosz, the Polish poet who defected in the forties, saying to me once that revolting though the Stalinist regime in his country certainly was, he and his friends had found themselves able to 'talk' to Party intellectuals, while the colonels and peasants were outside this café culture. As a result, in spite of the total divergence on all serious and essential issues between social democrats and communists, in spite of the far closer real ties between themselves and the non-intellectual masses, the tug of this temperamental 'feel' was strong enough often to cancel out the reality.

In every culture, especially in those going through change, there are temperaments available (or created by circumstance) which diverge in a 'revolutionary' way from the general trend of that society. Generally speaking, these emerge less from the supposedly exploited 'class' of a given period than from among disappointed members of the ruling establishment. They are, in fact, quite literally 'misfits'. It is, of course, arguable (at any rate, it is often argued) that a social order may itself be the deviant from the true line of human advance; in fact, that society may be the true 'misfit' while the individuals thus labelled represent the more admirable trend.

We may certainly feel that the rebel or deviant character may have something to contribute in producing change. But as a matter of shown experience, the vast bulk of rebel character appears to be in principle unsocialised, not amenable, or only barely, to the constraints of any type of social order whatever.

Thus we get in the novels of Doris Lessing accounts of the selfish incompetence of the private lives and conduct of English communist and communisant intellectuals, who are nevertheless represented as the political cream of society, capable of running a country as they cannot even run a kitchen.

On the other hand, we can see in Lenin the pure revolutionary, whose interest in the overthrow of the existing order was so intense that he did not spread his progressivism into any other fields, having nothing but contempt for modern art, free love, unorthodox medicine and all the other paraphernalia.

(In a sense Lenin is psychologically a simpler case than the generality of the revolutionary left. The single-minded, full-time, hard-working devotion to one aim is to be found in a variety of fields. The way in which, in Lenin's case, this was in the service of his particular projects, is a problem of a largely different character from that of the psychology of general revolutionary attitudes. The incompetent,

communal, obsessive living of almost all the old Russian revolutionaries contrasts markedly with Lenin's extreme tidiness and industry.
Indeed, his most extraordinary achievement was that he managed to
create a regimented organisation out of the misfits, whom he des-
pised but who were the only material he had to work with).

As has been shown by analysts of the revolutionary movements
of the Middle Ages, the leaders were mainly members of the lower
clergy (Spengler interestingly compares the revolutionaries of the
twentieth century with the mendicant friars), a few eccentric scions of
the lower nobility, together with obscure laymen who had somehow
acquired a clerical education: as Norman Cohn puts it, 'a recognisable
social stratum — a frustrated and rather low-grade intelligentsia'.
(And for their cannon fodder they did not recruit the poor as such,
but those of the poor, 'who could find no assured and recognised place
in society at all'.) And Cohn, noting all these resemblances to the
modern revolutionaries, adds that even in the medieval context, not
remarkable for tolerance or objectivity, the millenarians were 'ab-
normal in their destructiveness and irrationality — psychological
points.

Times of great stress produce both revolutionaries and mystics,
Zealots and Christians. It would be hard to define precisely the psychological differences between the types. And, indeed, there is
usually a good deal of movement from one view to the other; even in
the United States, one notes the political activitists of the sixties later
becoming involved in strange religious quietisms. Such changes are
explicable psychologically, but hardly sociologically.

To look at it from a different angle and to consider the concerns
of the 'progressive' intellectual to determine if the package they
form is a unity based on reason or a temperamental one, let us quote
the left-wing historian Professor E. J. Hobsbawm on the causes
pursued by the typical progressive figure a hundred years ago:
'natural philosophy, phrenology, free thought, spiritualism, tempe-
rance, unorthodox medicine, social reform, and the transformation
of the family' (*New Statesman,* 4 April 1970)--each supported with
just as much righteousness and certainty as the partially different
batch, containing a fresh lot of pseudo-sciences, now so much heard
of. The point is, clearly, that what comes out of the package is not
intellectual coherence, or the pursuit of interests, but a cast of mind.
There is no logical connection, no overriding ideological connection, between the views noted by Hobsbawm, but only the accidental

one of novelty and unorthodoxy, and the temperamental one of the *odium theologicum*. (It is hard to exaggerate the element of sheer lunacy in some of the 'progressive' thinkers who are still highly regarded. Fourier sincerely believed that under socialism the sea could be turned into lemonade; Saint Simon was mad; Robert Owen went mad.)

Now, modern men, though they might not agree on every point, would certainly grant that some of the opinions in Hobsbawm's package were totally crackpot and that others were penetrating anticipations. The difficulty, when one sees the similar package offered to the modern world, is that one cannot yet distinguish easily between what may prove to be a useful contribution to social or other progress and what will in a century be regarded with amusement as the strangest of aberrations. The unifying factor, in any case, is clearly not rational.

The millenarian revolutionary in a despotic society is a typical product of a *milieu* with little or no civic culture and thus cut off from all political realities. One can see how this also applies to a certain type of Westerner. He is typically a student, or an academic who has never in effect ceased to be a student. His experience has not included the give and take of ordinary political and civic life. He has come to Utopian or near-Utopian attitudes at an age when whatever he may have absorbed from the social ambience is at its weakest and his tendency to reject it at its greatest, and at a time when his own experience is virtually nil. He also, typically at least, comes from a family whose way of life has provided effective cushioning against the rough edges of reality.

The revolutionary-despotic (that is, the messianic) type of temperament exists in all societies, including those in which it does not necessarily find any outlet. For there are usually elements of each culture within the other: the survival of temperaments tending to the despotic is seen in the West (in addition to the seepage of despotic ideas and attitudes from other areas). Just as there are potential revolutionaries in situations in which they can never, or only rarely, emerge, there are also potential bearers of the civic and cooperative idea in despotic societies. And though our societies are not pure and abstract civic polities, nor are theirs seamless histories of despotism. Elements of civic life existed not only in pre-revolutionary France, but even in pre-revolutionary Russia. In neither case was revolution, in the catastrophic sense, quite inevitable.

Again, we can see immigrants into the civic culture who are, from the start, temperamentally identified with it. For example, Felix Frankfurter, an immigrant boy who had not heard a word of English until he was twelve, rose naturally to the Supreme Court, as a man of liberal principles who derived them from the empirical, anti-ideological tradition: 'I suppose I have a general predilection against pedantic, didactic, formalised, so-called ethical principles.' What counted he felt, was 'what is in the atmosphere . . . what kind of things instinctively, unconsciously enter your being'. What entered his was the American variant of the Anglo-Saxon culture.

Each regime projects, in a sense, a mesh of the right reticulation which, passed through society, pulls to the surface the politico-psychological type required and leaves the others unused. It is equally the case that on the breakdown of an order, the atmosphere and events of revolution similarly drag up, with a net of different mesh, a totally different ruling type, which replaces, within months, the older establishment.

One of the lessons of Nazism and the other totalitarianisms is that a reserve of people suited to the most abhorrent and horrible types of state are in existence in potential and are usable when the time comes. However hostile the view that might have been taken of Germany, few would have thought that quite such a criminal revolutionary element as eventually formed the ruling caste existed in its recesses. The same can be said of the Hungarian Rakosi regime. Again, in *The Gulag Archipelago* the moral-psychological type which Stalinism nourished and gave power to comes through very clearly indeed: not the iron executors of the laws of history, but the corrupt and selfish toadies of the *apparat*. Djilas tells us that Stalin had only one moral principle — objection to income from property. As far as the state he created is concerned, even that principle was of little account compared with the great driving force of mere self-interest, habit of mind, inability to think at all beyond closed formulae. But all were melded in the psychological product or catch. One can also recognise this phenomenon, at the moral level, in the brutal local operatives of the Jacobins. And Lenin, of course, not only made use of just such characters, but, with his usual clarity, justified the action: 'Party members should not be measured by the narrow standard of petty bourgeois snobbery. Sometimes a scoundrel is useful to our party, precisely because he is a scoundrel.'

One of the most curious and sinister of recent political phenomena has been the detail in which one can now explore the contrast in fanatical minds between the horrors of their political duty and the occasionally reviving feelings of the human being. One of the best illustrations is to be seen in Himmler's attitude when, under the influence of his masseur, he from time to time let a number of Jews out to Sweden. He was always deeply repentant of this gross lapse from duty, of this succumbing to easy temptations of undisciplined sentiment. In fact, we see a terrifying reversal of what we would regard as the natural order of things, by which failure to send innocent people to their death is regarded as a reprehensible piece of self-indulgence. We are also told that when Himmler actually watched some executions he was so nauseated that he felt it his duty never to do so again for fear of weakening his political conscience. Rather similarly, Marat was too sensitive to attend a post-mortem.

A messianic revolution is not the product of messianic supermen without earthly contamination, who have been sleeping in caves. It uses human material of the country it takes over. And, as we have said, political or general psychology is the product of generations.

In the Russia which the Bolsheviks seized they could rely on few who could in any real sense be said to have been their followers before the seizure (or the promise of the seizure) of power. As with all other seizures of power, it was a matter of the violent, the ambitious, the brutal, the criminal. But nor is this to say that the old underground party itself consisted simply of seagreen incorruptibles. When one thinks of Stalin, Kaganovich, Mekhlis, Yagoda, Shkiryatov, it is clear enough that the qualifications for underground membership did not exclude characters truly revolting by any standards whatever.

It is, of course, possible to be 'fanatical' about a major issue without that fanaticism being part of one's essential political make-up once the issue is resolved. The leaders of the majority faction in the Irish guerrilla or 'terrorist' war against Britain in the early twenties, once the settlement was reached, proved themselves ruthless in their suppression of the extremists and in setting up a peaceful political and civic order.

And we must, indeed, distinguish more generally between those who have so far gone into dogma that they are scarcely reconcilable in the short view to the libertarian culture and those who have gone part of the way with them, are impressed with them, are afflicted with the notion *pas d'ennemi à gauche* and so forth, but no more.

Many of those 'progressives' who accept formulae and connive at revolutionary cant are, all the same, not the mere products of running verbalisation but have also an element of genuine civic tradition. They can be reclaimed for civilisation. However, a danger remains, as the great American critic Lionel Trilling remarks in his *Manners, Morals and the Novel*: 'Some paradox in our nature leads us, once we have made our fellow men the objects of our enlightened interest, to go on to make them the objects of our pity, then of our wisdom, ultimately of our coercion.' In 'our' nature? Perhaps in all natures, unless checked by deeper self-awareness; in some natures, regardless. But which?

Sir Karl Popper argues at some length against what he views as the attempt of John Stuart Mill and others to reduce the study of society to psychology. Popper argues that men 'are, if anything, the product of life and society rather than its creators'. To the extent (not a very large one) that Mill implied that individual psychologies might be considered to exist separately, society being a sort of product of their interrelation, Popper is clearly right. But the question is not, or not so much, whether given drives and motivations take place in man-in-society, but whether these drives and motivations can be derived on any logical basis except from their temperaments. Of course, the temperaments are those of real men within, and to some degree moulded by, social order. But the notion that the individuals who are the levers for moving history are no more, or little more, than the products of large (and largely unconscious) mass motivation is one which fails to account for almost any given case.

Since Freud, it is a commonplace that conscious motives often conceal profounder, 'real' motives. Since Pareto, the fact that political ideals may also be rationalisations of quite different unconscious aims has been equally impossible to suppress.

In every society — but especially in those going through change — temperaments are available which are divergent from the broad norm of their culture. In different centuries different sets of views attract them; but the temperamental type attracted by extreme forms of theology in one century or economic theory in another remains the same, which certainly indicates that it is the extremity of a view, rather than its particular content, which is the attraction. C. S. Lewis notes of the extreme Puritans of Queen Elizabeth I's time:

> Unless we can imagine the freshness, the audacity, and (soon) the fashionableness of Calvinism, we shall get our whole picture

wrong. It was the creed of progressives, even of revolutionaries. It appealed strongly to those tempers that would have been Marxist in the nineteen-thirties. The fierce young don, the learned lady, the courtier with intellectual leanings, were likely to be Calvinists.

Temperament may, as we have said, be the product of 'social' circumstances, even if not in the fairly clear and rational way Marxism implies. For example, historians have pointed out the role of bored wives in the French Revolution. (Dickens shows what they became.) As Hermann Rauschning puts it, in his climb to power Hitler, too, made use of 'society ladies thirsting for adventure, sick of their empty lives'.

Yet psychological analysis, in the usual sense, also fails. Examination of the early lives even of the leading French revolutionaries shows, in most cases, happy homes and successful careers. The effects of Luther's mere personality on the events of the sixteenth century (and so of later centuries) would be hard to exaggerate. Yet the greatest psychoanalytical biography, Ericson's *Luther,* which suggests all sorts of possible causes of Luther's mental or physical-and-mental make-up, yet quite fails to prove that such factors were either necessary or sufficient to produce a Luther. None of the attempts to link political personalities with the types prescribed in psychological theory and to 'explain' them in this way seems very impressive.

When it comes to the sexual lives of revolutionaries, we are just not fully enough informed. But at any rate it is fairly clear that there are cases of men of power whose records refute the idea that there is a certain amount of libido available, and that thwarting it in a sexual sense is what drives it into channels such as power-seeking. A remarkable example is Kemal Ataturk, whose immense political and administrative energy did not prevent him from leading what many people might regard as a more than full-time sex-life.

It will be somebody's life's work to examine such problems properly. For the moment one is largely left, as in the preliminary period of any study, with odd and provocative details; and it would be hard to maintain that better political profiles than those of Plutarch are readily to be found in later and more 'expert' literature.

In general, when considering the association of psychological types with political attitudes one is not faced with the difficulty of choosing between the various systems of individual psychology which have been advanced during the present century. For none of them presents any worthwhile clues. The motivations of power considered by Adler and similar schools, the conception of the paranoiac and paranoid in traditional psychoanalysis, have their uses in the field but they do not differentiate in any substantial way between the political attitudes emerging.

A very prominent psychologist (now dead) once told me, rather indiscreetly, that of the MPs he knew there were two he would certify insane without further examination, and a third whom he would feel professionally obliged to check over a little more but who, without much doubt, could also be so listed. In spite of his prominence, I took it that he did not know huge numbers of MPs, as who does? He agreed, saying he probably knew twenty or thirty. This would imply something like 10 per cent of obtrusive lunacy in political life even of the Western type, in addition to any less obvious or less extreme symptoms.

When I asked if the condition he had diagnosed was paranoia, my acquaintance answered that this was, of course, the case. 10 per cent is a disturbingly high figure, to be sure, though no doubt it represents the potential revolutionary element. But the other 90 per cent had at least not such a heavy charge of mania. . . .

It is difficult enough to analyse the 'gift for politics', if one may use an extremely broad and vague expression. One often reads of people in all sorts of fields who take up what turns out to be their true vocation by chance. This may sometimes be true, but reading the biographies of writers, artists and scientists, as well as those of politicians, one is often struck by what seems a certain inevitability. The gift seems to create its opportunities. There is obviously some limitation on this. A man of the highest mathematical ability would not get very far in a Neolithic cave. A brilliant revolutionary politician will not be heard of in an epoch of social peace.

If we consider as a parallel to the complexities of politics those of war, we can find one important difference. With very few exceptions, the great generals have had a professional education in soldiering. It is only among the politicians of established cultures, civic or despotic, that anything resembling this has taken place. It is very rare for the actual leaders of a messianic revolution to have had any relevant experience or training except in the in-fighting of their little sects. (On the other hand, Marvell, in what is surely the best political poem ever written, greatly exaggerates Cromwell's lack of concern with politics.

It was dramatic, not true, to see him as torn from his private garden: but Cromwell was by no means a messianic revolutionary.)

Yet it can be argued that the 'political type' as such, in the very broadest sense, is already distinguishable from important sections of any population. It is true that there are, or have been in the past, people who have been thrust into politics by sheer heredity, as with particular kings and queens. In some cases, certainly, it might be argued that a fairly recent ancestor had been a voluntary politician in fighting his way to a throne, and that from him such monarchs might have inherited certain tendencies. But, in principle, the bulk of them have simply been sentenced to politics at birth.

Another semi-hereditary political caste might be seen in the Whig oligarchs in England. The ones who became really devoted politicians constituted a minority; even so, for leadership they often went to outsiders or socially minor figures. Nevertheless, there was a certain type of politician who, by family tradition and out of little more than a sense of duty, found himself assuming an important role in life. The sense of duty was not, of course, to abstract ideas so much as to a feeling of civic responsibility. One advantage of this type of political figure was that, not having much ambition, he was willing to resign or to provoke an election on a matter of simple principle. Whether one judges him right or wrong, Lord Hartington, Gladstone's Secretary for War during the siege of Khartoum, was a remarkable example of sheer conscientiousness overcoming all other considerations.

However, this sort of thing is fairly exceptional, especially nowadays. For better or worse, we have the full-time politician. In the past thirty or forty years in particular the remaining old trade union leaders on the Labour benches and squires on the Conservative ones have been replaced by a more strenuous crew, of whom the present stereotypes would be, rather, the sociology lecturer and the managerial whizz-kid respectively. Both tend to be manipulators of the people rather than representatives of the nation; both are more ambitious and so carry less moral ballast than their predecessors. At any rate, even in the West, politics has become much more a matter of state intrusion than ever before and has the political cadres suitable to this. Yet the older attitudes survive and are now beginning to show reserves of strength.

W. H. Auden effectively presents the distaste of many men of intellect for those who carry out the day-to-day work of administration, mythologising the two temperaments as 'Apollo' and 'Hermes':

but he commonsensically overrules the sentiment for practical purposes, admitting (so long as Apollo does not intrude into the private sphere):

> If he would leave the self alone,
> Apollo's welcome to the throne,
>   Fasces and falcons;
> He loves to rule, has always done it;
> The earth would soon, did Hermes run it,
>   Be like the Balkans.

After all, in a polity we need politicians. Yet we should not forget that a proportion of them are bound to be unduly attracted to the expansion of state power.

These discursive remarks about politicians in Western society seem to show that even the civic order, particularly if deviating in the *étatiste* direction, contains a psychology of weakly despotic type, perhaps capable of developing further in that direction if not halted. In considering the true revolutionary-despotic type we are to think of these illustrations from the civic sphere as inflated a hundredfold, to the point of becoming a fresh phenomenon. And, as we have seen, it is important to make the distinction.

Meanwhile, it seems important to stress again that radical movements in the West appear, in fact, to be divided between two main types of adherent. One has accepted, through immaturity or ignorance, the thesis that revolutionary change is necessary, but only for what might be called schematic reasons, retaining in his character (at a profounder level) the consensual assumptions of the Western culture; the other is a genuine revolutionary, for whom revolution rather than the supposed benefits emerging from it is the main point. This is not to say that, as in every field, these two categories may not contain borderline cases, capable of evolving from one to the other, given the right circumstances. Nevertheless, as general types, they are potentially different.

CHAPTER 14

Interest, Faction, State

It is, of course, a cliché of modern political thought that the economic interest of particular social groups is a decisive driving force in politics. Sometimes one would think that no one before Marx — or at best Taine or de Tocqueville — had ever come to this conclusion, though it is, a commonplace among ancient Greek political writers.

The truth of economic aspiration as a political force and of the importance of more or less definable 'economic' groups in politics is plain enough. Though the qualification 'economic *and social*' should always be applied: nor is this a quibble. Whoever speaks of interest groups is inclined to assume that they are (generally speaking) really working in their own interest. This is not necessarily the case. Even Marxism is always ready to say that the peasantry or petty bourgeoisie, for example, should, as a matter of *economic* rationality, see their future as bound up with that of the proletariat, but often do not do so, even while conducting a coherent group struggle.

Mass movements with short-term and often unconceptualised aims have often been taken over by pretenders to the throne, fanatical theologians and (in our own day) revolutionary intellectuals.

The idea of socialism in the early part of the nineteenth century had no special connection with the industrial working class. Only when this class came into being and intellectuals *already* holding socialist views saw it (in a way we can now hardly conceive) as a fantastically new and fresh phenomenon full of Utopian possibilities, as the last of all the classes in class society, did they project their idea upon it.

For, in any case, those who nominate themselves as 'representatives' of a given economic class are usually not really so in any rational sense: they represent, that is to say, not what will benefit those to whom they are supposedly devoted, but an ideological future in which not the real interests of the group in question, but the theoretical and messianic notion of its historical role prevails. In much the same way extreme nationalists (for example, the Nazis) set themselves up as the 'representatives' of their nation. The Nazis did indeed messianise or idolise the German nation. In their theory the nation played a far more sublime role than it did in the minds of many members of moderate parties in the German state. But few, I think, would argue that the Nazis' unrivalled devotion to nationality in fact operated in the real interests of the German people as against a less extreme view.

For 'interest groups' do not necessarily act so much in their own real interests as for some idea of those interests which they have wrongly been led to believe. It was always a conscious strategy of the Marxists to inculcate into the more or less spontaneous movements of the industrial working class the idea that socialism was its main, long-term interest. It is an ironic commentary on this that the great workers' risings have been in countries where capitalism had been overthrown, in cities like East Berlin, Poznan, Budapest, Plzen, Gdansk, Radom—to say nothing of Novocherkassk and Temir Tau.

One principle basic to all these regimes in that the parties concerned came to power while concealing from their rank-and-file supporters the inevitable sacrifices which would be asked of them. As Lenin put it in his *Works* (Russian edition, Moscow 1951, page 233): 'The victory of the workers is impossible without sacrifices, without a temporary worsening of their situation.'

Fifty years later Che Guevara was saying the same thing in his *Man and Socialism in Cuba*:

> The vanguard group is ideologically more advanced than the mass; the latter is acquainted with the new values, but insufficiently. While in the former a qualitative change takes place which permits them to make sacrifices as a function of their vanguard character, the latter see only by halves and must be subjected to incentives and pressures of some intensity; it is the dictatorship

of the proletariat being exercised not only upon the defeated class but also individually upon the victorious class.

The result of 'proletarian' revolutions has, at any rate, always been a lowering of the standard of living of the working class, together with the removal of their right to defend themselves against this in traditional fashion. More generally, as Academician Sakharov flatly points out, such a revolution in the Western countries 'does not appear to be an economically advantageous move for the working people', even apart from the bloodshed and the possibility of another Stalin.

The acceptance of sectarian doctrine on trust is always notable among the less intelligent adherents of one or another totalist party. The mobs of Byzantium and Alexandria who supported the homoousian, the strange fanatics of seventeenth-century London who interpreted Revelation obviously have much in common with the rank-and-file Nazi or Communist. I remember being told by the late Jacques Katel, once prominent in French communist circles, of how he attended a meeting of the Communist Party branch at the Renault works in 1934. A somewhat supercilious representative of the Central Committee was putting forward the new line of the 'United Front' with the Socialist Party. When he had finished one of the huge, loyal *militants* on whom the French Communist Party so strongly based itself got up and said, *'Comarade! Il y a une chose que je n'ai pas bien compris. Comment se peut-il que les Socialistes hier étaient des fascistes, et aujourd'hui ils sont des camarades?'* The representative of the Central Committee answered shortly, *'Camarade, c'est la dialectique.'* Upon which, somewhat to Katel's surprise, the militant said, *'Ah, oui, bien sur . . . ah, vous avez raison . . . oui, ç'est ça, la dialectique. . . .'* and sat down perfectly satisfied.

Marx's theory of classes has proved misleading. This has partly been due, as we all know, to his narrow definition of a class in terms of its ownership or non-ownership of the means of production. But the KGB and the Party *apparat* in the USSR have always formed 'interest groups' quite apart from the 'new class' of which they are components. So do the exploitative circles around certain Third World governments. For, of course, mere power groups, too, use their position to gain economic as well as other benefits.

As we noted earlier, in the nineteenth century economic forces were strong and political forces comparatively weak, at least by twentieth-century standards. The notion of the predominance of economic factors certainly stems from that temporary phenomenon—as dated as the crinoline.

It led to such notions as that which dominates Soviet theory: that economic circumstances determine consciousness, so that a change from above, as for example the collectivisation of agriculture, was not merely a product of miscalculation, nor a means for exerting direct control over the rural population, but, even more profoundly, a philosophical error. The destruction of the small farmer was necessary to produce a new 'consciousness'. As Solzhenitsyn puts it (in *Cancer Ward*): 'we thought it was enough to change the mode of production and people would immediately change with it. But did they? The hell they did! They didn't change a bit.'

More basically (in so far as one can meaningfully lean to one side or the other) it was politics that determined the great economic developments in England rather than vice versa. (Even Max Weber, while inclined to a certain economic determinism in more modern times, finds himself having to stress the 'Protestant ethic' as cause rather than effect in early capitalism.) Naturally this is not to deny mutual interaction: indeed, even to divide politics from economics in so formal a fashion is somewhat misleading.

Meanwhile, we may note that there are two ways in which 'special interests', operating *against* the general interest of the community, may act. They may seek so to weaken the executive that there is no power available to restrain them, as the barons did in Stephen's reign and as the unions, or some of them, are attempting to do now. Or they may seek to take over the executive, or at least reduce it to dependence on them in the manner of all partisan centralizes.

It would perhaps be generally admitted that the civic order in Western countries is now more at odds with the centralising bureaucratic element than has been the case for a century. The civic, consensual culture has always had to cope with attempts by the executive to increase its power as against the powers of the individual, the locality, the community. Recent troubles in Britain in particular may, in one respect, be viewed as galloping elephantiasis of the executive as it usurps new areas of decision—and this is true not merely of those theoretically committed to state socialism, but also of the managerialist, 'technocratic' Conservatives.

In particular, we may find that the current tendencies, excessive by all previous civic standards, to use the power of the Western executive arm in vast fields of internal affairs previously controlled by the communities (or guided rather than controlled) has imported into Western political thought and action attitudes which dispose its formulators to think, and wrongly, that the revolutionary polities are doing the same sort of thing. It would not be the first time that a sort of bureaucratic sympathy has determined attitudes. Lord Acton's controversy with Archbishop Creighton (the Catholic historian attacking and the Anglican defending the atrocities of the early popes) is convincingly attributed by Lytton Strachey to Creighton's instinctive sympathy with administrators dealing with refractory problems; the stake and the rack rather appeared to be side issues. . . .

In a somewhat different vein, academics in the West, as we have said, particularly to the extent that they are cut off from 'real' politics, are more than ordinarily inclined to systematising in concept and 'planning' in policy, beyond what the subject will bear, and this too leads to a tendency to see in totalist schemes just a variety of systematic politics. And, of course, these ideas are not confined to the academic world, but seep down, in even more debased form, to a larger audience. Serious-minded housewives by the millions absorb masses of horror-sociology, issued (in Britain) by Parrot Paperbacks.

The error is to see 'problems', work out 'solutions', and then turn to an agency for putting them into effect: the state. The idea that there are any limitations in principle to what the state, properly empowered, can do seems to evaporate. Yet this is to venture into action which time and again (and not necessarily through any malice) has brought the civic society into danger. Moreover, while to effect changes that go with the grain of a culture is comparatively easy, to the schematic mind one abstract change is as good as another and depends solely on its formal advantages.

David Hume deplored, two hundred years ago, the tendency of political parties to go beyond policy and to seek to be the bearers of a philosophy. Curiously enough (as Kenneth Minogue has noted),

> the less educated the market, the more susceptible it has often been to pseudo-philosophical rhetoric. An educated electorate decides between parties and policies in terms of complex and uncertain desirabilities, but ever since Marx and the ideologists of the nineteenth century, the uneducated have been bombarded with ideas about racial science or the 'correct' analysis of the present stage of dialectical evolution.

No thoroughgoing theory of society or history exists that is

capable of providing long-term predictions of the results of particular
policies. In fact, every attempt to reorganise society in accordance
with theory has proved disastrous. This is not to say that no general
view of the nature of politics can be taken. Such a view, if it is to be
helpful, cannot confine the future to programmatic formulae. It can,
however, suggest the open-ended, non-deterministic political system
and tradition within which solutions can be sought on their merits
rather than in accordance with dogma, and pursued or abandoned on
the basis of results rather than orthodoxy.

When one thinks of the results of the mass sociology boom of recent
years, with its output of alienated sub-Marxist students — including
a very high proportion of the German and Italian terrorists — it is
strange to recall that most of the pioneer masters of sociology have
taken a far more sceptical view of state action. Weber, Durkheim,
Tonnies, Simmel, more recently Nisbet, have all seen the disadvantages as well as the advantages of the change from the accepted community sense of traditional pre-modern society to the individualism
and rationalism which have marked modern progress. Nisbet, following
de Tocqueville, sees as the main trouble the weakening of all communal ties except that provided by the state. He points out that the
whole tradition of the liberation of the individual, from Rousseau on,
has been to make individuals independent of each other and of society
but more dependent on the state. As Nisbet points out, this is based
on an error: 'Centrality of sovereignty does not lead logically to
the centralisation of administration in public affairs...Decentralisa-
tion of administration is not merely feasible technically; it is a prime
necessity of free culture.'

Thus from the point of view both of the political stance I have
been illustrating, a concern with the survival of a flexible and 'open'
order, and of the tensions destructive of the individual, it seems
essential that strong limitations now be placed not so much on the
power as on the pervasiveness of the state.

As Irving Kristol puts it:

> The one way not to cope with this crisis in values is through orga-
> nised political-ideological action. Most of the hysteria, much of
> the stupidity and a good part of the bestiality of the 20th Century
> have arisen from efforts to do precisely this. Not only do such
> efforts fail; they fail in the costliest fashion. And if modern his-
> tory can be said to teach anything, it is that, intolerable as a crisis

in values may be, it invariably turns out to be far less intolerable than any kind of 'final solution' imposed by direct political action.

Indeed, let me repeat, the notion of the state as machinery which can effect any desired change whatever in human society is really a child's one, of the type 'If I were king I would . . .' or the teenage 'If I were dictator . . . .'

As Colin Clark has pointed out, the role of the state is to provide those services which by their nature benefit everyone, such as national defence, law and order, national parks and lighthouses; to which may be added certain social actions — for example, pollution or in which there is a divergence between various public interests.

Arthur Seldon suggested in his recent book *Charge* that all those benefits which could in principle be charged to the individual bene-ficiaries should be removed from the state budget, though a case would remain, often enough, for direct subsidies to individuals in case of need. Colin Clark holds that government expenditure could be reduced below the 25 per cent of net national product which he (sup-ported by Keynes long ago) estimated as the safe upper limit for taxation.

On this argument, regulation of the economy beyond a certain point is inevitably counter-productive. This has obviously been the case in the West whenever political intervention or highly organised and centralised demands from particular sections of the community, encouraged by theories or by factions, have involved economies (like that of Britain) in costs greater than the value of their products. But it is also the case that the more regulations, the larger the num-ber of people who are involved in organisation rather than the pro-duction of wealth. There is obviously a minimum point, even in the most 'liberal' economy, below which the number of regulators and persons involved in legal economic enforcement and the other ser-vices necessary to the maintenance of the state — itself economically as well as socially necessary — cannot be allowed to fall. Equally, there comes a point when the number of economic regulators and adminis-trators become parasitical on the economy and (even not allowing for any economic damage done by their specific action) it is simply too large a burden for the active productive forces to support.

At any rate, in the past generation we have entered a period in which the 'sovereignty of Parliament', itself in practice tending to mean the sovereignty of the Prime Minister, whose authority is asserted through his Whips, has been taken to dogmatic extremes; Parliament is made to take action in spheres in which, no doubt, it is theoretically competent, but in which its intervention in practice is destructive of civic society. The famous resolution of 1780, that the powers of the executive 'have increased, are increasing and ought to be diminished', is once again applicable. For as Dr Thomas Sowell has put it:

> The grand delusion of contemporary liberals [I would say of contemporary *étatistes* in general] is that they have both the right and the ability to move their fellow creatures around like blocks of wood — and that the end results will be no different than if people had voluntarily chosen the same actions.

When we speak of the executive, we should note that it is not distinguishable from the legislative in the same way as it used to be. The original role of Parliament was not to churn out legislation, but to prevent unwelcome innovations and usurpations on the part of the executive, by codifying (or interpreting in a particular way) the law, as it was supposed already to exist in principle.

As Giovanni Sartori puts it (in his *Liberty and Law*), parliaments were not originally 'assigned so much the task of changing the laws, but rather that of preventing the monarch from changing them unilaterally and arbitrarily'. And at present,

> When law is reduced to State law-making, a 'will conception' or a 'command theory' of law gradually replaces the common-law idea of law... There are many practical disadvantages, not to mention dangers, in our legislative conception of law. In the first place, the rule of legislators is resulting in a real mania for lawmaking, a fearful inflation of laws. Leaving aside the question as to how posterity will be able to cope with hundreds of thousands of laws that increase, at times, at the rate of a couple of thousand per legislature, the fact is that the inflation of law in itself discredits the law. Nor is it only the excessive quantity of laws that lessens the value of law, it is also their bad quality. Our legislators are poor lawmakers, and this is because the system was not designed to permit legislators to replace jurists and jurisprudence.

Nor does it seem so far-fetched to suggest that this trend towards excessive centralisation involves some trace of fellow feeling with, and hence amiable illusions about, despotic cultures proper; just as the

Stuart phase of executive usurpation went with a certain rallying to Bourbon tyranny on the Continent. At least *some* feeling of Burintern solidarity seems to play a role in the recent tendency to underrate the profound and principled hostility of communist culture to our own.

Thus we get the 'progressive' idea that there is nothing wrong with executive solutions to every sort of social and even moral problem, and hence that the revolutionary is really just a sort of rather impatient liberal — a fatal romanticising of what Richard Henry Lee defines as 'the fickle and the ardent, the right instruments for despotism'. The proponents of this view are as misguided as a sanguine topologist would have been in welcoming Alexander the Great as a fellow professional on the grounds of his having solved the problem of the Gordian knot.

Thus the centralising element, always necessary, shows signs of escaping from popular judgment. Perhaps this is seen less in major matters than in a tendency to override interests in favour of overall economic or other aims, insufficiently understood. This is an old story and certainly represents or includes one of the great social problems of the forthcoming period. What is clear, at any rate, is that it is only within the Western order that there is any prospect of the administrators and centralisers being criticised and controlled. Any notion that this can be done in some other fashion (that is, by a revolutionary dictatorship) is a leap from mildly uncomfortable frying pan into a particularly hot type of fire.

We can base ourselves on what we already have: the alternative, which constitutes the essential of our political culture. The failures have been failures of policy and of thought, not of our tradition as a whole. As we see, one may argue that the failures, or a great many of them, have frequently been due to an infection contracted from the autocratic tradition, a premature belief that social and political problems can be reduced to simple formulae and large-scale, set-piece solutions put in motion that are founded on insufficient study and insufficient intellectual modesty. Except for a fringe of those who would have us imitate supposedly progressive dictatorships set up in backward countries, and not particularly successful even there, most people in Britain and America would accept that our political and civic system has at least the right potentialities, that it is open-ended and capable of developing into a society in which present problems can be solved.

In thinking of our future we should look, first of all, at the profoundest point: the nature of the political and civic culture which we enjoy, which so many parts of the world do not, or only very precariously, and which, after all, carries with it all real hope of human advance.

None of this is to assert perfection. In fact, the assertion of perfection in politics is an invariable sign of a deadly flaw in the political mind. But it is not even to assert that the balance between state and citizen is, at a given moment, apportioned in a reasonable way.

The citizen benefits from both the civic and the administrative organisations within society. The triumph, or luck, of the British system is that it has managed to combine a strong state with a powerful and deeply rooted traditional civic order. It was a long and difficult evolution, with periods in which it seemed that despotism might emerge, either through the exaggeration of monarchic powers or through anarchy. Nor can it be said that it is out of danger yet. No one would say that Britain, or Australia, or the United States, are in any sense Utopias. Their problems and difficulties are very apparent. For some of those living in these countries and others of our culture it may sometimes seem that things could hardly be worse: but only if they have no knowledge of other political systems. At a time when students and academics are full of willingness to learn from the political experience of the world's most backward countries, it is perhaps not immodest to suggest that they should look at the lessons to be learnt from an area which has had more experience, and that, more varied and more relevant, than anywhere else.

More important still, our culture will face, probably in the next decade or so, the greatest threat to its mere survival that has ever arisen. Only the most rigorous understanding of the issues in all their profundity, the clearest view of the essential nature of Western culture and, even more, of the despotic culture now offering itself as an alternative and threatening a final confrontation, can save us from disaster.

Index

Index